American Red Cross

D0624737

Swimming and Water Safety

Dedicated to the memory of
David Earl Harbert

His commitment to the mission
of the American Red Cross and his
leadership role in water safety education
will never be forgotten.

American
Red Cross

Swimming
and
Water Safety

The following organizations provided expert review of the materials and support for American Red Cross Swimming and Water Safety:

StayWell

StayWell

Copyright © 2004 by The American National Red Cross

All rights reserved. No part of this publication may be reproduced, stored in a retrieval system, or transmitted in any form or by any means, electronic, mechanical, photocopying, recording, or otherwise, without prior permission from the publisher.

American Red Cross certificates may be issued upon successful completion of a Red Cross training, which uses this manual as an integral part of the course. By itself, the material in this manual does not constitute comprehensive Red Cross training. In order to issue American Red Cross certificates, your instructor must be authorized by the American Red Cross and must follow prescribed policies and procedures. Make certain that you have attended a course authorized by the Red Cross. Ask your instructor about receiving American Red Cross certification, or contact your local Red Cross chapter for more information.

The Care Steps outlined within this product are consistent with the Guidelines 2000 for Emergency Cardiopulmonary Resuscitation and Emergency Cardiovascular Care.

The emergency care procedures outlined in this manual reflect the standard of knowledge and accepted emergency practices in the United States at the time this manual was published. It is the reader's responsibility to stay informed of changes in the emergency care procedures.

The Girl Scout service mark is a registered trademark of the Girl Scouts of the USA.

Printed in the United States of America.

Cover design by Graphic World, Inc.

Composition by Graphic World, Inc.

Printing/Binding by Banta

StayWell

780 Township Line Rd.

Yardley, PA 19067

Library of Congress Cataloging-in-Publication Data

Swimming and water safety / American Red Cross

   p. cm

Includes index.

ISBN 1-58480-186-7

  1. Swimming. 2. Diving. 3. Aquatic sports—Safety measures. I. American Red Cross.

GV837.S933 2004

797.2'0028'9—dc22

04 05 06 07 08 / 9 8 7 6 5 4 3

Acknowledgments

The American Red Cross Swimming and Water Safety Program and supporting materials were developed through the dedication of both employees and volunteer staff. Their commitment to excellence made this possible.

The following American Red Cross national headquarters and USA Swimming staff contributed to the development, design, and review of this program and supporting materials. The Swimming and Water Safety project team included:

Mike Espino
Project Manager
Manager, Research and Product Development

Connie Harvey
Senior Associate, Research and Product Development

John E. Hendrickson
Senior Associate, Chapter Business Development and Sales Support

Tom Heneghan
Senior Associate, Program Administration and Support

Amanda Land
Manager, Program Communication and Marketing

Stephen Lynch
Senior Associate, Business Planning

Greta Petrilla
Manager, Program Communication and Marketing

Greg Stockton
Manager, Operations and Training

Dave Thomas
Sport Development Consultant
USA Swimming

Individuals supporting the Swimming and Water Safety project team included:

Casey M. Berg
Associate, Research and Product Development

Betty J. Butler
Administrative Support, Research and Product Development

Ted T. Crites, CHES
Manager, Research and Product Development

Nancy J. Edmonds
Associate, Research and Product Development

Tony Gallagher
Senior Associate, Evaluation

Jeff Grebinoski
Associate, Evaluation

LaKeva Lucas
Administrative Support, Research and Product Development

Marc D. Madden
Senior Associate, Research and Product Development

The following American Red Cross national headquarters staff provided guidance and review:

Pat Bonifer
Director, Research and Product Development

Steve Rieve
Director, Preparedness Product Management

The StayWell editorial and production team included:

Nancy Monahan
Senior Vice President

Doug Bruce
Vice President

Bill Winneberger
Senior Director of Manufacturing

Donna Balado
Director of Editorial

Paula Batt
Director of Sales

Reed Klanderud
Director of Marketing

Shannon Bates
Managing Editor

JoAnn Emenecker
Editorial Project Manager

Laura O'Leary
Senior Production Manager

Shawn Stout
Editorial Project Manager

Special thanks go to the following individuals for their assistance:

Graphic World, Inc.
Cover Designer

Vince Knaus
Photographer

Martin Simon
Photographer

Guidance, writing, support and review were provided by members of the American Red Cross Swimming and Water Safety Advisory Group:

Jim Beeson
Lucas County Educational Service Center
Toledo, Ohio

Tina Dittmar
Aquatics Supervisor
City of Laguna Niguel
Laguna Niguel, California

Kathie Edwards
Youth Safety Manager
Greater Kansas City Chapter
Kansas City, Missouri

Harriet Helmer
President
Aqua Smart Training and Consulting
Boise, Idaho

John Kaufmann
Division Officer, Aviation Survival Department
Naval Aviation Schools Command
NAS Pensacola
Pensacola, Florida

Stephen J. Langendorfer, Ph.D.
Associate Professor
School of Human Movement, Sports and Leisure Studies
Bowling Green State University
Bowling Green, Ohio

Robert Ogoreuc
Assistant Professor
Physical Education & Sport Management Department
Slippery Rock University
Slippery Rock, Pennsylvania

Murray Stephens
Head Coach
North Baltimore Aquatic Club
Baltimore, Maryland

Tony Trofimczuk
Aquatic Program Supervisor
City of Kirkland
Parks and Community Services
Kirkland, Washington

The following individuals also provided guidance, writing, support and review:

Tipton Ammen, ITCM (SEAL), USN
Navy Swim Program Manager
Aviation Survival Department
Naval Aviation Schools Command
NAS Pensacola
Pensacola, Florida

Tom Avischious
Program & Services Director
USA Swimming
Colorado Springs, Colorado

Carolyn Mayberry
Phoenix, Arizona

John Walker
Assistant Director
National Team Technical Support
USA Swimming
Colorado Springs, Colorado

John Waterhouse
Henderson, Nevada

External review was provided by the following individuals:

Craig Blaine, EMT-P
Gastonia, North Carolina

Scott Briscoe
Kansas City, Missouri

Jennifer Espino
Aquatics Director
Vandenberg Air Force Base, California

Joyce Fluegge, OTR
Special Projects Manager
Brooks Rehab Solutions
Grand Haven, Michigan

Vicki McGill
Heights Family YMCA
Albuquerque, New Mexico

Meg Pomerantz
Director, Physical Education Activities Program
Department of Exercise and Sport Science
University of North Carolina
Chapel Hill, North Carolina

M. Kathryn Scott
Committee Member
American Red Cross Advisory Council on First Aid and
    Safety (ACFAS)
Director, Physical Education Program
University of California
Berkley, California

NATIONAL ORGANIZATIONS

Steven Becker
Continental Consultant HPE&R
Jewish Community Centers Association
New York, New York

David Bell
National Health and Safety Committee
Boy Scouts of America
Ponca City, Oklahoma

Kathleen Cullinan
Camping Consultant
Safety and Risk Management
Girl Scouts of the USA
New York, New York

Rachel Falgout
Assistant Director, Health and Life Skills
Boys and Girls Club of America
Atlanta, Georgia

William S. Hurst
National Health and Safety Committee
Boy Scouts of America
Bowie, Maryland

Marc Meeker
Assistant Program Manager, Navy Fitness
Navy Personnel Command
Morale, Welfare, Recreation
Millington, Tennessee

Catherine M. Scheder
Manager, Learning Resources
American Camping Association
Martinsville, Indiana

Ed Woodlock
Director, Health and Safety Services
Boy Scouts of America
Irving, Texas

Special Acknowledgments

The American Red Cross would like to thank the following organizations and facilities that provided talent and locations for much of the photography in this manual:

City of Coral Springs
Coral Springs, Florida

Jillian Cicione
Allandale, Florida

Joya Cox
McLean, Virginia

District of Columbia
Department of Recreation and Parks
Washington, D.C.

Fairfax County Park Authority
George Washington Recreation Center
Oak Mar Recreation Center
Providence Recreation Center
Spring Hill Recreation Center

Fort Lauderdale Swim Team
Fort Lauderdale, Florida

George Washington University
Department of Human Kinetics and Leisure Studies
Washington, D.C.

George Washington University Hospital
Department of Cardiology
Washington, D.C.

Erik Hansen
Colorado Springs, Colorado

Lori Heisick
Colorado Springs, Colorado

International Swimming Hall of Fame Aquatic Complex
Fort Lauderdale, Florida

Lake Anna, Virginia State Park
Spotsylvania, Virginia

Tyler Page
Littleton, Colorado

Jean Skinner
Fairfax County Park Authority
Fairfax, Virginia

Southport Fitness Center
Alexandria, Virginia

Spotsylvania County Rescue Squad
Spotsylvania, Virginia

Timberlake
Oakton, Virginia

Phil Trinidad
Colorado Springs, Colorado

University of Maryland
College Park, Maryland

Waterful Aerobics, Waterful, Inc.
Coral Springs, Florida

The Red Cross also thanks Peak Performance Technologies, Inc., Centennial, Colorado, who provided the animated or kinematic motion measurement graphics.

Preface

Americans have made aquatic activities the number one recreational pursuit in the country. This can be traced, in part, to an increase in leisure time and the expanding availability of aquatic facilities and to the interest generated by the feats of world-class athletes. It is also a result of the growing variety of aquatic activities and the differing purposes—fitness, play, socializing—that are met in the water. Finally, it happens because entire groups of people, such as senior citizens, preschoolers and individuals with disabilities, have learned that they can perform well in the water.

This manual provides the best information available on a wide spectrum of aquatic activities. The six most widely used swimming strokes are explained in detail and reflect the latest research. A discussion of hydrodynamic principles (Chapter 2) and an application of them to each stroke (Chapter 4) will help you learn to swim or improve your skills. Other chapters cover topics such as the history of swimming and diving, safety guidelines and rescue techniques, diving, starts and turns and skills for all types of aquatic activities. If you are interested in fitness, Chapter 8 provides information to help you attain your personal goals. Training and competitive activities ranging from swimming to triathlons are covered. Regardless of your skill level, from novice to advanced swimmer, this manual can expand your knowledge, improve your skill and serve as a reference guide if you teach or plan to teach aquatic skills.

The goal of this manual is to integrate all of these interests with the common theme of safety in, on and around the water and to provide you with the information and resources to make participation in aquatic activities a lifetime pursuit.

Contents

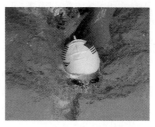
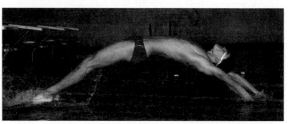

Swimming and

Diving: Then and Now

Chapter 1

eople love to swim. Swimmers can be found at pools and beaches all summer or in competition throughout the year. Others quietly swim their laps and mark their distance in personal notebooks or on public charts. Still others join teams for water polo, diving, masters swimming or synchronized swimming.

Other people swim to live. The lives, not just the livelihoods, of sailors and commercial fishermen depend on their ability to function in, on and near the water. Most of us fall somewhere between these two extremes. Some of us want to know how to swim well enough to be safe around the pool. Others might be curious about the new ways to do the strokes that were learned long ago. Still others have discovered the fitness advantages of doing aerobic exercise in the water.

Three fourths of the earth's surface is covered with water, so it is not surprising that evidence of swimming appears throughout history. However, most of the developments in stroke mechanics occurred in the last two centuries, with the most intensive research in the last three decades. This chapter reviews these developments and relates the current status of aquatics.

The Past: Swimming in History

Beginnings

Ancient civilizations left ample evidence of their swimming abilities. Bas-relief artwork in an Egyptian tomb from around 2000 B.C. shows an overarm stroke like the front crawl. The Assyrians showed an early breaststroke in their stone carvings. The Hittites, the Minoans and other early civilizations left drawings of swimming and diving skills. Even the Bible refers to movement through the water—in Ezekiel 47:5, Acts 27:42 and Isaiah 25:11. Competitive swimming is at least as old as 36 B.C., when the Japanese held the first known swimming races.

Among the first reasons humankind strived to perfect the art of swimming was to gain military advantage over a foe. Archeological evidence supports that ancient civilizations used swimming for military maneuvers thousands of years ago. The first known historical record of military use of swimming is found on Egyptian wall reliefs picturing the story of the route of the Hittites by Ramses II (1292-1225 B.C.) across the Orontes River in northern Syria. The reliefs show Hittites apparently swimming the breaststroke and elementary backstroke and an overarm stroke is shown in good detail, including breathing position, body position, kick, arm reaches and timing. Assyrian reliefs dated about 880 B.C. show figures swimming in an unmistakable hand-over-hand stroke. Several archaeological items reveal that ancient Greeks and Romans also used swimming for military operations.

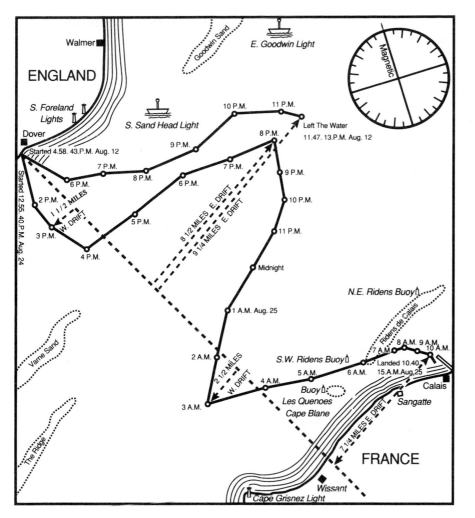

◄ Fig. 1-1

began in London, several indoor pools already existed. The National Swimming Society regulated competition. The breaststroke and the recently developed sidestroke were used. In 1844, Native Americans swam in a London meet. Flying Gull swam 130 feet in 30 seconds to defeat Tobacco and win a medal. Their stroke was described as thrashing the water with their arms in a motion "like a windmill" and kicking in an up-and-down motion. This early form of the front crawl was successful in that race, but the English continued to prefer the breaststroke for competition.

The English also liked to compete against nature. In 1875, Captain Matthew Webb first swam the English Channel (Fig. 1-1). While swimming the breaststroke, he swam the 21.26 miles in 21 hours and 45 minutes. The first woman to swim the channel was Gertrude Ederle in 1926. Marcus Hooper, the youngest person to complete the swim, swam the channel in 1979 at age 12. In 1987, Australian Clifford Batts swam the channel at the age of 67 years, 240 days, making him the oldest. This challenge continues to attract distance swimmers as the ultimate feat in this sport.

The earliest published work on swimming was written in 1538 by Nicolas Wynman, a German professor of languages. In 1587, Sir Evarard Digby of England wrote the Latin *De arte natandi* (The Art of Swimming). Years later, Melchisedec Thevenot translated or adapted Digby's work into French. After Thevenot's death, his version was published in 1696 with him as the sole author. After the English translation of Thevenot's French translation of Digby's Latin original, a process that took 112 years, the *Art of Swimming* became the standard swimming reference. It described a type of breaststroke done with the face out of the water and an underwater arm recovery. This stroke gave the swimmer good stability, even in rough water. The breaststroke was the most common stroke in Europe for centuries.

The Rise of Competitive Swimming

The English are considered the first modern society to develop swimming as a sport. By 1837, when modern competitive swimming

An Early Researcher

In the 1700s, Benjamin Franklin researched buoyancy, back floating and gliding, using his kite for propulsion and devising an early form of hand paddles and fins.

As he wrote, "When I was a boy I made two oval palettes, each about ten inches long and broad, with a hole for the thumb, in order to retain it fast in the palm of my hand. They much resembled a painter's palettes. In swimming I pushed the edges of these forward, and I struck the water with their flat surfaces as I drew them back. I remember I swam faster by means of these palettes, but they fatigued my wrists. I also fitted to the soles of my feet a kind of sandals; but I was not satisfied with them. ..."

Coach David Armbruster, who is credited in part with developing the butterfly, believed that the "fins" failed because Franklin was using a breaststroke kick.

Early Interest in Stroke Development

Throughout the 1800s, a series of swimming strokes evolved. The sidestroke was soon modified to become the overarm sidestroke. One arm was recovered above the water for increased arm speed. The legs were squeezed together in a scissors-like kicking action. In 1895, J. H. Thayers of England, using the overarm sidestroke, swam a record 1:02.50 for 100 yards. (Note: Swimming times are expressed in minutes, seconds and hundredths of seconds. So this record means the 100 yards were swum in 1 minute, 2 and 50/100 seconds. A time of less than a minute would be designated as 48.25—48 and 25/100 seconds. Times that last longer than an hour—as for a triathlon or a marathon—would be expressed 3:22:15.30, for 3 hours, 22 minutes, 15 and 30/100 seconds.)

John Trudgen developed a hand-over-hand stroke that became known as the trudgen. He copied the stroke from South American Indians and introduced it in England in 1873. Each arm recovered out of the water as the body rolled from side to side. The swimmer did a scissors kick with every two arm strokes. This stroke was the forerunner of the front crawl. Kick variations included different multiples of scissors kicks or alternating scissors and flutter kicks. F. V. C. Lane showed the speed of the trudgen in 1901 by swimming 100 yards in 1:00.0.

Recent Times: Swimming in the Twentieth Century

The American Red Cross and Water Safety

The American Red Cross became involved in swimming and water safety largely because of one person, Wilbert E. Longfellow. At the turn of the century, Longfellow was one of the first to become concerned with the number of drownings in the United States. He anticipated that the increasing death toll might soon assume the proportions of a national tragedy unless drownings were curbed. He saw the need for a nationwide program of swimming and lifesaving instruction. His vision combined with his aquatics skills, teaching abilities, showmanship and enthusiasm made him the natural leader of this enterprise.

Eager to do what he could to prevent the loss of life, Longfellow carefully studied the literature on aquatics trends, activities and safety procedures. He wrote features

▲ Fig. 1-2

month the Red Cross Life Saving Corps, forerunner of the present-day Red Cross water safety courses, came into being. Longfellow was appointed to organize the lifesaving program. He was awarded Red Cross Lifesaving Certificate Number One and the lifesaving emblem that has since been earned and proudly worn by millions (Fig. 1-3).

on water safety, waterfront rescues and steps taken to safeguard swimmers. He became highly proficient in various swimming styles and lifesaving skills (Fig. 1-2). He also offered his spare-time services to the U.S. Volunteer Life Savings Corps, a young organization in New York City, and began sharing his aquatics knowledge and skills with other swimmers. Soon he was organizing his more talented pupils into volunteer crews for safeguarding the lives of swimmers. Under his direction, the position of lifeguarding gradually spread to nearby towns and cities.

In 1905, in recognition of his already noteworthy achievements, Longfellow was awarded the title of "Commodore" by the Life Savings Corps. In 1910, the Corps appointed him to the salaried post of Commodore in Chief. In recognition of his abilities and achievements, he was designated general superintendent of the organization.

Based on his successes in water safety and lifesaving education, "Commodore" Longfellow began planning his most ambitious program yet, "the waterproofing of America." However, the Life Saving Corps decided it could not afford a nationwide expansion of its activities because of the large amount of additional funds required. Looking for a way to accomplish his great purpose, Longfellow presented his plan to the Red Cross in 1912.

A committee representing several national organizations prepared a plan, which the Red Cross adopted for a nationwide program in January 1914. The following

▲ Fig. 1-3

Soon the big fellow with the Red Cross emblem on his swimsuit began to appear at beaches and swimming pools all over the country. Everywhere he was recognized as an expert in aquatic arts and lifesaving skills (Fig. 1-4).

The Commodore put the lifesaving plan into operation in a simple way. In each community, he gathered together talented swimmers, trained them in lifesaving and resuscitation skills, organized them into a volunteer corps and asked them to supervise swimming activities in the community. He then persuaded owners and operators of swimming facilities to staff their beaches and pools with these trained lifeguards.

▲ Fig. 1-4

The next step, which was more difficult and perhaps more important, was to provide sound, large-scale swimming instruction in the communities. Longfellow selected outstanding swimmers from each corps that he organized, gave them additional training and authorized them to teach swimming. In this way, swimming instruction multiplied swimmers many times over.

Finally, it was necessary to consolidate public interest and support, which the Commodore did with amazing success. He gave talks and demonstrations, wrote for newspapers and periodicals, created and produced water pageants and, with the advent of radio in the 1920s, put his message on the air. The water pageants illustrated very well the Commodore's philosophy of teaching, which was to "entertain the public hugely while educating them gently." Under Longfellow's guidance, a pleasurable activity for participants and spectators alike became a solid educational experience.

He was always the cheerful crusader, the self-styled "amiable whale," the man whose mission was to lure Americans to the water, to teach them how to be at home in it, how to have fun in it and how not to drown.

"Water is a good friend or a deadly enemy," the Commodore often told his pupils. "After you have been properly introduced to it, keep on good terms with it. Don't slap it; try hugging it—an armful at a time!"

From 1914 until his retirement and then death 3 months later on March 18, 1947, Longfellow worked with intense devotion and great enthusiasm in the nationwide water safety program of the Red Cross. The results of his efforts were astonishing. The Commodore saw the nation's drowning rate cut dramatically—from 8.8 people per 100,000 in 1914 to 4.8 in 1947. He also wit-

TABLE 1-1 Drowning Rates (per 100,000 population)

YEAR	RATE
1903	11.4
1910	9.4
1914	8.8
1920	5.7
1930	6.1
1940	4.7
1947	4.8
1950	4.1
1960	3.6
1970	3.9
1980	3.1
1990	1.9
2000	1.3

Source: National Safety Council

preventing serious injuries and loss of life by promoting aquatic safety.

Recreational Swimming

Swimming for recreation has become tremendously popular since late in the nineteenth century. The first municipal pool in the United States was built in Brookline, Massachusetts, in 1887. Soon after that, New York City built public facilities, then called "baths." In the 1920s, the first boom for swimming pools occurred, with several thousand pools built in this country. At the same time there was a great rise in "estate pools," as residential pools were first called. Construction of all types of swimming pools has not slowed since and shows little sign of ending.

Today, pools are everywhere. Most hotels and motels, private associations, apartment buildings and condominiums, schools, universities and municipalities have pools. Water theme parks with rides, fountains,

slides and artificial waves attract millions of participants each year. Most swimmers use pools, although swimming in oceans, lakes, rivers, canals and quarries continues to be popular.

Just as the number of places for swimming has increased, so have the kinds of activities people enjoy in and on the water. Boating and water skiing, snorkeling and scuba diving, surfing and sailboarding, fishing and an unlimited number of games—from tag to water polo—are all increasingly popular. The variety of relaxing water pastimes, such as hot tubs, saunas and whirlpools located at swimming facilities or at residences, also are growing in popularity.

Recreational swimming has great social value. Family and neighborhood ties are strengthened by weekends at the beach, vacations by mountain lakes, pool parties and just "having the neighbor kids over to use the pool" (Fig. 1-5).

nessed a tremendous upsurge in the popularity of swimming, boating and other water activities. It reached the point where an estimated 80 million Americans were participating in some form of aquatic recreation. Thanks to the dedication and untiring efforts of those who followed his example and continued his work, by 2000 the drowning rate dropped further, to 1.3 per 100,000 (Table 1-1).

The Commodore's efforts, enthusiasm and foresight are carried forward now by his successors, who face the never-ending challenge of

▶ FIG. 1-5

Sutro Baths

The increased popularity of swimming and diving in the early 1900s led to construction of water recreation facilities. The Fleishhacker Pool in San Francisco was the world's largest outdoor swimming pool. It was 1,000 feet long, 90 feet wide and contained 800,000 gallons of water. The 450-foot bathhouse was designed in Italian Renaissance style.

In 1896, San Francisco Mayor Adolf Sutro opened a series of private swimming pools called Sutro Baths. The large, glass-roofed building had seven swimming pools with varying water temperatures, a skating rink, several restaurants and a museum. The pool shells were 499.5 feet long and 254 feet wide and contained 1,804,962 gallons of crystal clear water. Equipment included 9 diving boards, 7 slides, 3 trapezes, 30 swinging rings, a raft and several high diving platforms. The bathhouse had 517 private dressing rooms. There were 7,400 seats for water shows. The Sutro Baths were said to be the largest glass-roofed building in the world. The admission price was 50 cents to swim or 10 cents to watch from the observation deck. The Sutro Baths were closed in 1966.

Fitness and Aerobics

The therapeutic power of water has long been recognized. Ancient cultures, such as Greece and Rome, had their "baths." The Romans wrote that "health comes from water" on the walls of their public facilities. Natural mineral springs and hot springs have always been popular sites for resorts.

In our own time, the importance of aerobic exercise and the advantages of exercising in water are well known. Water exercise leads to less stress on and fewer injuries to tendons and joints (Fig. 1-6). Research on conditioning and aerobics in the 1960s revolutionized the world of water and most other sports.

The emphasis changed to cardiovascular conditioning rather than simply developing muscles. Physical fitness now focuses on heart rate, progressive resistance, overload, metabolism and other aspects of fitness. Chapter 8 discusses fitness swimming and aquatic exercise in detail.

Aquatics in the Military

Today, swimming is an integral part of the United States and foreign armed forces. Entry-level swim skills are required by most services, and advanced swimming and aquatic skills are taught to personnel in special forces, aviation, rescue and diving specialties.

◀ FIG. 1-6

The Development of Modern Competitive Strokes

Although people have been swimming since ancient times, swimming strokes have been greatly refined in the past 100 years. Competitive swimming—notably the modern Olympic Games, which began in Athens, Greece, in 1896—increased interest in certain strokes. Scientific stroke analysis has helped produce new and modified strokes, greater speeds and a better understanding of propulsion through the water.

Research and Training Techniques

Unlike walking and other locomotor activities, swimming is a less natural activity for the human body because it takes place in the water. A standing position on land does not translate easily to a horizontal swimming position. People throughout history have experimented with different ways to swim better. Our ability to use a variety of swimming techniques is due in part to the flexibility and range of motion allowed by the ball-and-socket joints of our shoulders and hips.

Early swimmers experimented by trial and error and watched others. In 1928, David Armbruster first filmed swimmers under water to study strokes (Fig. 1-7). The Japanese also photographed and studied world-class athletes, using their research to produce a swim team that dominated the 1932 Olympic Games. This marked the beginning of research into stroke mechanics.

At the same time, others advanced the role of conditioning. The 1956 Olympic Games in Melbourne, Australia, showed the clear value of conditioning. The host team for those Games had fantastic success, due in large part to their training program, not their stroke technique. American swimming coaches began adopting training methods like those used by track coaches to help runners break the 4-minute mile.

Current research focuses on the forces that act on a body moving through the water. The main points of this science, hydrodynamics, are presented in Chapter 2. Dr. James Counsilman, Charles Silvia and Dr. Ernest Maglischo, among others, have revolutionized stroke mechanics with their pioneering and painstaking work.

The increased understanding of stroke mechanics has helped researchers and coaches improve swimmers' times in competition. American swim researchers included C. H. McCloy and Robert Kiphuth,

▼ Fig. 1-7

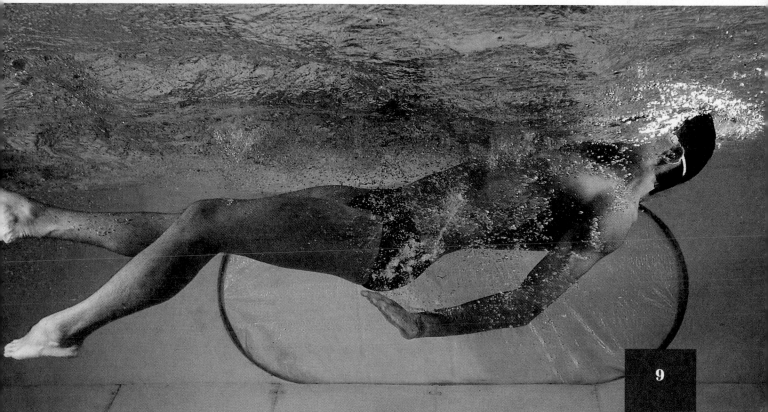

who was awarded the Medal of Freedom, the United States' highest civilian award, by President Johnson in 1963. They and others gave swimmers new techniques, drills and training methods based on these scientific principles.

Front Crawl

The inefficiency of the trudgen kick led Australian Richard Cavill to try new methods of kicking. He used a stroke that he observed natives of the Solomon Islands using, which combined an up-and-down kick with an alternating overarm stroke. He used the new stroke in 1902 at the International Championships to set a new world record (100 yards in 58.4 seconds). The stroke he used became known as the "Australian crawl."

The Australian men's swimming team introduced a front crawl stroke that took advantage of body roll at the 1956 Olympic Games in Melbourne. This roll increased speed through the water and soon became common.

Backstroke

Before 1900, swimming on the back was not done in competition. Because the breaststroke was still the stroke of choice, the recreational backstroke was done like an upside-down breaststroke. As the front crawl became popular, swimmers tried the alternating overarm style on the back. Combined with a flutter kick, this created a

fast and efficient way to swim on the back. In 1912, the backstroke became a competitive event. The continued effort to gain greater speed, along with studying and experimenting with the stroke, led to the back crawl as we know it today.

Breaststroke and Butterfly

Swimming research has helped the breaststroke evolve. Other strokes are faster, but the breaststroke is still used in competitive events. Until the 1950s, the breaststroke was the only stroke with a defined style. The underwater recovery of both arms and legs in the breaststroke is a natural barrier to speed.

Early Champions

The front crawl was further changed by "Duke" Kahanamoku, a Hawaiian, who learned the stroke by watching old Hawaiian swimmers (top right). His sprint crawl stroke was characterized by a truly vertical six-beat flutter kick. The Duke was an Olympic record holder and an Olympic gold medal winner for the 100-yard front crawl in both the 1912 and 1920 games.

Johnny Weissmuller, who portrayed Tarzan in the movies, also influenced the evolution of the front crawl stroke (right). He dominated sprint swimming in the period including the 1924 and 1928 Olympic Games. In 1927, Weissmuller swam 100 yards in 51 seconds flat over a 25-yard course, setting a record that existed for

almost two decades. His style featured a strong kick, which allowed the chest and shoulders to ride higher; a rotating of the head for inhalation that was coordinated with the action of the arms; and an underwater arm action in which the elbow was bent slightly for greater leverage.

The popularity of Duke Kahanamoku, Johnny Weissmuller and Buster Crabbe, another Olympic swimming champion (in 1932), who succeeded Weissmuller as Tarzan in the movies, contributed greatly to the popularity of the front crawl (bottom right). Their popularity and records led to the front crawl becoming the stroke most commonly taught to beginners in North America.

In 1934, however, David Armbruster, coach at the University of Iowa, devised a simultaneous overarm recovery out of the water. This "butterfly" arm action gave more speed but required greater training and conditioning. Then in 1935, Jack Sieg, a University of Iowa swimmer, developed the skill of swimming on his side and beating his legs in unison like a fish's tail. He then developed the leg action face down. Armbruster and Sieg combined the butterfly arm action with this leg action and learned to coordinate the two efficiently. With two kicks to each butterfly arm action, Sieg swam 100 yards in 1:00.2. This kick was named the dolphin fishtail kick (Fig. 1-8).

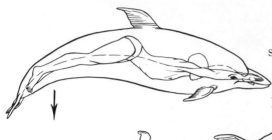

▲ Fig. 1-8

Even though the butterfly breast-stroke, as it was called, was faster than the breaststroke, the dolphin fishtail kick was declared a violation of competitive rules. For the next 20 years, champion breaststrokers used an out-of-water arm recovery with a shortened breaststroke kick. In the late 1950s, the butterfly stroke with the dolphin kick was legalized as a separate stroke for competition. Many swimmers say the "wiggle" is the key to the stroke and that a swimmer who undulates through the water naturally can more easily perform the butterfly.

Competitive Swimming

As competitive swimmers and coaches refine strokes or make changes, one of the best ways to see if the new stroke is an improvement is to use it in competition. This is why so much attention is paid to speed and endurance records.

Variety of Events

The first modern Olympic Games had only four swimming events, three of them freestyle. The second Olympics in Paris in 1900 included three unusual swimming events. One used an obstacle course; another was a test of underwater

swimming endurance; the third was a 4,000-meter event, the longest competitive swimming event ever. None of the three was ever used in the Olympics again.

From the humble beginning with four swimming events, the Olympics have expanded to 32 swimming races, 16 for men and 16 for women.

Women in Competitive Swimming

For a variety of reasons, women were excluded from swimming in the first several Olympic Games. In 1896, women could not participate because the developer of the modern games, Pierre de Coubertin, held firmly to the assumption, common in the Victorian era, that women were too frail to engage in competitive sports. In 1900, the committee organizing the Paris games allowed women to participate in golf and tennis, because these were popular sports in Europe. (Until the International Olympic Committee was formed, events at Olympic Games were chosen by the host committee).

The 1904 games in St. Louis were dominated by the President of the Amateur Athletic Union (AAU), James E. Sullivan, who allowed women to participate only in archery, a demonstration sport. Women's swimming made its debut in the 1912 games at the prompting of the group that later became the International Olympic Committee. As early as 1914 in this country, the Women's Swimming Association of New York, another outgrowth of the U.S. Volunteer Life Saving Corps

▲ Fig. 1-9

(Fig. 1-9), provided the first opportunity for women to train for national and international competition.

Competitive Swimming Today

Today, swimmers can engage in competitive swimming in various settings, usually related to age, school affiliation or ability. Many organizations promote and conduct swimming events. One or more of the organizations described below offer programs that may meet most swimmers' needs. Some organizations are more prominent in certain geographical regions than others.

USA Swimming

USA Swimming, Inc., is the national governing body for amateur competitive swimming in the United States.

United States Swimming was founded in 1980, based on the passage in 1978 of the Amateur Sports Act, which specified that all Olympic sports would be administered independently. Before this act, United States Swimming was the Competitive Swimming Committee of the Amateur Athletic Union (AAU). In 1998, United States Swimming officially changed its name to USA Swimming.

As the national governing body, USA Swimming conducts and administers competitive swimming in the United States. USA Swimming makes rules, implements policies and procedures, conducts national championships, gives out safety and sports medicine information and selects athletes to represent the United States in international competition. USA Swimming is organized on three levels:

▶ *International.* The international federation for amateur aquatic sports is the Federation Internationale de Natation Amateur (FINA). USA Swimming is affiliated with FINA through United States Aquatic Sports (USAS), which regulates the four aquatic sports of swimming, synchronized swimming, diving and water polo.
▶ *National.* USA Swimming is a member of the United States Olympic Committee (USOC) and has voting representation in the USOC House of Delegates.
▶ *Local.* Within the United States, USA Swimming is divided into Local Swimming Committees (LSCs), each administering USA Swimming activities of local clubs in a specific geographical area. Each LSC has its own bylaws for local operations.

USA Swimming has the following classifications for competitions:

▶ Senior—for all registered swimmers
▶ Junior—for all registered swimmers 18 years of age and younger
▶ Age Group/Junior Olympic—for all registered swimmers grouped by ages 10 and under, 11–12, 13–14 and either 15–16 and 17–18 or 15–18. An 8-and-under age group competition may be conducted.
▶ Post Age Group—for all registered swimmers older than 18 years of age whom an LSC elects to include in its age group program
▶ Masters—for all swimmers 19 years of age and older who register with United States Masters Swimming
▶ Long Distance—for all registered swimmers

Events in a Swim Meet

The following table gives typical swimming events grouped by age for swimmers up to age 18. The actual events held in a meet depend on the sponsoring organization.

AGE	DISTANCE*	STROKE
10 and under	50	Freestyle
	100	Freestyle
	100	Individual medley
	50	Backstroke
	50	Breaststroke
	50	Butterfly
	200	Freestyle relay
	200	Medley relay
11–12	50	Freestyle
	100	Freestyle
	200	Individual medley
	50	Backstroke
	50	Breaststroke
	50	Butterfly
	200	Freestyle relay
	200	Medley relay
13–14	50	Freestyle
	100	Freestyle
	200	Freestyle
	200	Individual medley
	100	Backstroke
	100	Breaststroke
	100	Butterfly
	400	Freestyle relay
	400	Medley relay
15–16	50	Freestyle
	100	Freestyle
	200	Freestyle
	200	Individual medley
	100	Backstroke
	100	Breaststroke
	100	Butterfly
	400	Freestyle relay
	400	Medley relay
17–18	50	Freestyle
	100	Freestyle
	200	Freestyle
	200	Individual medley
	400	Individual medley
	100	Backstroke
	100	Breaststroke
	100	Butterfly
	400	Freestyle relay
	400	Medley relay

*May be yards or meters.

▲ FIG. 1-10

In USA Swimming, as in other organizations that promote competitive swimming, athletes learn about perseverance and determination, goal setting, achievement, dedication, loyalty and commitment. Each swimmer is a valuable part of the team, and swimmers learn cooperation with teammates and adults. Above all, they learn that competitive swimming is fun (Fig. 1-10).

United States Masters Swimming

United States Masters Swimming (USMS) is an umbrella organization with responsibility and authority over the Masters Swimming Program in the United States. Through its local Masters Swimming Committees and swim clubs, USMS offers competitive swimming to swimmers 19 years of age and older.

Competitions are organized by age groups of 5-year spans (and one 6-year span) (19–24, 25–29, 30–34 and so on, up to 95 and over). Events include 50, 100, 200, 500, 1,000 and 1,650 freestyle (400, 800 and 1,500 in meters); 50, 100 and 200 backstroke, breaststroke and butterfly; and 100, 200 and 400 individual medley (an event in which each quarter of the total distance is swum using a different stroke in a prescribed order—butterfly, backstroke, breaststroke, freestyle). There are also freestyle and medley relays for men, women and mixed teams. In a medley relay, each member of a four-member team swims one quarter of the total distance and then is relieved by a teammate. Open-water swims are held in many locations in the summer, ranging from 1 to 10 miles.

Masters Swimming's credo is fun, fitness and competition (Fig. 1-11). Masters swimmers enjoy the benefits of swimming with an organized group, participating in structured workouts and developing friendships with other adult swimmers. Members participate in a wide range of activities from noncompetitive lap swimming to international competition. Socializing at meets is another reason that Masters Swimming is popular.

Coaching and officiating opportunities, paid and volunteer, are available at all levels of USMS. Contact a local Masters Swimming club or USMS for details.

YMCA of the USA Competitive Swimming and Masters Swimming

YMCA Competitive Swimming trains individuals of all ages to compete in YMCA programs that may lead to cluster, field and national championships (Fig. 1-12). YMCA age group competition is organized in four age groups: 10 and under, 12 and under, 14 and under and senior. Competition is organized at four levels:

▶ Interassociation meets
▶ Cluster, league and district championships
▶ State or field championships
▶ National championships

▼ FIG. 1-11

▲ FIG. 1-12

YMCA Masters Swimming is an age-grouped competitive program for adults, starting at age 20. Groups are divided by 5-year spans 20–24, 25–29, 30–34 and so on, with no top age limit. Some YMCAs also sponsor competitive teams in springboard diving and synchronized swimming. YMCAs may register with U.S. Masters Swimming and represent the YMCA in regional and national competition.

National Collegiate Athletic Association

The National Collegiate Athletic Association (NCAA) is the organization for U.S. colleges and universities to speak and act on athletic matters at the national level. The NCAA is also the national athletics accrediting agency for collegiate competition.

Founded in 1905 when 13 schools formed the Intercollegiate Athletic Association of the United States, the NCAA has grown to more than 1,000 member institutions. The NCAA enacts legislation on nationwide issues, represents intercollegiate athletics before state and federal governments, compiles and distributes statistics, writes and interprets rules in 12 sports, conducts research on athletics problems and promotes and participates in international sports planning and competition (in part through membership in the U.S. Olympic Committee).

The NCAA sponsors the following national championships:

▶ Division I Men's Swimming and Diving Championships
▶ Division I Women's Swimming and Diving Championships
▶ Division II Men's Swimming and Diving Championships
▶ Division II Women's Swimming and Diving Championships
▶ Division III Men's Swimming and Diving Championships
▶ Division III Women's Swimming and Diving Championships

The National Junior College Athletic Association

The National Junior College Athletic Association (NJCAA) was founded in 1937 to promote and supervise a national program of junior college sports and activities consistent with the educational objectives of junior colleges. The NJCAA interprets rules, sets standards for eligibility, promotes academics through the Academy All-American and Distinguished Academic All-American programs, publishes a monthly magazine, provides weekly polls and distributes sport guides.

The NJCAA first sponsored track and field events, which drew participants only from California schools. Today, there are member institutions throughout the United States, ranging in enrollment size from 500 to 25,000 students. The NJCAA sponsors 50 national championships, 25 for men and 25 for women. At the Men's and Women's National Swimming and Diving Championships each year, the NJCAA presents All-American Awards, Swimmer/Diver of the Year Award and Swimming/Diving Coach of the Year Award.

The National Federation of State High School Associations

The National Federation of State High School Associations consists of the high school athletic associations of the 50 states and the District of Columbia. Also affiliated are 10 Canadian provinces, the Bermuda School Sports Federation, the Guam Interscholastic Activities Association, the Philippine Secondary School Athletic Association, the St. Croix Interscholastic Athletic Association and the St. Thomas–St. John Interscholastic Athletic Association.

The federation began in Illinois in 1920 and is a service and regulatory organization for its members. It provides central record keeping, publishes rule books and a journal and conducts conferences. It oversees more than 30 interscholastic sports and lists swimming and diving among the 10 most popular sports (Fig. 1-13). Its goal is to promote the educational value of interscholastic sports.

▼ FIG. 1-13

Local Options

Many national caliber swimmers started as "summer" swimmers. As their love of the sport grew, they sought out more challenging teams. Finding a local competitive team to join is usually easy. The lifeguard at the local pool can often provide information. Local swim clubs and public recreation departments often sponsor teams or rent space to teams. Many locations have outdoor pools with seasonal teams that welcome beginning competitors. Leagues group swimmers by skill level and often provide instruction.

Phil Cole / ALLSPORT

▲ Fig. 1-14

Competition for People with Disabilities

Swimming competition for people with disabilities has a long history. In 1924, the Comite International des Sports des Sourds (CISS [the International Committee for Sports for the Deaf]) held the first Summer World Games for men and women who were deaf. Athletes with cognitive disabilities first joined in international swimming competition in 1968, with the International Summer Special Olympics. At the 2003 Special Olympic World Games, more than 600 athletes participated in aquatic events (Fig. 1-14).

In 1948, Sir Ludwig Guttmann organized a sports competition in Stoke Mandeville, England, involving World War II veterans with spinal cord injuries. Four years later, competitors from Holland joined the games and the international movement, now known as the Paralympics, was born. Olympic-style games for athletes with a disability

were organized for the first time in Rome in 1960. In the 1960 Games, there were nine swimming events each for men and women.

Today, the Paralympics are elite sport events for athletes from 14 different disability groups—10 for functional disabilities, 3 for visual disabilities and 1 for cognitive disabilities. They emphasize the participants' athletic abilities rather than their disabilities. The number of athletes participating in Summer Paralympic Games increased from 400 athletes in Rome in 1960 to 3,843 in Sydney in 2000. In Sydney, a record 122 countries (123 delegations including independent athletes from East Timor) participated at the Paralympics, making this the largest Games in Paralympic history. In Sydney, there were 16 swimming events each for men and women.

For the first time at the FINA World Swimming Championships, exhibition events were held for athletes with disabilities. In 2003 in Barcelona, Spain, 44 of International Paralympics Committee Swimming's top athletes demonstrated to spectators that swimmers with disabilities can compete at an elite level.

Triathlon

Since the first known swim-bike-run triathlon was held in San Diego in 1974, the sport has grown tremendously. An estimated 200,000 to 300,000 active triathletes in the United States now compete regularly. The triathlon became an Olympic sport in the 2000 Olympic Summer Games in Sydney, Australia. This sport has encouraged cross-training and led to technological improvements in clothing and equipment.

▲ FIG. 1-15

Participants from age 15 to over 70 compete in 5-year age groups at regional, zone and national levels. Some triathlons are team efforts. For beginners, completing the course is seen as a tremendous personal achievement (Fig. 1-15). Fitness enthusiasts engage in the sport to gain the benefits of cross-training. Some career triathletes compete as often as 25 times a year.

Part of the appeal of the triathlon is its variety. Doing three types of aerobic exercise can be both challenging and rewarding. Different sports use different muscle groups. Therefore, training for and compet- ing in a triathlon can lead to greater overall fitness. Moreover, proficiency in one sport can make up for some weaknesses in another.

Most triathlons with a swimming component are held in open water (ocean, bay, tidal river or lake). Salt water gives more buoyancy, but ocean waves and currents in bays or rivers can be a problem. Fresh water is easier on the taste buds but gives less buoyancy, and some muddy or grassy lake bottoms can be unpleasant.

USA Triathlon

USA Triathlon is the national governing body for the multi-sport disciplines of triathlon, duathlon, aquathlon and winter triathlon in the United States. USA Triathlon is a member federation of the U.S. Olympic Committee and the International Triathlon Union. USA Triathlon's membership is comprised of athletes of all ages, coaches, officials, parents and fans striving together to strengthen multi-sport. USA Triathlon recognizes four distance categories:

▶ *Sprint.* These events vary greatly, depending on local organizers, and are often called training triathlons. The national championship event is a 0.5-mile swim, 13.5-mile bike race and 3-mile run.

▶ *International and Olympic.* This category, also called "short course," uses the distances proposed for an Olympic event: 1.5-kilometer swim, 40-kilometer bike race, and 10-kilometer run.

▶ *Long course.* With a 1.2-mile swim, 56-mile bike race and 13.1-mile run, this category is half the ultra distance.

▶ *Ultra.* This category includes the world-famous Ironman race, first held in Hawaii, comprising a 2.4-mile swim, a 112-mile bike race and a full 26.2-mile marathon.

More than 2,000 triathlons are held in the United States each year. Three quarters are in the International distance category.

Open-Water Swimming

Open-water swimming is defined as any competition that takes place in rivers, lakes or oceans. The first modern Olympic Games in Athens, held in 1896, included open-water swimming events. Hungary's Alfred Hajos won the 1,200-meter freestyle at those Games by being the first swimmer to reach shore after a boat had left everyone in the waters of the Mediterranean. In early Olympic Games, swimming competitions were held in open water and included unusual events such as underwater swimming (1900), 200-meter obstacle swimming (1900) and plunge for distance (1904). The swimming venues ranged from the Bay of Zea in 1896 to Paris's River Seine in 1900 to a little lake in St. Louis in 1904. A swimming pool was first used for the 1908 Olympic Games, where a 100-meter pool was constructed inside the track.

In 1986, FINA, the world governing body of swimming, officially recognized open-water swimming. The first official competition was staged at the 1991 World Swimming Championships in Perth, Australia. Open-water swimming is roughly divided into long-distance swimming, with distances of less than 25 kilometers, and marathon swimming, with distances of more than 25 kilometers. Typically, events are held for both men and women at distances of 5, 10 and 25 kilometers.

Competitive Diving

People may have been diving throughout history, but written reports date from 1871 when divers plunged from London Bridge and other high places. Springboard diving began as an Olympic event in the 1904 Games in St. Louis. American Jim Sheldon won gold medals in the

1-meter and 3-meter events. An event called distance plunging also was held. Each diver performed a racing dive into the pool, followed by a prone glide for distance. W. E. Dickey won the gold with a plunge of 62 feet, 6 inches in the only Olympics that included this event.

Men's platform diving (10 meters) began in the 1908 games in London, and women's diving events started in the next two Olympic Games— platform diving in 1912 and springboard diving in 1920. The Olympic Games were not held in 1916 because of World War I.

Diving grew out of the gymnastic movement in Germany and Sweden. As a result, athletes from these countries won most of the early competitions. However, the United States has dominated Olympic diving competition since 1920, when Americans won gold medals in three events.

Eight U.S. divers have won 20 Olympic gold medals, each winning at least two. Al White (1924), Pete Desjardins (1928) and Victoria Draves (1948) won double gold medals in springboard and platform events at the same Olympics. In the platform event, Dorothy (Poynton) Hill (1932 and 1936), Sammy Lee (1948 and 1952) and Bob Webster (1960 and 1964) won gold medals in back-to-back Olympic Games. Most impressive, however, were Pat McCormick (1952 and 1956) and Greg Louganis (1984 and 1988) (Fig. 1-16) who were the only divers to sweep gold medals at consecutive Olympics.

Several coaches also have helped the United States achieve supremacy in diving. Ernst Bransten is known as "the father of diving in the United States." He emigrated from Sweden just before 1920, bringing a thorough knowledge of diving fundamentals and revolutionary ideas for developing divers. One notable contribution was the construction of a "sand pit," a diving board mounted

Alvin Chung / ALLSPORT

▲ Fig. 1-16

over sand (Fig. 1-17). This allows divers to practice basic diving movements, such as approach and takeoff, more efficiently.

Mike Peppe, the swimming and diving coach at Ohio State University from 1931 to 1963, had a phenomenal coaching record. From 1938 on, his divers won 150 of 200 possible titles in the Big Ten Conference of the NCAA and the AAU. In two years (1947 and 1956), Peppe's divers placed 1-2-3-4 in both the 1-meter and 3-meter springboard events at the NCAA championships. His pupils did equally well in Olympic competition, winning two gold, five silver and three bronze medals from 1948 through 1960.

Peppe treated his divers and swimmers with equal importance and thus led other schools to emphasize diving more—just so they could compete with his teams. His influence led to improved diving facilities, more practice time, greater respect for the sport and the birth of the diving coach. For this reason, Peppe might be designated the "father of collegiate diving in the United States."

Before 1960, college diving was strictly for men. Women trained at private clubs, such as the Dick Smith Swim Gym in Phoenix, Arizona. In the Big Ten Conference, two coaches, Hobie Billingsley at Indiana University and Dick Kimball at the University of Michigan, opened the door for women in varsity diving programs.

▲ Fig. 1-18

Billingsley also contributed to diving by applying the principles of physics. He analyzed dives in terms of Newton's laws of motion. One of the divers he coached, Cynthia Potter, is a 28-time U.S. champion.

Kimball was the foremost proponent of the overhead-mounted safety belt system for spotting divers over the trampoline and dry board (Fig. 1-18). This training aid allows the diver to repeat a dive many times in a short period.

Ron O'Brien followed in Peppe's footsteps at Ohio State University. He won the Mike Peppe Award for the outstanding Senior Diving Coach in the United States every year from 1979 to 1988. As the list of competitive dives has evolved to add a third somersault and twist, O'Brien has been an advocate of maintaining aesthetic qualities of the sport. The stylized performance of his Olympic gold

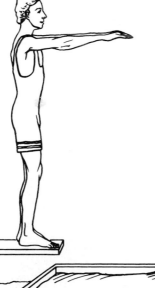

► Fig. 1-17

Development of The Diving Board

Important in diving history is the evolution of the diving board. Changes improved safety and allowed for greater variety and difficulty in dives. Before the mid-1940s, diving boards were wood planks covered with cocoa matting to prevent slipping. They were mounted on a fixed fulcrum and sloped slightly upward.

Since then, diving boards have become lighter and thinner and are made of an aluminum alloy with a nonskid surface. These are mounted level on movable fulcrums, which allow divers to achieve a greater height. Thus, divers can more easily complete rotations and twists and travel a safe distance from the diving board.

In the early days, there were only 14 platforms and 20 springboard dives. Competitors and coaches have now assembled about 90 different dives from the basic "ingredients": forward, backward, reverse or inward takeoffs; handstands and twists; somersaults and reverse dives—performed in a straight, pike, tuck or free positions from 1-meter or 3-meter diving boards or from platforms at various heights. Even the difficulty of dives has changed greatly. In 1904, a double somersault from a platform was considered dangerous; today, world-class divers routinely perform the reverse three-and-one-half somersault. What lies in store for tomorrow is anyone's guess, but millions of diving fans and enthusiasts are watching eagerly to see.

medalists Jennifer Chandler (springboard, 1976) and Greg Louganis (double gold medals, 1984 and 1988) defined the standard for grace.

Competitive Diving Today

Competitive diving has grown rapidly in the past few years. Dives once considered difficult even on the 3-meter board are now done regularly on the 1-meter board. This progress results in part from technological advances in the way diving boards and stands are manufactured. Training has also improved with the use of trampolines, dry-land diving facilities with overhead spotting belts, individualized weight training and flexibility programs and improved coaching.

The unification of rules through the concerted efforts of United States Diving, the NCAA and FINA has standardized requirements and equipment. As a result, training has also been standardized.

Synchronized Diving

Once only used in aquacades and diving shows, synchronized diving (or synchro diving) has become one of the most popular diving events in the world. In synchro diving, two divers of the same gender perform the same or complementary dives from the same level board. On the platform, divers take off from opposite sides of the platform. On the springboard, divers take off from adjacent boards. The sport was introduced internationally at the 1995 FINA World Cup and debuted as a full-medal sport at the 2000 Olympic Games with four events: men's synchro 3-meter, men's synchro platform, women's synchro 3-meter and women's synchro platform.

United States Diving

United States Diving, Inc., is the national governing body of diving. United States Diving is a member of United States Aquatic Sports, Inc.,

the U.S. member of FINA. United States Diving—also known as USA Diving—is organized through local diving associations (LDAs) encompassing clubs nationwide. United States Diving is organized into three programs:

- ▶ Junior Olympic—provides a developmental diving and physical fitness program for the youth of the United States and teaches fundamentals of diving and benefits of participation in competitions
- ▶ Senior—further develops and identifies U.S. divers of national and international caliber to compete in National Championships, Olympic Games, World Championships, Pan American Games and other national and international competition
- ▶ Masters—provides a continuing physical fitness program for diving enthusiasts 21 years of age and older who no longer compete in the Senior program

▲ FIG. 1-19

The mission of United States Diving, Inc., is to conduct and promote the sport of diving in a manner that allows each participant to achieve the peak of excellence afforded by his or her ability, effort, desire and dedication. All divers have the opportunity to realize the poise, maturity, grace and strength inherent in diving and to reach their personal goals (Fig. 1-19). For some, satisfaction comes from knowing they have done their best; for others, it is international recognition. Coaching and officiating opportunities are available at all levels of United States Diving.

The YMCA of the USA, NCAA and National Federation of State High School Associations, which are described in the earlier section on competitive swimming, also promote diving.

Water Polo

Water polo is a team sport that combines soccer and rugby skills and is played in deep water. It requires tremendous stamina and skill. It was made a sport in 1885 by the Swimming Association of Great Britain and became an official Olympic sport in 1908. Today, it is played as recreation and is a popular high school, college and Olympic sport (Fig. 1-20). Even beginners who make their own rules can enjoy themselves and the activity.

Water polo evolved from its "anything goes" reputation of the early years to the skilled, fast-moving sport of today. The old-style game let players take both the ball and each other under water. Makeshift water polo contests were held in Great Britain as far back as the 1860s. The game was first played in open water with boats or rafts as goals. Goal frames were introduced in 1887, and water polo came to the United States in 1888 from England.

Water polo was a demonstration sport in the 1900 Paris Olympics and was officially added to the 1908 London Games. Of the 14 teams in the 1920 Olympics, the Hungarians dominated when they introduced ball passing in the air. Underwater play was still permitted and continued to result in many injuries. The underwater action was less exciting for spectators, and the sport fell out of favor in the United States. Many rule changes and injuries later, surface play returned in the late 1940s. National championships for women began in 1961.

The sport's popularity continues to grow, as ball handling skills and speed-swimming elements make it exciting to watch and challenging to play. Water polo is popular with coaches of swim teams. The sport is used for conditioning early in a season and to provide variety to training later in a season.

▶ FIG. 1-20

USA Water Polo

USA Water Polo, Inc. (USWP) is the national governing body for water polo in the United States. Local clubs compete in matches and may progress to regional and zone competition. Qualifying teams from geographic zones compete in national championships. Teams compete in indoor and outdoor tournaments at the junior and senior levels. Age-group competition is organized as 13 and under, 15 and under and 17 and under, although many teams mix ages. Coed teams and leagues are sanctioned but do not have national competitions.

Synchronized Swimming

Synchronized swimming is a creative sport for swimmers at any level. It may be purely recreational or competitive (Fig. 1-21). Beulah and Henry Gundling, founders of the International Academy of Aquatic Art, deserve much credit for its development. The term synchronized swimming was first used in a water show at the 1933 Chicago World's Fair. Before this, swimmers used floating patterns and transitions with minimal swimming in performances that were called water ballets.

Esther Williams, who was inspired by Eleanor Holmes, popularized synchronized swimming in the movies

Playing Water Polo

A water polo team has seven players who play both offensive and defensive roles, much as in soccer. Players generally specialize in particular positions. Shooters generally do the scoring. Drivers are the quickest swimmers and move continually to receive or block passes. Holemen take position in front of the goal and are key members of the offense. They often are under the most physical attack. The goalie is the only player allowed to use two hands or a closed fist and to stop on or jump from the bottom.

The ball is passed from player to player and thrown into the goal past the defending goalkeeper to score one point. Players, except for the goalie, cannot touch the bottom or sides of the pool and must tread water, swim or kick throughout the game. Players may dribble the ball ahead of them as they swim, using the waves made by their arms and chest to move the ball. Players use a strong rotary kick to rise high in the water to make or receive a pass or block a shot.

Games are 34 minutes long, divided into four 7-minute periods with three 2-minute breaks. Two referees and two goal judges enforce the rules. Major violations include seriously kicking or holding an opposing player and can result in 45-second penalties for the offending player. Minor fouls include deliberate face splashing, play interference or using a clenched fist or two hands to play the ball. Most offensive fouls are penalized with loss of ball possession.

Rectangular goals are set at water level at the ends of a 30- by 20-meter pool. Regulation games are played in a minimum depth of 2 meters. The nonslip rubber ball is slightly smaller than a volleyball and weighs 15 ounces for men. The women's ball is slightly smaller in size and weight. For identification, players wear blue and white numbered caps, and goalies wear a red cap with number 1. The close-fitting cloth caps must have plastic cups built in to protect the ears. Strong players can hurl the ball more than 40 miles an hour, and players without protection could receive ear injuries.

▲ Fig. 1-21

(Fig. 1-22) and teamed with Johnny Weissmuller in the 1940 San Francisco World's Fair Aquacade. In competition, swimmers are judged on intricate skills and synchronization of routines set to music. In January 1991, the United States Synchronized Swimming National Team became the world champions.

The rhythmical water activity is performed in definite patterns in time with music. Duets, trios and teams also perform in synchronization (Fig. 1-23). Competition in synchro, as it is sometimes called, requires both figure and routine events. Routines are judged on technical merit and artistic expression. The combination of scores for figures and routines determines final placement.

The synchronized swimmer learns skills like those of the gymnast and dancer. The sport requires tremendous strength and endurance to give the appearance of graceful, effortless movement through the water.

▼ Fig. 1-22

Archive Photo

▲ Fɪɢ. 1-23

A synchronized swimming routine lasts 3½ to 5 minutes. The swimmer needs the same cardiorespiratory endurance as a middle-distance swimmer. The artistic quality of movement gives the sport great spectator appeal. Like dancers, synchronized swimmers move in specific directions to specific beats with a personal manner of presentation.

United States Synchronized Swimming

United States Synchronized Swimming, Inc. (USSS) is the national governing body of synchronized swimming. USSS was founded in 1979 to promote and support all competitive and noncompetitive levels of the sport. It also selects and trains athletes to represent the United States in international competition.

Registered members, who range in age from 6 to 80, belong to registered clubs. Masters swimming for USSS includes participants who are 20 years old and older, and for international Masters competition, participants are 25 years old and older, based on rules set by FINA. There are clinics, camps and training programs for every level of swimming ability. There is also a training and certification program for coaches.

Three synchro events are recognized internationally: solo (one swimmer), duet (two swimmers) and team (up to eight swimmers). Synchronized swimming premiered at the 1984 Olympic Games in Los Angeles, with Americans Tracie Ruiz and Candy Costie winning the first medals in the duet event. Tracie Ruiz also won the gold medal in the solo event. The

team event debuted in the 1996 Olympic Games in Atlanta—replacing the solo and duet events. The 2000 Olympic Games in Sydney included the team event, as well as the duet event. There are also compulsory figure competitions. USSS competitions also include the trio event (three swimmers) for junior national, age group, U.S. open and collegiate events.

Synchronized swimming combines skill, stamina and teamwork with the flair of music and drama. Coaches, psychologists, physiologists, nutritionists, dance specialists and former champions all contribute their expertise. This sport is increasingly popular with both spectators and participants. Noncompetitors can participate as coaches, volunteers and judges.

Synchronized Swimming

Facilities and Equipment

A large, deep pool is best, but many aspects of synchronized swimming can be taught and enjoyed in any pool. A minimum depth of 8 feet is needed for good vertical descent. Clear water, a light-colored pool bottom and good lighting enhance viewing.

The musical accompaniment may use any type of equipment at poolside. Underwater speakers are critical, and portable underwater speakers can be used in facilities without permanent equipment.

The swimmer's equipment includes a comfortable suit and a nose clip. This clip squeezes the nostrils together to prevent water from entering the nose and sinuses while inverted under water.

Strokes and Figures

The swimmer can modify the basic strokes in endless creative ways to enhance the routine's composition and appeal. Many strong swimmers are attracted to synchronized swimming because of the creative possibilities, which require great strength and excellent swimming skills.

The synchro swimmer uses versions of the front crawl, elementary backstroke, sidestroke, back crawl and breaststroke to move from place to place within the routine. To modify the strokes, various parts of the recovery can be held, accented or modified to fit the music's mood and tempo. Hybrid strokes use parts of different strokes. The routine typically covers all areas of the pool.

The swimmer often adapts strokes in the following ways:

- ▶ The face is kept above the water. Facial expressions are an appealing part of the routine.
- ▶ Arms are carried higher during recoveries.
- ▶ The kick is deeper to avoid splashing.
- ▶ Only the head and arms are above the water.
- ▶ Each phase of the arm stroke is carefully planned and synchronized to the music and the other swimmers.

Figures are movements in the water composed of basic positions, their variations and transitions from one position to another. Basic positions include prone, supine and vertical layouts (a position in which the body is straight), the pike and the tuck.

Sculling is a basic skill developed more highly in synchronized swimming. Sculling provides support and balance for the body and is used for propulsion in figures and strokes. U.S. Synchronized Swimming describes eight basic sculling positions:

- ▶ Back layout position, arms at sides, direction of head
- ▶ Back layout position, arms at sides, direction of feet
- ▶ Back layout position, arms overhead, direction of head
- ▶ Back layout position, arms overhead, direction of feet
- ▶ Front layout position, arms at sides, direction of head
- ▶ Front layout position, arms at sides, direction of feet
- ▶ Front layout position, arms overhead, direction of head
- ▶ Front layout position, arms overhead, direction of feet

The rotary, or eggbeater, kick is used in synchro swimming because it helps the swimmer keep a high vertical position. It leaves the swimmer's hands free to create various movements.

Summary

▲ FIG. 1-24

▲ FIG. 1-25

An estimated 103 million people a year swim for survival, recreation or competition. Interest in swimming and diving continues to grow. Comprehensive facilities, such as the Indiana University/Purdue University Natatorium in Indianapolis, the King County Aquatic Center in Seattle and the Coral Springs Aquatic Complex in Florida (Fig. 1-24), are examples of excellent multifunction aquatic facilities. Public and private facilities also are expanding to accommodate the number and kinds of water activities available. Wave pools and water parks are enjoying a large share of the dollars spent on recreation (Fig. 1-25).

Aquatic research continues worldwide and will help develop swimming and diving skills and techniques in the future. Numerous organizations now govern competitive aquatics. The Federation Internationale de Natation Amateur (FINA [the International Federation of Amateur Swimming]) was founded in 1908 and continues as the world governing body for competitive swimming and diving. Many aquatic organizations support swimming and diving programs throughout the country.

Photo courtesy City of Coral Springs

27

Hydrodynamics

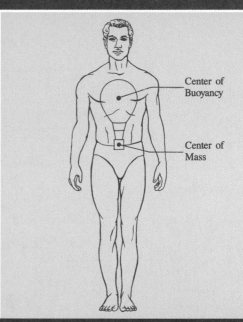

Center of
Buoyancy

Center of
Mass

Chapter 2

One might ask, "Why is it important to know anything about physics to be a good swimmer?" To become a better swimmer, one might simply use trial and error and practice, practice, practice. But good swimmers do not rely on practice alone. They mix practice with a basic knowledge of the science of matter and energy, also known as physics. Combining practice with knowledge allows one to learn something more easily than with trial-and-error practice.

Water density increases resistance to movement and makes inhaling more difficult but makes the body feel lighter in the water than on land. Students must adapt their breathing and movements in the water environment. Instructors should be aware of some basic physical principles and how they affect a swimmer's movement.

Researchers have spent years trying to learn—and continue to study—how the human body moves through the water and find ways to help people gain even a small advantage in swimming. Their study builds on a long history of exploring the world of hydrodynamics, as the physics of fluids is called. In this chapter, main physics principles are related to aquatics and how a person swims.

The more swimmers understand why things happen in the water, the better they will be at what they do in the water or how they teach. This chapter describes principles related to being in and moving through the water. It uses exercises to help one understand and get a "feel" for the principles. It is important to realize that in most cases—whether in the exercises or while moving through the water—more than one physical principle is at work. These exercises are intended mostly for beginners, but even experienced swimmers and divers might want to do them for fun or to review basic principles.

Why Some Things Float

Archimedes' Principle

Imagine three containers of the same size and shape. Each weighs 1 pound and can hold 10 pounds of water. Leave the first container empty, seal it and put it in water. It bobs high in the water, with most of the container above the surface. Now put 8 pounds of pebbles in the second container, seal it and put it in water. This container also floats, but it is low in the water, most of it submerged. Finally, put 11 pounds of pebbles into the third container, seal it and put it in water. It sinks even if it has air inside. If the third container was lifted while it was still under water, however, it would seem to weigh only 2 pounds. (The container weighs 1 pound plus 11 pounds of pebbles minus 10 pounds of displaced water.) The effect shown on all three containers is called Archimedes' principle. Archimedes' principle states that a body in water is buoyed by a force equal to the weight of the water displaced (Fig. 2-1).

Now consider three different people: one with lots of body fat, another with normal body fat and a third with little fat who is heavily muscled. These bodies will act similarly to the containers. Archimedes' principle explains why most people float. Like containers, the body displaces water. This can be seen when someone sits in a bathtub and the water level goes up. (In fact, this is reportedly what Archimedes was doing when he discovered this famous principle.) When the weight of the water that is displaced is more than

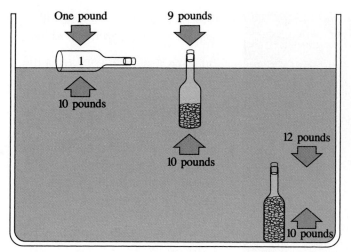

▲ FIG. 2-1

the body weight, flotation occurs. The force of buoyancy in this case is greater than the force of gravity. This is like the first two people in the previous example who will float in water.

Buoyancy

Because of buoyancy, the upward force that the water exerts on an object, many swimmers weigh less than the water displaced and can spend most of their energy producing forward movement. This may be valuable for persons with disabilities who find it hard to move on land or who depend on a wheelchair. They often can get around in water much more easily because the buoyancy of water does most of the work supporting them.

The amount of buoyancy of a body is determined by that body's specific gravity. The first two containers floated at different heights in the water even though buoyancy pushed both up. Even though they both displaced the same amounts of water, they had different weights, or specific gravities. Specific gravity is the ratio of the weight of a body to the weight of the water it displaces.

Pure water has a specific gravity of 1. The specific gravity of other objects is the ratio of their density to that of water. Objects with a specific gravity of less than 1 float; objects with a specific gravity greater than 1 sink. The first container, which weighs 1 pound but displaces 10 pounds of water, has a specific gravity of 0.1 and floats high on the surface. The second container, which

weighs 9 pounds (the container weighs 1 pound plus 8 pounds of pebbles) but displaces 10 pounds of water, has a specific gravity of 0.9 and floats with only a small part (1/10) above the surface. The third container, which weighs 12 pounds (the container weighs 1 pound plus 11 pounds of pebbles) but displaces 10 pounds of water, has a specific gravity of 1.2, so it sinks.

What does all this mean for swimming? For one thing, it explains why some people can float easily while others do not. Specific gravity among humans varies because of different amounts of muscle mass and body fat and bone density. Adipose tissue (body fat) has a specific gravity less than 1.0, thus promoting floating. Bone and muscle tissue have a specific gravity slightly greater than 1.0, causing sinking. Most people tend to float at or near the surface of water, depending on their specific gravity. People with lots of muscle and a heavy bone structure and with little body fat do not float easily and may even sink. Some individuals will not float, even with a full breath of air, while executing a survival float. Those with more body fat will float more easily. Because the average female has 21 to 24 percent body fat and the average male has 15 to 20 percent body fat, females, as a group, tend to float more easily than males.

The old saying that everyone can float is not entirely correct because true floating depends on one's body composition. But inhaling deeply and holding that breath lowers specific gravity, which enhances the ability to float. Wearing a life vest also increases buoyancy because it displaces a lot of water while only minimally increasing weight. Floating postures may have to be augmented with arm sculling and a slight kick to keep at the surface one who tends to sink. Conversely, one who tends to float may need more time to master techniques to stay under water.

To check for buoyancy:

1. Move into a tuck float position (Fig. 2-2).
   - ▶ Lean over and tuck up the knees.
   - ▶ Hold the knees against the chest until the body stops rising or sinking.
2. Recover to a standing position.
3. Return to the tuck float position, but take a big breath of air, hold it and move into a tucked position.
4. Recover to a standing position.

▲ FIG. 2-2

those who are more buoyant will assume a more horizontal position.

A body's specific gravity is not the only factor that affects buoyancy. The water can also make a difference. Salt water has more buoyant force. If one floats easily in fresh water, one will float even higher in salt water. If a person has trouble floating in fresh water, floating in salt water may be easier.

Center of Mass and Center of Buoyancy

It has been demonstrated how the specific gravity of a body affects how high it floats. Two other factors affect the position a floating body takes in the water: the center of mass (sometimes called the center of gravity) and the center of buoyancy.

The center of mass is an imaginary point around which an object's mass is balanced. It is the point at which all forces act on the body as a whole. It also acts like the fulcrum, or pivot

5. Return to the tuck float position, then slowly let air out through the mouth and nose.
6. Recover to a standing position.
7. Move into a back float with the arms at the side.
8. Recover to a standing position.

If the back rose above the surface at step 1, the swimmer normally floats easily. If the back rose during step 3, the swimmer will likely float in a diagonal position. In step 5, the swimmer sinks easily if the body drifted down during the exhale. In step 7,

Density Characteristics

Because water is much heavier than air, breathing takes more effort when a person's chest is surrounded by water. The swimmer must inhale more deeply (attempt to expand the lungs more) to compensate. Efficient air exchange, or "breath control," is an essential but relatively easy skill for swimmers to master. Blowing bubbles, bobbing, floating and rhythmic breathing activities help the student develop good breathing habits.

The pressure on the chest and sinuses increases as a swimmer goes deeper. A swimmer's snorkel is not much longer than 12 inches because it is not effective if it is longer than this. Beyond this depth, the diaphragm muscles can seldom overcome the water pressure around the chest needed to get sufficient breath from a snorkel. Instead, the increased pressure forces air out if one opens the mouth. Scuba equipment overcomes this problem by using a regulator that adjusts the pressure in the lungs as needed. Swimmers most often notice this density effect as ear discomfort when surface diving.

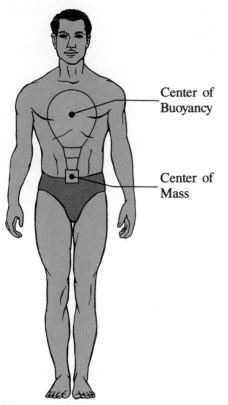

▲ Fig. 2-3

point, of a lever, as the center of rotation of the body. When standing, the center of mass is usually located near the hips. The position of the center of mass actually changes as a person changes the body shape, such as by raising the arms or lifting a leg. Land movements are coordinated by keeping the center of mass balanced over the base of support. This is usually done unconsciously, except when moving in an unfamiliar way or when assuming an awkward or unusual position.

An object's center of buoyancy is a point around which the buoyancy forces are balanced. Because the lungs provide a large buoyant volume of air, the center of buoyancy is usually located in the chest.

The center of mass is below the center of buoyancy. Think of this like a hot-air balloon. The basket (where the center of mass is) always hangs below the center of the balloon (where the center of buoyancy is) (Fig. 2-3).

When a person of average build tries to float horizontally on the back with arms along the sides of the body, the center of mass is nearly level with the center of buoyancy. Many people have more body weight in their legs and hips because of the high proportion of muscle tissue there, so their center of mass is near the hips. Thus when trying to float in a horizontal position, gravity pulls the hips and legs downward while the buoyant force of the water pushes the chest area (center of buoyancy) upward. The body rotates until the center of mass is directly below the center of buoyancy, resulting in a diagonal body position. At that point, the person should float motionless.

A person's natural floating position (vertical, diagonal or horizontal) in the water depends on the position of the center of mass relative to the center of buoyancy. It is important to realize that the center of mass can be altered relative to the center of buoyancy (Fig. 2-4). Shift the center of mass by moving the arms and legs to redistribute weight. This means that someone who floats diagonally when the arms are at the side and the legs are straight out might be able to float horizontally with a few changes. The goal is to move the center of mass toward the center of buoyancy by shortening the leg length and increasing the arm length. As the center of mass moves closer toward the center of buoyancy, a body will float more horizontally.

The following steps demonstrate how to alter the center of mass:

1. Float on the back with the arms at the side.
2. Move the arms above the head.
3. Flex the wrists so the hands are out of water.
4. Bend the knees (Fig. 2-5).

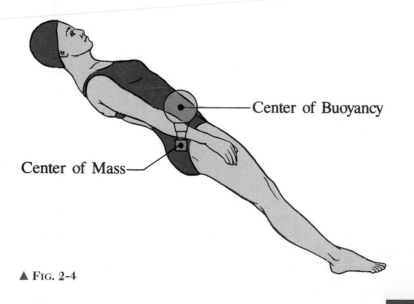

▲ Fig. 2-4

Resistance to Movement in the Water

Because water is denser and more viscous than air, the swimmer experiences much more resistance to movement than on land. This resistance is known as drag. An object's shape, or form, wave action and surface friction contribute to the resistance to its movement through the water.

Form drag is resistance related to a swimmer's shape and body position when moving through the water. A tight, narrow shape experiences less form drag through water than a broad shape because it has to push less water aside. The goal is to reduce the amount of frontal surface area that is pushing through the water and to have a pointed, rather than blunt, front end. Being in a streamlined position in the water reduces the frontal surface area and the resistance caused by the swimmer's form. To attain a streamlined position, swimmers need to narrow

their shape (Fig. 2-6). Smooth, even strokes and arm entries with little splash also help to reduce form drag. Avoiding excessive side-to-side or up-and-down body motion also helps to reduce form drag.

Waves caused by the swimmer's movement through the water produce resistance to swimming. Swimmers can seldom control waves but can reduce resistance caused by waves that they produce

▲ Fig. 2-6

by paying strict attention to skill and technique. Turbulence caused by other swimmers and lots of activity in the water can also cause drag. Lane lines have been designed to reduce turbulence. Wave drag is also reduced, but not completely eliminated, when the swimmer moves under water, for instance, during starts and turns and in underwater swimming.

The body surface of the swimmer causes friction, which produces resistance to movement through the water (frictional drag). This resistance is increased dramatically by wearing loose clothing while swimming. To reduce frictional drag, competitive swimmers wear swimming caps and smooth, tight-fitting swim suits. Some competitors even shave their body hair to reduce friction.

Experience how resistance affects swimming by performing the following activities:

Activity 1

1. Wear a T-shirt while swimming. Notice the slower speed (Fig. 2-7).

Activity 2

1. Stand in chest-deep water. With elbows at the side and palms down, bring hands together and apart several times.
2. Repeat with thumbs up and palms facing.

In step 2 there was a greater resistance, and therefore it was more difficult. This resistance is part of what makes water aerobics effective.

Activity 3

1. Push off under water in streamlined position (arms extended overhead, hands clasped together with arms against ears, legs extended together behind) and glide as far as possible.
2. Push off under water with hands apart and glide as far as possible.
3. Push off under water with arms in streamlined position but with legs apart and glide as far as possible.
4. Push off under water with both arms and legs separated and glide as far as possible.

5. Push off under water in streamlined position, then bring the arms down and straight out, even with shoulders, and separate legs.

Each step in this activity increases drag. In the first step, the swimmer is in the most desirable position to achieve the farthest glide.

Propulsive Forces

Research and analysis of stroke mechanics has shown that swim strokes use a combination of drag and lift forces to move forward. Research and analysis is ongoing, however, to determine which form of propulsion is dominant.

Drag propulsion is based on Isaac Newton's law of action and reaction, which states that for every action there is an equal and opposite reaction. For example, a canoe is moved forward by the backward push of the paddle blade. This motion is called paddle, or drag, propulsion. In swimming, the limbs act as paddles to push water backward, which results in moving the swimmer forward.

Lift forces act in a direction to the perpendicular direction of fluid flow over a curved surface. The principle of laminar flow, discovered by Daniel Bernoulli, has been the foundation of fluid mechanics for more than two centuries. The basic principle is that as a fluid moves around an object, its molecules either speed up or slow down so that they can stay parallel to the molecules on the other side of the object. Molecules

▼ Fɪɢ. 2-7

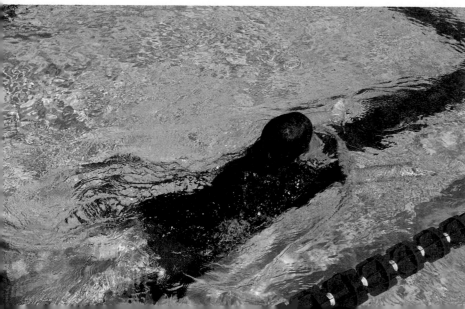

that slow down, because of drag resistance, create pressure against the object, while those that speed up pull the object toward them. Lift forces may also be generated by pushing water backward using intermediate angles of pitch. In swimming, the curved surface is the hand. The effect of this principle is that during the stroking phase of the front crawl, sculling actions of the hand are used.

To experience lift, try the following exercises:

Activity 1

1. Stand in chest-deep water.
2. With palms open and facing downward, scull back and forth (an action similar to leveling sand or waxing a car).
3. Continue to scull and lift the feet off the bottom.

 Fig. 2-8

Activity 2

1. Stand in chest-deep water with one arm extended forward from the elbow and the palm cupped and facing upward. Relax the arm muscles; there will be some buoyancy, causing the hand to drift upward.
2. Sweep the hand several times at different speeds horizontally through the water. Lift forces pull the hand deeper under water (Fig. 2-8).

Newton's Laws of Motion and Swimming Efficiency

Isaac Newton discovered three laws of motion: the law of inertia, the law of acceleration and the law of action and reaction. These are also important for swimming efficiency. Experimenting with these laws can improve swimming, but it is important to see how each works and how they interact to help a person swim.

Law of Inertia

The law of inertia states three things: An external force is needed to get a body at rest to begin moving. An external force is needed to stop a moving body. An external force is needed to change the direction of a moving body. All three parts of this law affect swimming in positive or negative ways.

Understanding the law of inertia can promote efficient swimming. More energy is needed to start a stroke than to keep a stroke moving. It is

more efficient to keep moving than to start and stop repeatedly. This is why continuous strokes, like front crawl and back crawl, are most efficient. Once moving, inertia allows the swimmer to rest during the glide portion of a stroke. But if a glide is too long, the swimmer may slow down so much that it requires more work to perform the next stroke. The second aspect of inertia related to swimming explains that a swimmer who keeps a streamlined position needs less force to keep moving than one who creates more drag.

The third part of the law of inertia is that force is needed to change the direction of a moving body. When swimming, inertia keeps a person going in the direction that he or she is moving. The faster the swimmer is moving, the more force is needed to change the direction. To change the direction of travel, force must be applied to change the direction of the body. If a swimmer is not swimming in the desired direction, incorrect body position or improper stroke mechanics are probably causing forces that overcome the desired direction of travel. It is not uncommon for a beginning swimmer to be unable to swim in a straight line.

Law of Acceleration

The law of acceleration states that the change in speed of an object is dependent on the amount of force applied to it and the direction of that force. This law has relevance for swimming in two ways. First, the more force used in a stroke in the chosen direction, the faster one will swim. Second, swimming is more efficient when one stays in the chosen direction and when all the propulsive force is in that direction. If forces are applied in directions other than that to support forward movement, the motion will change direction and additional sideways force will be needed to get the body motion readjusted back to its intended direction. Likewise, to exert force at an angle away from the intended direction, the body will be pushed somewhat off course and more force is necessary to get back on track.

The following activities help illustrate this law:

Activity 1

1. Forcefully push off the pool wall and move into a streamlined position. Do not kick or stroke with the arms, but allow the body to slow to a stop.
2. Once again, forcefully push off the pool wall and move into a streamlined position. Start swimming the front crawl as fast as possible.

Forcefully pushing off the wall causes a rapid acceleration from a static position to a full glide speed. As the swimmer glides with no kicking or arm action, the glide slows to a stop because of drag resistance. In the second step, when the front crawl is added and maximum speed is reached, the additional acceleration produced by the arms and legs is counterbalanced by the deceleration caused by drag resistance. The net effect is no acceleration, and that is why the swimmer moves with constant speed through the water.

Activity 2

1. Swim the elementary backstroke one length of the pool as fast as possible.
2. Return using only one arm for each stroke (alternate arms, keeping the arm not used at the side).

In the first step, the swimmer is likely able to stay in a straight line and move rather quickly. In the second step, the swimmer is likely moving in a zigzag pattern. As a result, much of the swimmer's application of force becomes focused on adjusting the direction of motion rather than accelerating forward.

Law of Action and Reaction

The law of action and reaction states that every action has an equal and opposite reaction. For example, when a parked vehicle is struck from behind by a second moving vehicle, that second vehicle transfers some of its motion and direction to the stationary vehicle. But the stationary vehicle "pushes back" by transferring some energy and momentum. This might be enough force to stop the moving vehicle.

This law is evident in aquatics. During paddle propulsion swimming strokes, as the arm pushes against the water, the water pushes back, providing resistance, which allows the swimmer to move forward. When diving from a diving board, the board reacts to the force of the feet acting against it, to allow taking off for the dive (Fig. 2-9).

To experience this law, try the following:

▶ Stand at end of diving board. Push down on the end of board (jump). The board will then lift the body into the air.

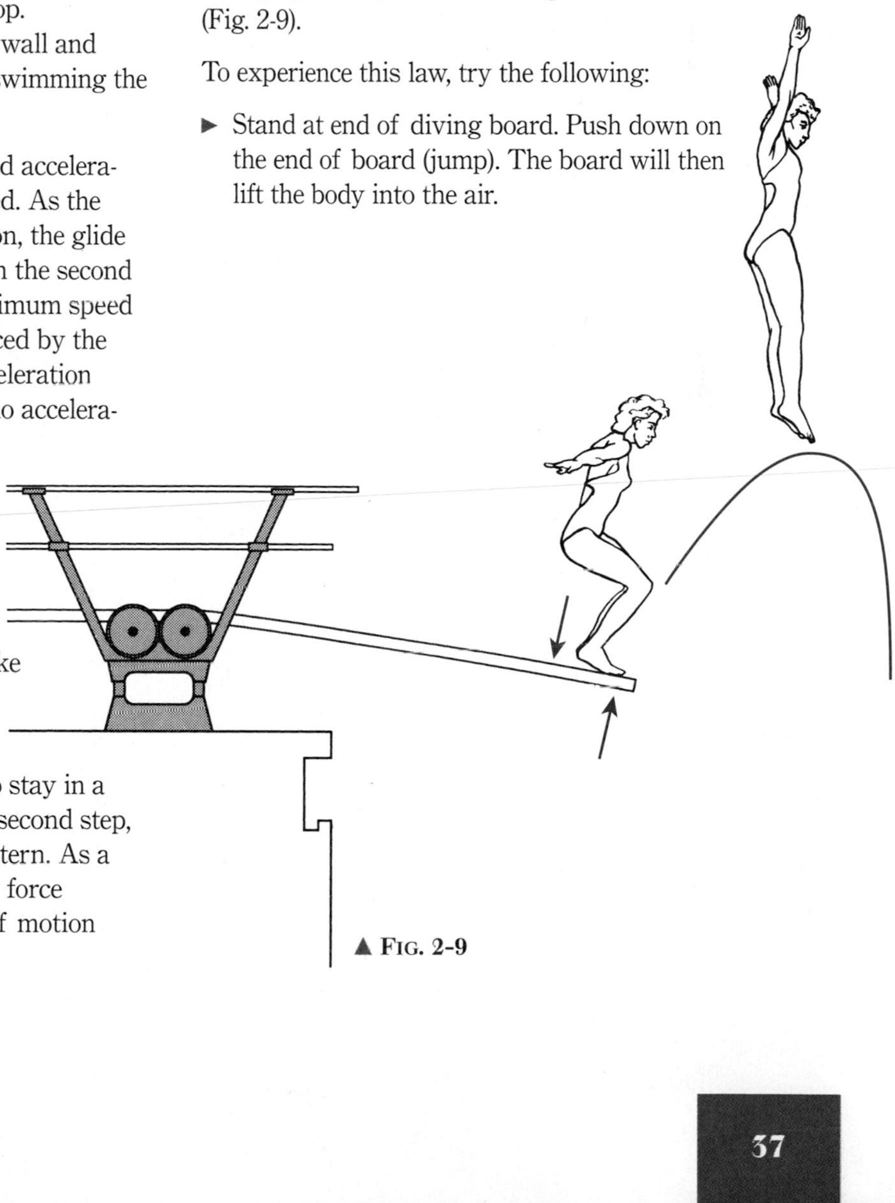

▲ Fig. 2-9

Law of Levers

Applying the law of levers has helped researchers analyze strokes to find the best limb positions and motions for effective swimming. A lever consists of a pivot point and one or two rigid parts called arms. A common example of a lever is a seesaw. The pivot point is in the center, and the arms extend on each side. The weights of two children riding the seesaw are the forces acting on the lever. The law of levers states that the product of the force and force arm is equal to the product of the resistance and resistance arms.

The law of levers relates four components:

▶ Force applied (the weight of the first child)
▶ Resistance encountered (the weight of the second child)
▶ Force arm (the distance between the first child and the pivot point)
▶ Resistance arm (the distance between the second child and the pivot point)

When swimming the crawl stroke, the arm acts as a lever with the shoulder as the pivot point. The shoulder muscles are the applied force and the length of bone between the shoulder and muscle attachment is the force arm. Encountered resistance is water resistance against the arm, and the resistance arm is the distance from the shoulder point to the middle of the forearm. In the crawl stroke, bending the elbow shortens the resistance arm, reducing the force

needed to propel the swimmer forward. For the same reason, bending the arms during treading water provides more upward force than straight arms (Fig. 2-10).

Try this exercise to better understand the law of levers:

▶ Stand in shallow water near the edge of the pool.
▶ With arms straight, try to lift out of the water without pushing off from the bottom of the pool.
▶ Try the same exercise, but this time try bending the arms at the elbows to try to lift out of the water. This shortening of the resistance arm should make it easier to lift the body from the water.

Applying the law of levers has helped swimming researchers analyze all types of strokes to find the best limb positions and motions for each. These results are part of the description of swimming strokes in Chapter 4.

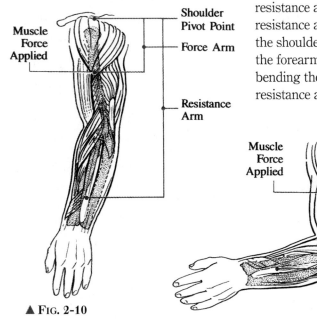

Muscle Force Applied

Shoulder Pivot Point

Force Arm

Resistance Arm

▲ FIG. 2-10

The Swimming Treadmill

The swimming treadmill, or "flume," at USA Swimming headquarters, located on the grounds of the United States Olympic Training Center in Colorado Springs, Colorado, is the centerpiece of research for evaluating swimming technique. The steel flume weighs nearly 1 million pounds. It is 25 meters long, is 4 stories high and holds 50,000 gallons of water. Its 265-horsepower pump moves the water at speeds up to 3.0 meters per second, which is equal to a 33-second, 100-meter freestyle swim. Because the world record for this event is 47.89 seconds, the flume will still be able to test swimmers for years to come.

The environment of the swimming channel can be fully controlled. Scientists can simulate altitudes from sea level to 8,000 feet above sea level and regulate the temperature between 65° and 104° F (18° to 40° C).

With this impressive treadmill, coaches and scientists run controlled tests on swimmers for training and research purposes. Often swimmers work on their technique in the flume. Using computers and the latest video/DVD imaging technology, coaches and scientists can evaluate the motion of an athlete within an hour of a test. This study has helped improve understanding of how physical principles affect stroke mechanics.

Summary

Even after reading this chapter, one might not be interested in the discoveries of Archimedes, Bernoulli or Newton, but whether a beginner or an experienced swimmer, everyone is interested in swimming faster and more efficiently and not being sore or tired afterward.

Being aware of and understanding the forces that act on swimmers in the water and knowing how to overcome them will help improve swimming skills. Consider one principle at a time and the way it applies to strokes. Just as swimming researchers do, watch swimmers with good technique to see how these scientific principles are working as they swim. What researchers have learned through their curiosity is applied in the following chapters.

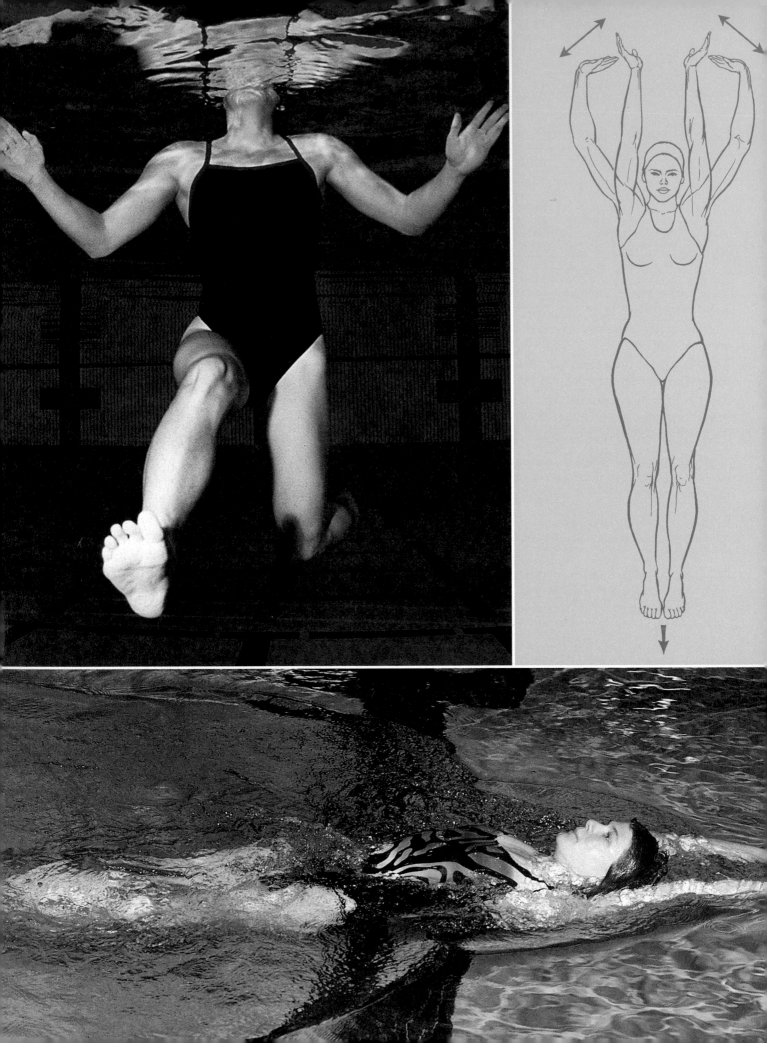

Basic Aquatic Skills

Chapter 3

W hen asked to think of swimming, some people imagine the arm-over-arm motion of the front crawl, whereas others envision the explosive power and beauty of the butterfly. Others recall how pleasantly they have used the sidestroke to move peacefully and smoothly through the water.

Swimming requires many other skills besides performing strokes. These include safety skills, starts, turns and dives. This chapter describes many of these fundamental skills, starting with entering the water and getting adjusted to it. It also addresses different ways to float. As a person becomes used to the water, they learn skills for moving around. This allows independence in the water. Treading water, surface diving, finning and sculling are basic ways to hold and change position and move in the water. Changing directions and rolling over to a back float are important safety skills that also help build confidence. This chapter also discusses how to start basic swimming movements in the water.

It is not necessary to learn all the skills in this chapter immediately, but the safety skills and the fundamental skills needed for learning strokes are important. Although this information can be used for self-instruction, a trained and certified instructor can make the process much easier by guiding learners through progressions and providing tips, encouragement and a helping hand. Check with the local Red Cross chapter for course offerings. Instruction is tailored to different ages and skill levels.

Basic Skills

Physical and Mental Adjustment

When entering the water for the first time, gradually adjust physically and mentally. Swimming pool water is much cooler than bath water. Even relatively warm water (80° to 82° F, 26.7° to 27.8° C) may feel cool and may make breathing speed up. When up to the neck, either wading or crouching, breathing may seem harder because of the added pressure of the water on the chest. A swimmer may also feel somewhat lighter because of the effects of buoyancy. (See Chapter 2.) Take the time to get used to the effects of temperature, pressure and buoyancy. As a swimmer becomes more comfortable and relaxed, these effects may no longer be noticeable.

Entering the Water

Getting wet gradually will help the body get used to the cooler water temperature (Fig. 3-1). Accomplish this by:

► Entering on the steps, ramp or slope until thigh-deep and scooping water with the hands to wet the arms, chest, neck and face.
► Sitting on the edge of the pool and scooping water onto the body.
► Acclimating to the water temperature before getting in all the way.

▲ Fig. 3-1

To bob:

1. Hold on to the side of the pool in chest-deep water.
2. Take a breath, bend the knees and submerge the head.
3. While going down, gently exhale and then straighten the legs to return to the surface.
4. Inhale when the mouth rises above the surface of the water.
5. Exhale through the mouth and nose, and make the bobbing movement smooth and steady.
6. Repeat this movement over and over until comfortable, then move to chin-deep water away from the wall and practice some more.

Deep-water bobbing is a good self-rescue skill. If suddenly in water over the head, the swimmer can keep breathing and, while bobbing, push off the bottom at an angle toward shallow water, until out of deep water and able to stand.

Bobbing and Breath Control

Coordinated breath control is necessary to swim well. Holding the breath for a long time is not critical, but it is important to be able to breathe in and out rhythmically and steadily while swimming. A good method to practice breath control is called bobbing (Fig. 3-2).

▼ Fig. 3-2

43

Staying Afloat

Everyone needs to feel confident and safe in the water. Confidence helps prevent panic and allows for clear thinking. This is even more important for the beginner or nonswimmer. The ability to stay on the surface and move calmly, however slowly, is an important safety skill.

Floating is an easy way for many people to stay near the surface. Chapter 2 explains why and how a person floats. Learning to float is easier if using those principles and if the person is comfortable in the water. Remember that not everyone floats easily. Reread Chapter 2 if experiencing trouble floating.

Jellyfish Float

A

The jellyfish float helps demonstrate buoyancy and how water provides support (Fig. 3-3, *A*).

1. In chest-deep water, submerge to the neck.
2. Take a deep breath of air and hold it.
3. Bend forward at the waist and put the head in the water.
4. Flex the knees slightly to raise the feet off the bottom.
5. Let the arms and legs hang from the body.
6. Hold the breath and relax as much as possible.
7. Allow the back to rise to the surface of the water.
8. To recover, simply drop the feet and stand up.

◀ Fig. 3-3, *A*

Tuck Float

The tuck, or turtle, float is similar to the jellyfish float. Use this float to check buoyancy (Fig. 3-3, *B*).

1. In chest-deep water, submerge to the neck.
2. Take a deep breath of air and hold it.
3. Bend forward at the waist and put the head in the water.
4. Flex the hips and knees and draw them toward the body.
5. Hold on to the legs at mid-calf.
6. Hold the breath and relax as much as possible. Sinking a few inches is possible before getting into position, but there should then be a slow rise until the shoulders are just above or below the surface. Very few people lack enough buoyancy to float in this position.
7. Allow the body to rise to the surface.
8. To recover, let go of the legs, drop the feet and stand up.

▲ Fig. 3-3, *B*

Front Float

The front, or prone, float helps one become comfortable in a position that involves holding the breath. It is easy to learn this skill in water shallow enough to put the hands on the bottom.

1. Start by lying face down with the hands on the bottom.
2. Take a breath and place the face in the water until the ears are covered.
3. Relax and slowly lift the hands off the bottom.
4. Extend the arms in the water above the head.
5. To keep the nose from filling with water, lift the chin slightly and blow some air gently out through the nose.
6. If the toes are still on the bottom, relax the legs and gently push up off the bottom to see if they will rise. Do not be alarmed if the toes return to the bottom. This only means that the water is not deep enough for the body to rotate to its normal (diagonal or vertical) floating position.

7. To recover, lift the head, bend the hips, press the arms down and place both feet on the bottom at the same time.

Learn the front float in chest-deep water.

1. Flex the knees until the shoulders are submerged, extend the arms on the surface, take a deep breath, place the face in the water, lean forward and gently push the toes up off the bottom.
2. If the normal floating position is near vertical, the toes will return to rest on the bottom.
3. To stand from this floating position, pull the knees under the body and move the arms toward the bottom. Lift the head and stand up.

Another way to experience buoyancy is to combine several face-down floats. In chest-deep water, begin with the jellyfish float, move to the tuck float and extend to the front float. Then reverse the process and recover to a standing position.

Back Float

▲ Fig. 3-4, *A–C*

Learn the back, or supine, float by letting the body rise to its natural floating position.

1. Stand in shoulder-deep water.
2. Take a deep breath, lay the head back, arch the body gently at the hips, relax, bend the knees and hold the arms out from the shoulders, palms up. The water will support the body when laying all the way back. Do not push off the bottom but let the feet move to the floating position that is comfortable—vertical, diagonal or horizontal (Fig. 3-4, *A–C*).
3. Breathe in and out through the mouth every few seconds.
4. Keeping the lungs full of air helps one float.

If the natural floating position is diagonal or vertical, floating more horizontally is possible by moving the arms in the water above the head, lifting the hands out of the water and bending the knees (Fig. 3-5). If floating motionless is difficult, use sculling motions or small finning motions to help stay on the surface with only a little effort.

▲ Fig. 3-5

To recover to a standing position:

1. Exhale, tuck the chin toward the chest and bring the knees forward by bending at the hips.
2. Sweep the arms back, down and forward in a circular motion to bring the body back to vertical, and then stand placing both feet on the bottom at the same time.

This motion is like pulling up a chair to sit in.

Treading Water

Treading water keeps one upright in deep water with the head out of the water. This is an important personal safety skill for all swimmers. Swimmers must master treading water before taking a lifeguarding class. Tread water using the arms only, the legs only or arms and legs together. Use the scissors, breaststroke or rotary kick along with sculling or finning movements of the arms and hands, as described below. Treading water should be performed in a relaxed way with slow movements. Move the arms and legs only enough to keep the body vertical.

To tread water with the scissors or breaststroke kick:

1. Stay nearly vertical, with the upper body bent slightly forward at the waist (Fig. 3-6, *A*).
2. Make continuous broad, flat, sculling movements with the hands a few inches below the surface in front of the body, palms facing downward. Keep the elbows bent.
3. Do the sculling movements with a much wider reach than used to hold position when back floating.
4. Kick with just enough thrust to keep the head above water (Fig. 3-6, *B*).

The rotary or "egg beater" kick is also effective for treading water. It gives continuous support because there is no resting phase. This strong kick is used in water polo, synchronized swimming and lifeguarding.

▶ Fɪɢ. 3-6, *A-B*

A

B

A

B

To tread water with the rotary kick:

1. Stay in the same position as treading water with other kicks.
2. Keep the back straight.
3. Keep the hips flexed so that the thighs are comfortably forward (Fig. 3-7, *A*).
4. Flex the knees so that the lower legs hang down at an angle of nearly 90 degrees to the thighs.
5. With the knees slightly wider than hip distance apart, rotate the lower legs at the knees, one leg at a time.
6. The left leg moves clockwise and the right counterclockwise. Make a large circular movement with the foot and lower leg.
7. Reach as far sideways and backward as possible while keeping the body position.
8. As each foot moves sideways and forward, extend it sharply (Fig. 3-7, *B*). The power of the kick comes from lift forces created by the inward sweeping action of the foot (Fig. 3-8).
9. As soon as one leg completes its circle, the other starts. Kick just hard enough to keep the head out of the water.

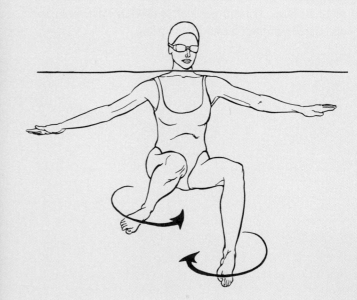

▲ FIG. 3-8

Movement in Water

Once comfortable floating or treading water, learn how to move in the water. Many swimming strokes can be used and are described in Chapter 4. The following sections describe basic skills to help move or change direction in the water.

Sculling

Sliding the hands back and forth through the water creates a force perpendicular to the direction of motion (lift). This action is known as sculling. Sculling is a way to move through the water or to stay in position while floating on the back or treading water. When sculling, the wrist is rotated so that the palm presses against the water in both directions. It is like spreading sand on a hard surface. At the start, equal pressure is applied in both directions. Once you get the feel of it, minor, almost automatic, changes in pitch and speed allow the force to be directed as needed to stay still, move or change direction.

1. Move into a back float with the head back and arms at the side. Hands are flat, fingers are together and wrists are loose and flexible.
2. Using constant pressure, swing the arms away from the shoulders rotating in a rapid back-and-forth pattern, sweeping the palms in and out.

From this position, sculling is possible in three different ways: the flat, head-first and feet-first scull.

Flat Scull

The flat scull is used to provide additional support, with minimal movement, while back floating. The object is to use just enough energy to keep the face comfortably above the surface of the water. To scull:

1. From the starting position, rotate the hands slightly to put the thumb down and move the hands outward just beyond shoulder width.

2. Keep the elbows loose.
3. Rotate the hands to put the thumbs up and palms facing inward.
4. Move the hands toward the hips. The hands lead and the forearms follow. The motion is smooth and continuous (Fig. 3-9).

As each hand sweeps from side to side, water passing over the back of the hands creates lift that raises the hand in the water. This force, combined with the leverage of the shoulder, helps maintain position in the water.

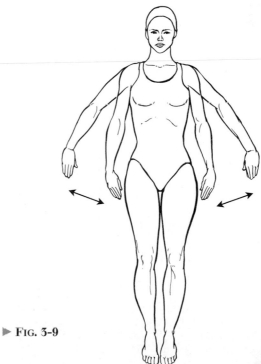

► FIG. 3-9

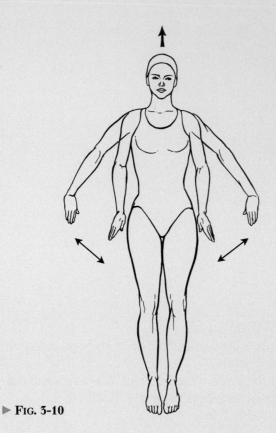

Head-First Scull

The head-first scull is used when back floating. The motion is similar to the flat scull, but a different pitch of the hands directs the force forward to move the whole body headfirst.

1. Extend the wrists so the fingers point up slightly, with the palms of the hand facing toward the feet.
2. Do the sculling motion with the thumb side of each hand pitched slightly toward the head during the inward press and the little finger of each hand pitched slightly toward the head during the outward press (Fig. 3-10).
3. The back-and-forth motion may be horizontal, as in the flat scull, vertical (up and down) or anywhere in between.

► FIG. 3-10

Feet-First Skull

The feet-first scull is also used when back floating.

1. Flex the wrists so that the fingers point slightly down toward the bottom of the pool with the palms open toward the head.
2. Do the sculling motion with the thumb side of each hand pitched slightly toward the feet during the inward press and the little finger of each hand pitched slightly toward the feet during the outward press (Fig. 3-11).
3. The back and forth motion may be horizontal, as in the flat scull, vertical (up and down) or anywhere in between.

► FIG. 3-11

50

Advanced Sculls

To perform the canoe scull (left), the body is streamlined in the prone position. To maintain a horizontal position, the swimmer must slightly arch the back, press up gently with the heels and press down gently with the shoulders. This will keep the heels, buttocks and head at the surface of the water. The face may either be in or out of the water. The arms and hands move freely between the shoulders and hips either to propel the swimmer forward or to keep him or her stationary.

elbows. The hands are flat and fingers are close together with the thumb alongside the forefinger. The movement of the arms and wrists resembles leveling sand on a hard surface.

The execution of the torpedo scull (center) is similar, but the body is in the supine position, and the swimmer moves feetfirst. The body is streamlined, with the face, hips, thighs and feet at the surface. The movement of the arms and wrists is identical to that of the canoe scull, but the swimmer gently slides the arms up the sides of the body to a position above the head, keeping the wrists and elbows relaxed.

The support scull (right), which is extremely important in synchronized swimming, is a stationary scull that allows the swimmer to lift the legs out of the water and maintain an inverted position. Once in the inverted position, the swimmer begins with forearms and hands at waist level and perpendicular to the body. The hands are flat and the palms almost face the bottom of the pool. The outward rotation is identical to that of the other sculls, but because of the inverted position, it is extremely difficult to do and creates a strain on the forearms. Even the strongest swimmers will have difficulty with the outward rotation.

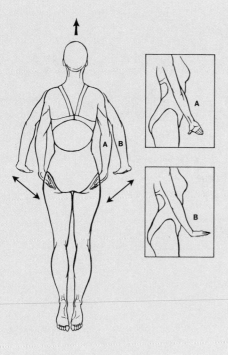

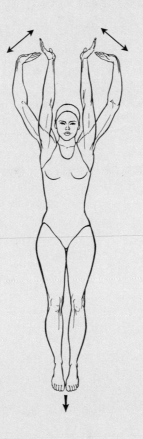

Lead with the wrists, palms outward, away from the body, sweeping the water out by outwardly extending the elbows 12 inches. Immediately turn the palms inward and sweep the hands back toward each other by bending the

Finning

Finning is a way to move through the water using a pushing motion with the arms under water or to stay at the surface of the water while floating on the back.

1. Move into a back float with the head, back and arms at the side. Hands are relaxed under the surface of the water with palms facing the bottom of the pool.
2. Bend the elbows and slowly move the hands out from the side.
3. Flex the wrists and push the water with the palms toward the feet in a short stroke. Movement may be simultaneous or in slight opposition to one another.

Turning Over

It is helpful to know how to turn over to change strokes. The momentum from the stroke will help complete the turn. To turn over while swimming on front:

▸ Lower one shoulder and turn the head in the other direction.
  • To turn to the right, lower the right shoulder and turn the head to the left.
  • To turn to the left, lower the left shoulder and turn the head to the right.

If too tired to keep swimming, float or scull gently on the back. To turn over while swimming on the back:

1. Lower one shoulder and turn the head in the same direction.
2. Keep the arms under water while turning, and reach across the body in the direction of the turn until in a position on the front.

Changing Directions

Being able to change directions while swimming is an important safety skill. When swimming on the front:

1. Reach an arm in the desired direction.
2. Look toward that arm and pull slightly wider with the other arm in the new direction.

To change directions while swimming on the back, tilt the head in the desired direction and stroke harder with the opposite arm.

Starting

When first learning strokes, one needs to know how to start and resume swimming while in the water. Starting from a standing position in shallow water, or holding to the side in deeper water, are both options. Starting from a dive is a more advanced skill that is described in Chapter 5.

Starting Facedown

1. To start facedown from the side of the pool, grasp the overflow trough or the pool wall with one hand.
2. If holding on with the right hand, rotate the body and lean forward slightly so that the left shoulder and arm are under the surface.
3. Hold the feet together and place them against the pool wall, with the right foot closer to the surface (Fig. 3-12, *A*).
4. While pushing off the wall with both feet, lift the right hand up and extend the arm above the head.

5. As the right arm extends, rotate the body to a prone position and submerge so that both arms are under water and extended over the head (Fig. 3-12, *B*).
6. Interlock the thumbs or index fingers or overlap the hands to stay safe and streamlined. Glide until the momentum slows to the swimming speed and then start swimming.

Use this technique with the front crawl and the breaststroke. This start is better than just plunging forward in the water because it helps assume a streamlined position for starting the strokes. This start is appropriate regardless of the pool depth.

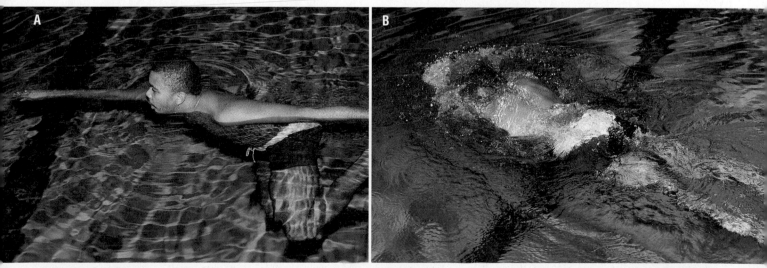

▲ FIG. 3-12, *A-B*

Front Glide

Use the front glide to start from the pool wall or a standing position.

1. Begin as for a front float, and push off the side or bottom with the feet to move forward in a front streamlined position.
2. Begin the swimming stroke.

Starting on the Side

1. To start a sidestroke, use the same body position as for facedown strokes but do not rotate the body.
2. Extend in front the arm closer to the bottom of the pool.
3. Push off with both feet and place the other arm against the thigh.
4. Glide until the speed slows and then start the sidestroke.

▼ Fig. 3-13, *A-B*

Starting on the Back

1. To start swimming on the back, hold the pool wall with both hands about shoulder-width apart.
2. Tuck the body and put the feet about hip-width apart against the wall just under the surface.
3. Bend the arms slightly and put the chin on the chest (Fig. 3-13, *A*).
4. Pull the body closer to the wall, take a breath and lean the head backward to slightly arch the body.
5. Let go, bring the hands close to the body and push strongly off the wall.
   ▶ If starting the back crawl, move into the streamlined position with the body stretched and the arms over the head with hands touching, glide just under or at the surface of the water until speed slows and then start the flutter kick followed by the first arm pull (Fig. 3-13, *B*).
   ▶ If starting the elementary backstroke, glide with the hands at the sides and begin the stroke as speed slows.

Back Glide

Use the back glide to start from the wall or a standing position.

1. Begin as with a back float, and push off the bottom or side with the feet and move in a streamlined position.
   ▶ For the back crawl, start with the flutter kick followed by the first arm pull.
   ▶ For the elementary backstroke, begin the recovery phase for the arms and legs followed by the power phase.

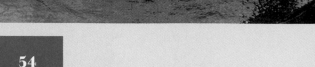

Underwater Skills

Surface Diving

Surface diving is used to go under water when swimming on the surface. This skill is used to retrieve objects from the bottom, to rescue a submerged victim and to go under water in activities such as skin diving. Surface diving is the quickest way to descend accurately under water.

A surface dive can be either feetfirst or headfirst. The head-first dive may be in a tuck (curled) or pike (bent at the hips) position. To avoid injury by hitting an object when descending (going down) or ascending (coming back up), keep the eyes open and arms above the head. In all surface dives, exhaling through the nose while descending prevents water from entering the nose.

The key to an effective surface dive is to raise part of the body above the surface so that the weight out of the water forces the body downward. If ear pain or uncomfortable pressure is experienced during the descent or when swimming under water, pinch the nostrils and gently attempt to blow air out through the nose. If this does not relieve the discomfort, swim to shallower water or to the surface to prevent damage to the ears.

Feet-First Surface Dive

A feet-first surface dive is the only safe way to go down into murky water or water of unknown depth.

1. Start by treading water vertically.
2. Simultaneously press both hands down vigorously to the sides of the thighs and do a strong scissors or breaststroke kick. These movements help you rise in the water for a better descent (Fig. 3-14, *A*).
3. Take a deep breath at the top of the rise.
4. As you start down, keep the body vertical and in a streamlined position.
5. When the downward speed slows, turn the palms outward, then sweep the hands and arms upward to get more downward propulsion (Fig. 3-14, *B*). The sweeping action should occur completely under water. The timing is off if the arms break the surface.
6. When at the desired depth, tuck the body and roll to a horizontal position.
7. Extend the arms and legs and swim under water.

▼ Fig. 3-14, *A-B*

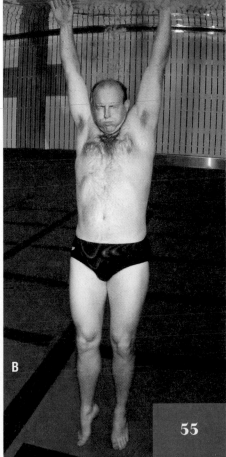

55

Tuck Surface Dive

The tuck surface dive is a head-first surface dive.

1. First, get forward momentum with a swimming stroke or glide.
2. Take a breath, sweep the arms backward to the thighs and turn the palms down.
3. Tuck the chin to the chest, bend the body at a right angle at the hips and draw the legs into a tuck position (Fig. 3-15, *A*).
4. Roll forward until almost upside down (Fig. 3-15, *B*).
5. Extend the legs upward quickly while pressing the arms and hands forward, palms down, toward the bottom (Fig. 3-15, *C*).
6. For greater depth, do a simultaneous (breaststroke) arm pull after the initial descent slows.
7. If depth of the water is unknown or it is less than 8 feet, keep one arm extended over the head toward the bottom.

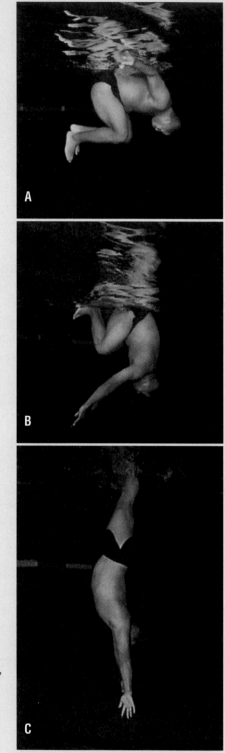

▶ Fig. 3-15, *A-C*

Pike Surface Dive

The pike surface dive is similar to the tuck surface dive, except the legs are kept straight and the pike position is used.

1. Use a swimming stroke or glide to gain forward momentum.
2. Sweep the arms backward to the thighs and turn them palm down.
3. Tuck the chin to the chest and flex at the hip sharply while the arms reach forward and downward toward the bottom (Fig. 3-16, *A*).
4. Lift the legs upward, straight and together.
5. The body is now fully extended, streamlined and almost vertical (Fig. 3-16, *B*).

The weight of the legs and the forward momentum usually take one deep enough without more arm movement.

▲ FIG. 3-16, *A-B*

57

Swimming Under Water

Safety Precautions

Swimming under water allows one to recover lost objects, avoid surface hazards and explore the underwater world. This skill is easy to learn, but safety precautions must be followed to prevent injury. Keep at least one hand extended in front when descending and ascending. Always swim with the eyes open. These precautions help avoid obstructions and provide information about how deep one is.

When swimming under water, do not hyperventilate. This is dangerous because even an accomplished swimmer may black out under water and possibly drown.

Underwater Strokes

Although no one stroke is always best for underwater swimming, a modified breaststroke is generally used. Modify the breaststroke for underwater swimming in several ways:

▶ Use a breaststroke, scissors or flutter kick (Fig. 3-17).
▶ Extend the arm pull backward to the thighs for a longer and stronger stroke. Another method is to use the arm pull and kick together followed by a glide with arms at the sides.
▶ If visibility is poor, shorten the arm pull or do not use it at all.
▶ Keep the arms stretched out in front to feel for obstacles.

To change direction or depth while swimming under water, raise or lower the head and reach the arms in the desired direction while pulling. Flexing or extending the hips directs the body up or down.

▲ FIG. 3-17

Summary

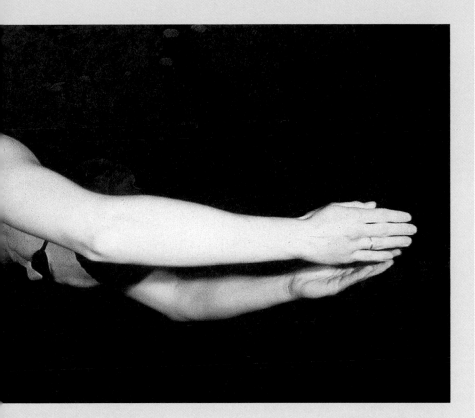

Various water skills are used when swimming. The beginner should first get used to being in and moving in the water. The fitness swimmer may be looking for ways to swim more efficiently, and the competitive swimmer is always looking for techniques to swim faster. Most of us also want to improve our skills to have more fun. This chapter presents various skills to learn and practice. Knowing how to turn over and rest on the back, or to change directions to swim back to shallow water, helps one become safer and more confident in the water. As new strokes are learned, these skills will be even more useful. As a swimmer becomes more accomplished, many of these basic skills will be taken for granted.

Stroke Mechanics

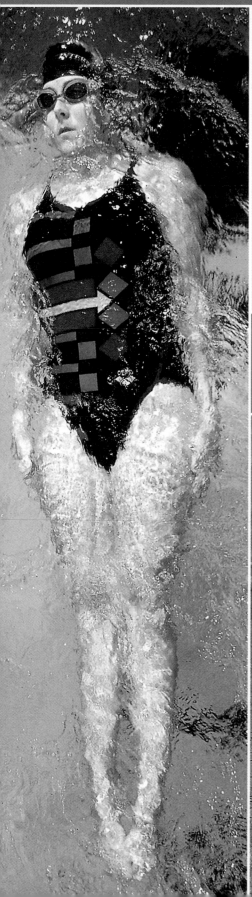

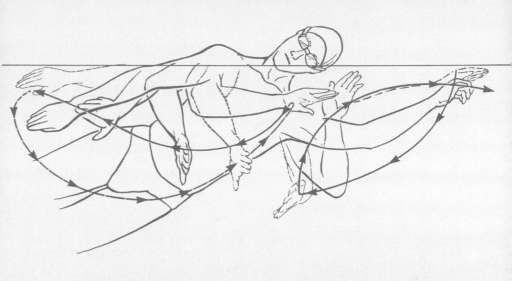

Chapter 4

Throughout history, swimmers have developed many strokes to improve their speed and mobility in the water. Although new developments still occur, the focus in recent years has been on improving the basic swimming strokes that have endured over time. The science of stroke mechanics has led to new and more efficient ways to propel through the water.

In the past, swimmers and their coaches used trial-and-error methods to improve their performance, but now stroke mechanics has advanced, with a greater understanding of hydrodynamics (Chapter 2) and the use of underwater video and computer analysis.

This chapter describes in detail the six basic strokes: front crawl, elementary backstroke, breaststroke, sidestroke, back crawl and butterfly. Less commonly used strokes are described in summary form: trudgen, trudgen crawl, double trudgen, overarm sidestroke and inverted breaststroke. Each stroke is described simply enough for the beginner to evaluate progress and in enough detail to benefit an experienced swimmer.

A clear, consistent approach is used to describe all strokes. The different movements that make up each stroke are analyzed in their different aspects and phases:

▶ One or two hydrodynamic principles involved in the stroke

▶ Balance, body position and motion

▶ Arm stroke

▶ Kick

▶ Breathing and timing

The purpose of this chapter is to help improve swimming strokes. Whether swimming for recreation or competition, propelling oneself easily and efficiently through the water is the goal. This chapter focuses on how to propel through the water efficiently and effectively with each stroke. Other factors, such as size, strength, body composition and flexibility, influence individual stroke performance. This chapter does not try to promote one "perfect" way to swim a stroke. Instead, it gives the basics that can be adjusted for individual circumstances. The better one understands the components of the strokes, the better swimmer one will be.

Front Crawl

The front crawl, sometimes called freestyle, is the fastest stroke. Most people think of the front crawl when they imagine swimming, and most expect to learn it first. Like all strokes, it has three characteristics:

► The goal is efficiency of motion.

► The stroke depends on principles of hydrodynamics.

► Stroke components, such as body position, arm and leg action and breathing, are critical for success.

Hydrodynamic Principles

Almost all hydrodynamic principles are involved in the front crawl, but two are prominent. The front crawl, like other strokes, is a "feel stroke" in that the more one "feels" the water, the better one swims. The resistance is generated by propulsive forces from the arms and legs. The focus of stroke mechanics is on sweeping arm motions combined with body roll.

It is also important to keep the body aligned in this stroke. Good body alignment makes strokes much more efficient. Any lateral movement of part of the body away from the long axis increases the resistance of the water against the body. An improper body position caused by holding the head too high has a similar effect. In either case, energy is expended to correct body position instead of using it to propel forward.

Balance, Body Position and Motion

In this stroke, the body is prone and straight. The front crawl uses much body roll, however. Body roll is a rotating movement around the long axis, an imaginary line from head to feet that divides the body equally into left and right parts. With body roll, the whole body rotates, not just the shoulders (Fig. 4-1).

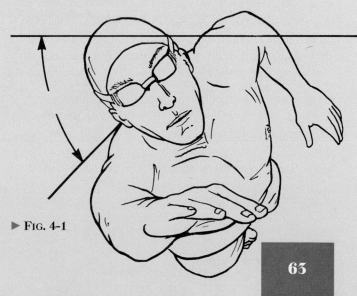

► FIG. 4-1

▲ Fig. 4-2

Body roll is important for almost all aspects of the front crawl. It allows for a relaxed and high elbow recovery and improves arm propulsion. Body roll helps keep good lateral body position (the position in relation to the midline). It also helps one breathe rhythmically and keep an overall rhythm in the stroke.

Head position is an important part of overall body position. Most swimmers keep the water line between the eyebrows and hairline, depending on their buoyancy (Fig. 4-2). Someone with little buoyancy may have to lower the head a little to raise the hips to the best level.

Head movement also is critical. As is commonly said, "Where the head goes, the body follows." If the head moves from side to side, the body will move laterally. If the head bobs up and down, the hips will do the same. In both cases, the resulting body motion is slower.

Finally, the legs also affect body position. Poor body position can cause a poor kick, and a poor kick can cause poor body position. In an efficient and effective kick, the heels just break the surface of the water. The legs roll with the rest of the body.

Arm Stroke

Power Phase

To begin the power phase of the arm stroke, the hand enters the water in front of the shoulder, index finger first. Keep the elbow partly flexed so that the point of entry is about three fourths as far as the arm could reach if straight. Use a smooth entry, with the elbow higher than the rest of the arm and entering the water last (Fig. 4-3). Think of it as the forearm going through a hole that the hand makes in the water's surface. After fully extending the arm, the fingertips are pointed downward and the palm of the hand is pitched slightly outward. This is called the catch because it feels like grabbing a semi-solid mass of water (Fig. 4-4, *A*).

▲ FIG. 4-3

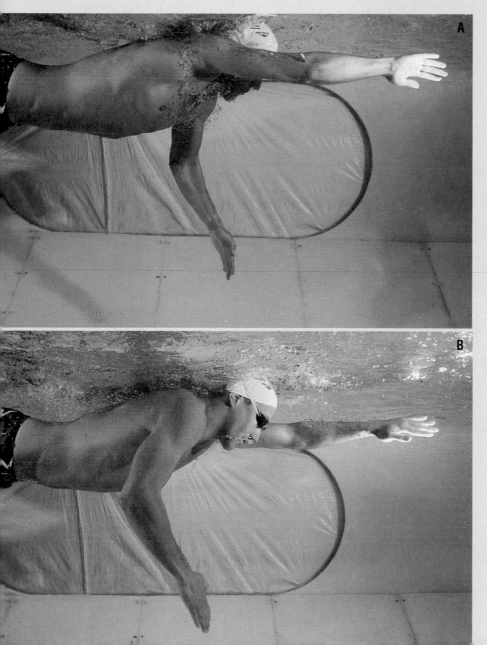

The power phase starts with the catch. With the arm extended and the wrist slightly flexed, sweep the hand down and slightly out to just outside the shoulder. The elbow should be higher than the hand at the start of the pull and stays higher throughout. The catch seems to lead one to move forward. It happens automatically if the hand is pitched effectively and the body is allowed to roll properly. There is tension in the wrist and pressure on the palm.

As the power phase continues, the elbow bends to a maximum of 90 degrees and the hand and arm sweep inward and upward toward the chest (Fig. 4-4, *B*). As the inward and upward sweep of the arm and hand is initiated, the body starts to rotate along the long axis. During the power phase, when using one arm, the body rotates so that the opposite hip rotates toward the bottom of the pool. The hand should not cross the midline of the body. In this sweep, pitch the hand in and keep the fingertips pointed toward the bottom and the wrist nearly flat.

◀ FIG. 4-4, *A-B*

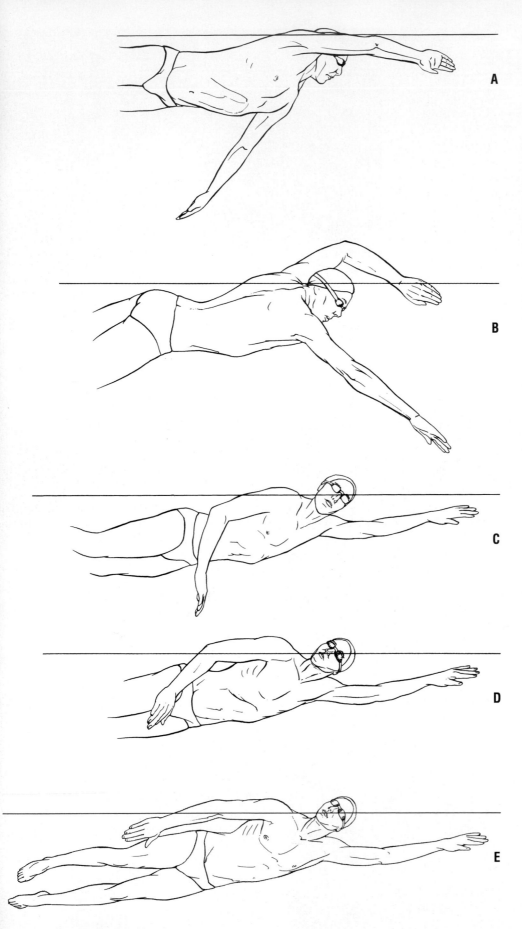

A

In the finish of the stroke, the hand is pitched slightly outward and moves upward as the arm extends. The body completes its rotation along the long axis, which allows the hand to exit the water without obstruction. Extend the wrist (bend it back) to keep the palm pressing toward the feet while the fingertips remain pointed toward the bottom. Keep this action going until the arm is nearly extended—the arm should reach full extension. The hand has accelerated from the catch through the finish of the stroke and is at its highest speed (Fig. 4-5, *A-E*).

B

Recovery

The recovery is not propulsive; it simply puts the hand in a position to pull again. The most important point is that the recovery should be relaxed. While the arm recovers to the starting position, its muscles can rest. If the arm, hand and fingers cannot relax, they do not benefit from this brief rest and will tire more quickly. The recovery will also be stiff and mechanical.

C

D

E

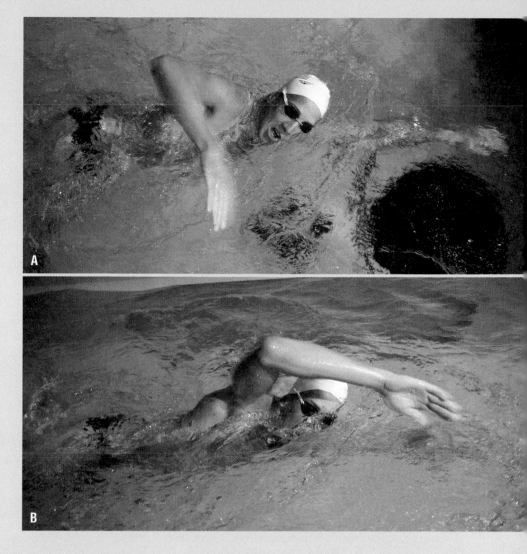

Make a smooth transition from the finish of the power phase to the beginning of the recovery. In the recovery, lift the elbow high out of the water. The body roll is at a maximum. Lift the elbow high and relax the arm with the forearm hanging down (Fig. 4-6, *A*). As the hand passes the shoulder, let it lead the rest of the arm until it enters the water (Fig. 4-6, *B*).

For many recreational swimmers, the arms are always in opposition. That is, one is back, the other forward. However, during a competitive recovery, the recovering arm can catch up with the pulling arms so that, for only a moment, both arms are in front of the head. Some coaches emphasize a more pronounced glide with the leading arm extended for a longer period while the other arm recovers.

Kick

The propulsion from the kick (called a flutter kick) is less than from the arms, but the kick is still important. In fact, without a good kick, one will not have proper stroke mechanics.

The position of the ankles is essential in this kick. They should be relaxed and "floppy" to be most effective. If the ankles are loose and relaxed, the kick will be moderately effective even if other aspects of the kick need work (Fig. 4-7).

► Fig. 4-7

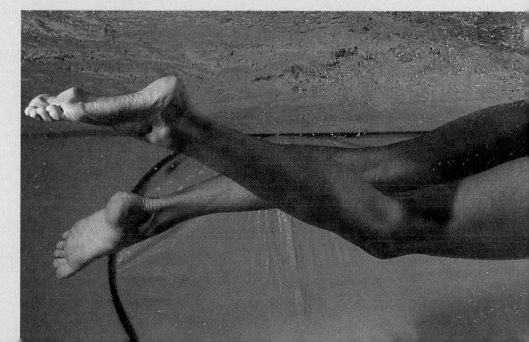

The kicking motion starts at the hip, with the thigh starting downward even while the calf and foot are still moving upward. For most of the downbeat, keep the knee slightly flexed (Fig. 4-8, *A*). The propulsion occurs when the leg straightens. This motion continues through the whole leg, and the feet follow through. The feet are turned slightly inward (pigeon-toed). The foot snaps downward, completing the motion, as though kicking a ball (Fig. 4-8, *B*).

The kicking action continues throughout the rotation of the body along the long axis. In the upbeat, raise the leg straight toward the surface with little or no flexion in the knee (Fig. 4-8, *C*), until the heel just breaks the surface. The leg must stay straight in the upbeat. The knee is flexed for most of the downbeat, and extends forcefully at the end of the kick.

The size of the flutter kick, the distance the leg moves up and down, is not great. The overall leg movements of the flutter kick are illustrated in Fig. 4-9, *A* and *B*.

Use different cadences or "beats" with the front crawl. The number of beats is measured for one arm cycle: from the time one arm starts to pull on one stroke to the time it starts to pull on the next stroke. Cadences vary from a six-beat kick to a two-beat kick. One way is not more correct than another. They are used at different times and at different speeds. Usually more beats are used for shorter distances, fewer for a longer swim. All kicks have a rhythm corresponding to the arm stroke, and most swimmers fall into a cadence that suits them.

▶ Fig. 4-8, *A-C*

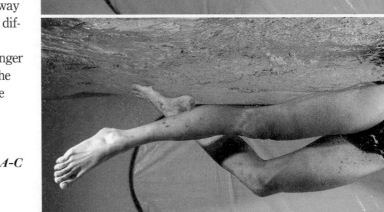

▲ Fig. 4-9, *A-B*

Trudgen, Trudgen Crawl and Double Trudgen

The trudgen family of strokes uses a shortened scissors kick by itself or combined with a flutter kick along with the breathing and arm pull of the front crawl. In this scissors kick, the knees do not recover as far as in the sidestroke. An alternative is a wider flutter kick, as occurs naturally with greater body roll. The table below presents the details of the three strokes.

	Trudgen	**Trudgen Crawl**	**Double Trudgen**
Body Position	Prone; accentuated roll to breathing side	Same as trudgen	Prone; greater body roll away from the breathing side to accommodate second kick
Kick	Scissors kick during final phase of arm stroke on breathing side; legs trail between kicks	Same as trudgen, with addition of two or three flutter kicks between scissors kicks	Two scissors kicks for each arm cycle
Arm Stroke	Similar to front crawl (more body roll to breathing side)	Same as trudgen	Catch-up stroke: Each arm does a complete stroke and recovery before opposite arm strokes
Breathing and Timing	Leg on breathing side kicks as arm on breathing side finishes power phase; inhalation at start of arm recovery	Same as trudgen	Same as trudgen; may breathe to alternate sides

69

Breathing and Timing

Swimmers may breathe either each arm cycle (e.g., each time their right arm recovers) or every 1½ arm cycles (alternating the side on which they breathe). Either method is acceptable, although most people learn this stroke by breathing every cycle. Coordinate breathing so that there is no pause in the stroke to breathe. It is not necessary to inhale a large amount of air with each breath because the next breath is coming soon.

Start turning the head to the side as that arm starts its pull. The mouth clears the water at the end of the pull; inhale just as the recovery starts. Body roll makes it easier to turn the head to the side. Look to the side, keeping the forehead slightly higher than the chin. The opposite ear stays in the water. In this way the swimmer breathes in a trough made by the head as it moves through the water (Fig. 4-10). After inhaling, return the face to the water.

Proper head motion for breathing lets the head remain low in the water, which helps maintain good body position. Return the face to the water, then the arm moves forward. Exhale slowly through the mouth and nose between breaths.

▲ Fig. 4-10

Computer Analysis of Swimming Strokes

Images created by computer can tell us more than meets the eye about our strokes. These images, called "hand force curves," provide detailed information about the stroke. They can also further understanding of the overall patterns of strokes and how to make them more efficient. The hand force curves shown in this chapter are part of a series of images generated by computer analysis of videotape. The total force produced is shown in yellow. The force used to produce forward motion, the effective force, is shown in black. The closer these two lines are to each other, the more efficient the swimmer. Points where the line drops below the zero line of the graph indicate drag and are red.

Examine the graph from left to right to see that the entry not only produces no forward motion, it creates drag, decreasing the efficiency of the swimmer. The first "peak" is the catch, where the swimmer begins to move forward. Each peak and valley represents changes in hand pitch and motion. The highest peak represents the finish, the most powerful part of the stroke.

The differences between swimmers give each force curve a slightly different shape, but the overall patterns remain the same. This knowledge can assist in making a stroke as efficient as possible. Remember, however, that hand movement is only one component of a complex interaction. For greatest efficiency, all parts of the body must respond together.

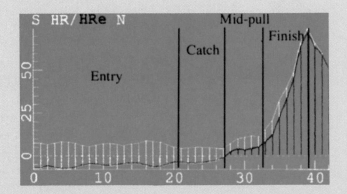

Back Crawl

This stroke, which developed from the inverted breaststroke and the trudgen, was introduced in 1902. The body position generally allows unobstructed breathing and clear vision above water. It is one of the four competitive strokes and is the fastest stroke on the back. For this reason, it is often called the backstroke. It is also used in recreational swimming, primarily for exercise.

Hydrodynamic Principles

Similar to the front crawl, in the back crawl, the arms and legs provide resistance forces. The focus of stroke mechanics is on maximizing propulsive movements while maintaining efficient body position.

Also as with the front crawl, it is important to keep the body aligned in this stroke. Good body alignment makes strokes much more efficient. Any lateral movement of part of the body away from the long axis increases the resistance of the water against the body. An improper body position caused by holding the head too high has a similar effect. In either case, energy is expended to correct the body position instead of using it for propulsion.

Body Position and Motion

In this stroke, a swimmer lies on the back in a streamlined, horizontal position. As in the front crawl, there is a lot of body rotation along the long axis. It is important to keep the head still and aligned with the spine. Because the face is out of the water, it is not necessary to roll the head to breathe. For most swimmers, the water line runs from the middle of the top of the head to the tip of the chin, with the ears under water. The best head position depends on one's proficiency, speed through the water, body composition and buoyancy. Keep the back as straight as possible. Flex the hips slightly to let the feet churn the surface.

Arm Stroke

The arms move continuously in constant opposition to each other, one arm recovers while the other arm pulls (Fig. 4-11). Except for differences of speed between the power phase and the recovery, each arm is always opposite the other arm.

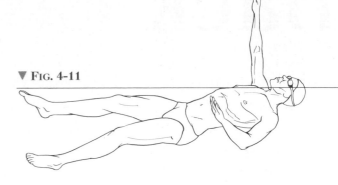

▼ Fig. 4-11

Power Phase

With the arm straight, one hand enters the water just outside the shoulder, little finger first. The palm is to the outside and the wrist angled slightly down (Fig. 4-12, *A*). Keep the body streamlined. With the head steady, roll the body to the side of the entry arm just before the hand enters the water. At the same time, lift the other arm toward the surface to start its recovery.

The entry hand slices downward 8 to 12 inches and slightly outward to the catch, where the propulsive action starts (Fig. 4-12, *B*). Sweep the hand outward and down-

ward as the elbow is bending. This elbow must point toward the bottom of the pool.

About one quarter through this sweep, the mid-pull starts. Keep bending the elbow and rotate the wrist slightly so that the hand presses upward. The elbow is bent most (about 90 degrees) at the midpoint of this movement as the forearm passes the chest (Fig. 4-12, *C*).

For the finish of the power phase, the hand speeds up as it sweeps downward and toward the feet, with the wrist extended so that the palm faces the feet. This phase ends with the arm straight and the hand below the hips (Fig. 4-12, *D*).

▼ Fig. 4-12, *A-D*

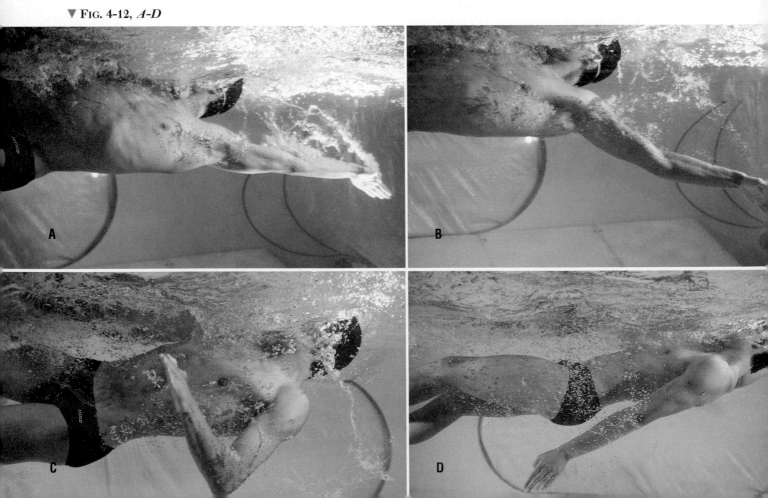

Recovery

Start the recovery by lifting the arm from the water, shoulder first, palm inward (Fig. 4-13, *A*). Relax the wrist so that the thumb and the back of the hand leave the water first. This position of the arm when it leaves the water allows the large muscles on the back of the upper arm to relax more. In the recovery, the arm moves almost perpendicular to the water (Fig. 4-13, *B*). Body roll makes this easier. Keep the arm straight but relaxed in the recovery. Rotate the hand so that the little finger enters the water first (Fig. 4-13, *C*). Remember that the arm muscles should rest in the recovery.

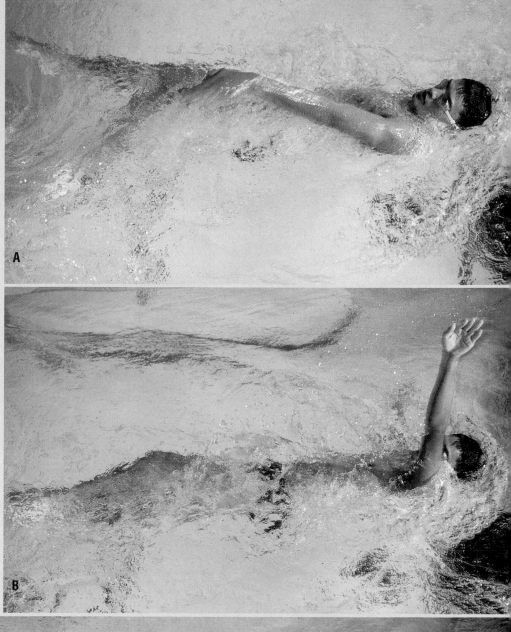

A

B

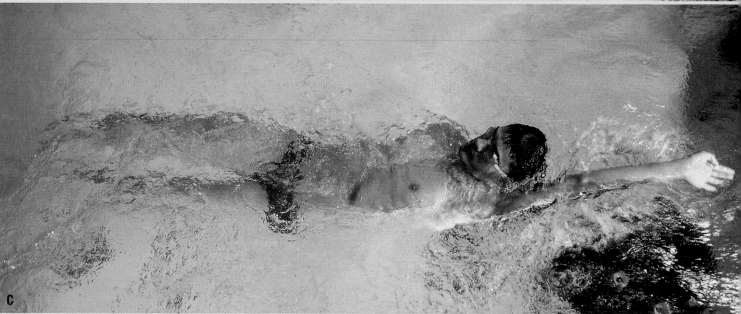

C

Kick

The kick is like the flutter kick used in the front crawl but is a little deeper in the water. It is a continuous, alternating, up-and-down movement that starts from the hips. Keep the ankles loose and floppy, the feet slightly pigeon-toed and the legs separated slightly so that the big toes just miss each other. Most of the propulsive force comes from the upward kick, which is like punting a football with the tip of the foot. The downward movement of the sole of the foot against the water also helps propulsion. The kick also helps stabilize the swimmer by counteracting the motion of the arms and the rolling of the body.

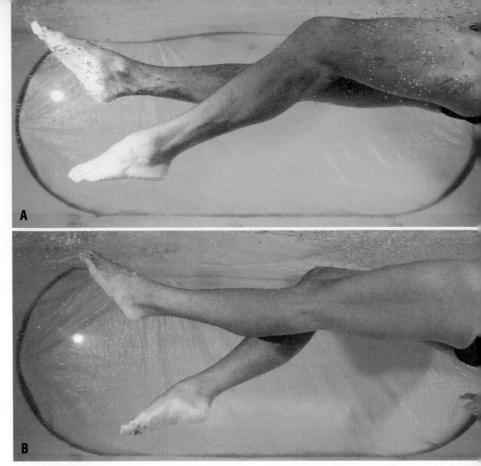

▲ Fig. 4-14, *A-B*

At the start of the upward kick, flex the knee to gain the most propulsion from the upper surface of the lower leg and foot. Bring the thigh and knee near the surface, but keep whipping the foot upward until the leg is straight and the toes reach the surface. Keep the leg nearly straight in the downward kick. At the end of the downward movement, bend the knee and start the upward kick. The thighs should pass each other and the knees should stay relaxed (Fig. 4-14, *A* and *B*).

The depth of the kick depends on the length of the legs, the hip and ankle flexibility, the pace with the stroke and the amount of body roll. Remember that if the kick is too deep, the greater form drag will cancel out the kick's added propulsion.

Breathing and Timing

Use a regular breathing pattern during each stroke. Inhale when one arm recovers and exhale when the other arm recovers.

Start the body roll to the side of the entry arm as it starts to enter the water. The body continues to roll as the entry hand reaches the catch and the other arm lifts toward the surface to start its recovery. The propulsive action of one arm and the recovery of the other arm start at the same time.

This stroke uses a continuous kick. Although most swimmers use a six-beat kick for each full arm cycle, the beat depends on the individual. Find the best timing by slightly adjusting the stroke mechanics until the stroke is smooth and effective.

Butterfly

Many people think of the butterfly as a difficult stroke that is useful only for competition. As a result, many swimmers, even those good at other strokes, do not try to learn it. But even beginning swimmers can learn the butterfly by practicing timing and technique. The key to this stroke is relaxing and using the whole body in a flowing motion. This stroke offers a rewarding feeling of power and grace.

Hydrodynamic Principles

Many hydrodynamic principles make the butterfly work. In the stroke as a whole, the power of each stroke maintains the speed of the body. But in the wavelike motion, the separate actions of the head, torso, hips and legs each build on the change in momentum of the preceding part for forward progress. If the swimmer does not use this momentum well, the stroke becomes awkward or does not work at all.

Balance, Body Position and Motion

Leg and body motions give this stroke a unique dolphinlike feeling. In a prone position, the body moves in a constantly changing, wavelike motion in which it rolls forward through the water. The wave motion starts with the head and continues to the ends of the feet. The kick, breathing and pull are very closely related. For this reason, body motion is described in the section on breathing and timing, after understanding how the kick and pull are done.

Arm Stroke

Power Phase

The power phase of the butterfly arm stroke consists of the catch, the mid-pull and the finish. Each individual arm motion is like that of the front crawl, except that now the arms move together and the sweep out and sweep in are exaggerated, tracing a pattern like a keyhole (Fig. 4-15). The press back is very much like the front crawl.

The catch is an outward sculling motion that starts with the arms extended in front of the shoulders. It ends with the hands spread slightly wider than the shoulders (Fig. 4-16, *A*). With the elbows high, flex the hands slightly down and pitch them to the outside in this phase.

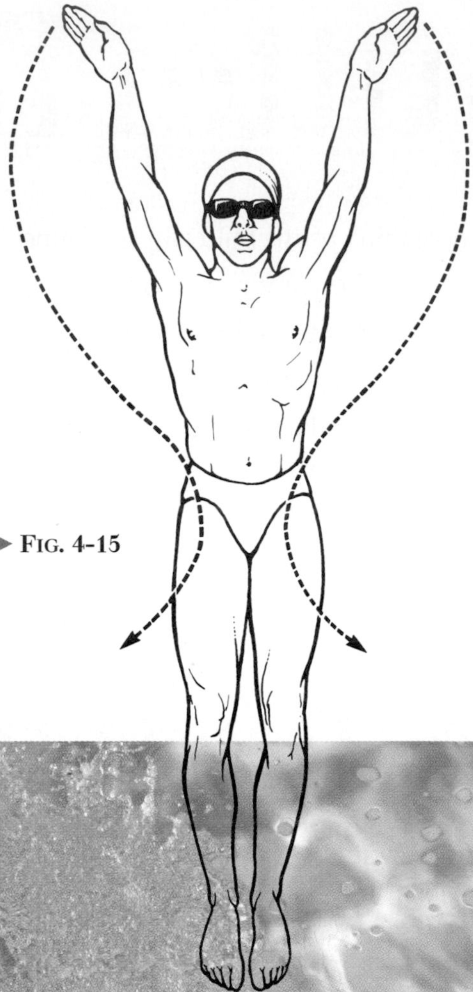

► FIG. 4-15

► FIG. 4-16, *A-E*

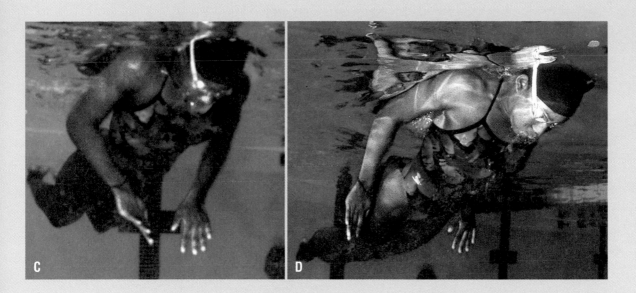

In the mid-pull, continue the sculling action and sweep inward and backward from the end of the catch to a point near the midline of the body. Change the pitch of the hands from outward to inward (Fig. 4-16, *B*). Start to bend the arms after the catch to a maximum of about 90 degrees at the finish of the arm pull. As the arm reaches this maximum bend, the hands are very close together under the torso (Fig. 4-16, *C*). As the hands sweep together, the elbows stay higher than the hands, as in the front crawl.

As the inward sweep of the hands ends and a backward press starts, finish the power phase (Fig. 4-16, *D*). Continue to press the hands back, past the hips, and exit the water past the hips (Fig. 4-16, *E*). As in the front crawl, speed up this motion from the start of the stroke to the finish, especially at the end. Action-reaction forces are dominant in the end of the power phase.

Recovery

Relaxed arms are still important, but the recovery takes more effort than in the front crawl because there is no body roll to help and the arms stay nearly straight. The recovery is easier if acceleration is hard through the finish of the stroke and then the head is lowered as the arms recover.

The recovery starts as the hands finish their press toward the feet and the palms turn toward the hips. Bring the elbows, slightly bent, out of the water first (Fig. 4-17, *A*). Then swing the arms wide to the sides with little or no bend in the elbows (Fig. 4-17, *B*). Move the arms just above the surface to enter in front of the shoulders (Fig. 4-17, *C*). Keep the wrists relaxed and the thumbs down through the recovery.

The entry ends the recovery. With the elbows still slightly flexed, the hands enter the water directly in front of or slightly outside of the shoulders. After the entry, extend the elbows to prepare for the next arm stroke. Pitch the hands out and down for the catch of the next stroke.

Kick

The power of the dolphin kick, the kick used in this stroke, comes from the same dynamics as the flutter kick. The leg action is the same as in the front and back crawl, but the legs stay together in the dolphin kick. The kick starts at the hips and makes the same whiplike motion as the front crawl. Most of the power comes from the quick extension of the legs. Bend the knees slightly through most of the downbeat and straighten them on the upbeat (Fig. 4-18, *A* and *B*). Relax the ankles. Let the heels just break the surface at the end of the recovery.

Compared with the front and back crawl, the hip muscles are used much more in the dolphin kick, moving up and down in the stroke (Fig. 4-19, *A* and *B*). Raising the hips at the right time in the stroke makes the follow-through of the legs a natural continuation of the motion. Thus, the dolphin kick involves the whole body, not just the legs.

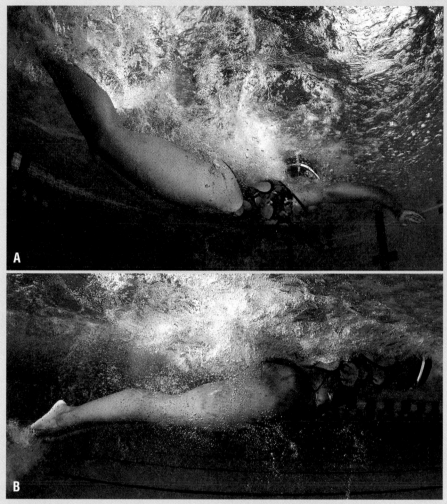

▲ Fig. 4-18, *A-B*

▼ Fig. 4-19, *A-B*

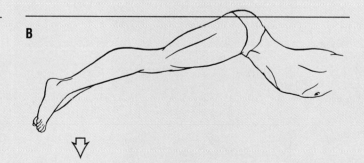

Breathing and Timing

The butterfly uses two kicks at specific moments in each arm stroke. With the right timing, this stroke is graceful. With the wrong timing, the stroke is awkward and very difficult. The timing of the butterfly depends on the relation of the kicks to the entry and finish of the arm stroke. As the hands move into the water to start the catch, raise the hips and start the downbeat of the first kick (Fig. 4-20, *A*). As the hands press through the finish of the power phase, start the downbeat of the second kick (Fig. 4-20, *B*). End the second kick just as the pull finishes (Fig. 4-20, *C*).

Inhale at the end of the second kick, before the arms start

their recovery. To be ready, exhale fully during the underwater pull and raise the head as the hands press toward the hips (Fig. 4-20, *D*). Thrust the chin forward (not upward) as the face just clears the water (Fig. 4-20, *E*). Inhale and start the arm recovery, lowering the head to return the face under water (Fig. 4-20, *F*). Some swimmers learn to breathe only every two or more strokes to gain efficiency.

For the butterfly, one learns to use a wavelike movement of the body. In the downbeat of the first kick, the hips go up and the head goes deeper. As the head comes up during the mid-pull phase, the hips drop and the legs recover. As the arm stroke finishes, the hips go up again and the head and shoulders go down to help the arms clear the water in recovery.

▼ Fig. 4-20, *A-F*

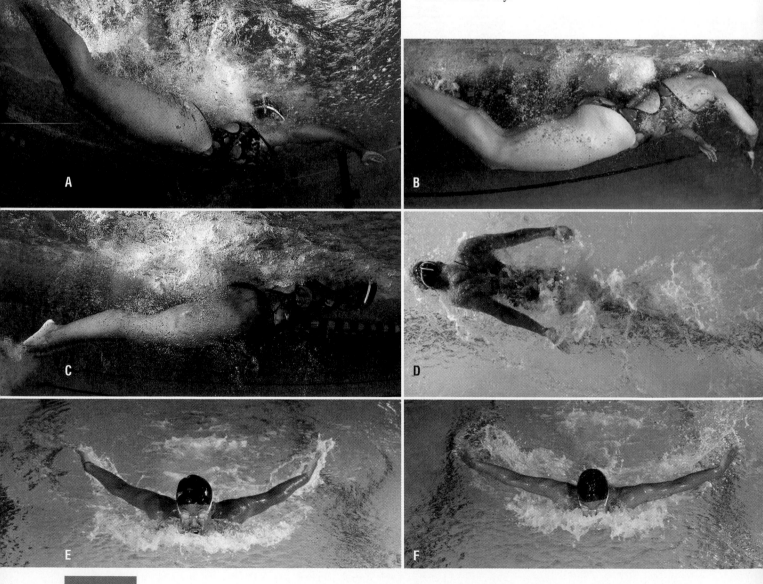

A

B

C

D

E

F

Breaststroke

Hydrodynamic Principles

Correct body alignment is important for all strokes. It is easier to keep aligned with the strokes that involve symmetrical movements (breaststroke, elementary backstroke and butterfly), because propulsive forces are naturally balanced. Because the arm and leg actions of both sides are performed together, force components that would otherwise push the body out of line (accelerate it in one direction) are counteracted by the same forces from the other side of the body.

Body Position, Motion and Balance

The breaststroke is the oldest known swimming stroke used in organized competition. Although still used in competitive swimming, it is very popular for recreational swimming. The head can be kept up, making vision and breathing easy, and the swimmer can rest momentarily between strokes. Swimmers can use it for survival swimming and in modified form in some lifesaving situations.

In this stroke, the arms and legs move symmetrically. In the glide, the body is flat, prone and streamlined, with legs together and extended. Extend the arms in front of the head. Keep the palms down and below the surface. Position the head with the waterline near the hairline. Keep the back straight and the body nearly horizontal, with hips and legs just below the surface.

Arm Stroke

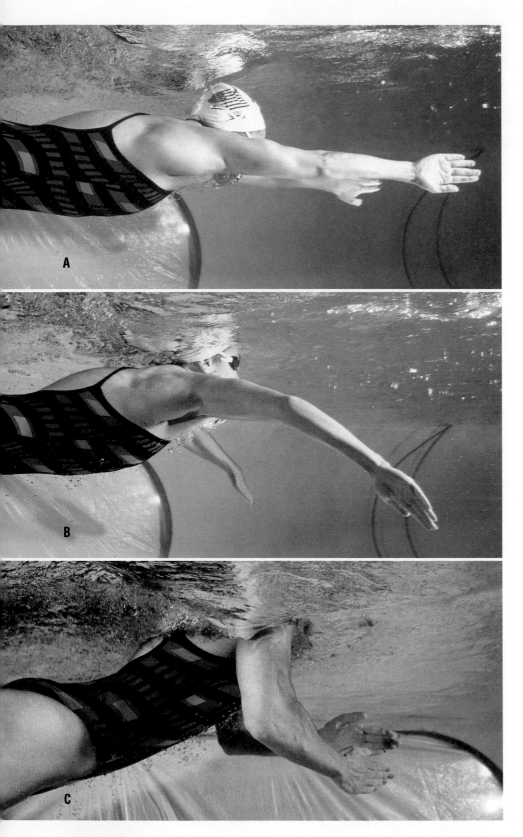

A

B

C

Power Phase

In the glide position, angle the hands slightly downward and turn the palms outward at 45 degrees to the surface of the water (Fig. 4-21, *A*). With the arms slightly bent, press the palms directly out until the hands are spread wider than the shoulders. From this catch position, sweep the hands downward and outward (Fig. 4-21, *B*) until they pass under the elbows with forearms vertical. At this point, sweep the hands inward and upward, until the hands are below the chin, facing each other and almost touching (Fig. 4-21, *C*).

Elbow position is important for good propulsion. Throughout the power phase, the elbows should be higher than the hands and lower than the shoulders. They should also point outward, not backward, and should not pass back beyond the shoulders.

◀ Fɪɢ. 4-21, *A-C*

A

Recovery

Start to recover the arms immediately after the power phase. After sweeping the hands in together, keep squeezing the elbows toward each other. Then, with palms angled toward each other, extend the arms forward to a glide position below the surface and rotate the wrists until the hands are palms down. The entire breaststroke pull pattern is illustrated in Figure 4-22, *A-G*.

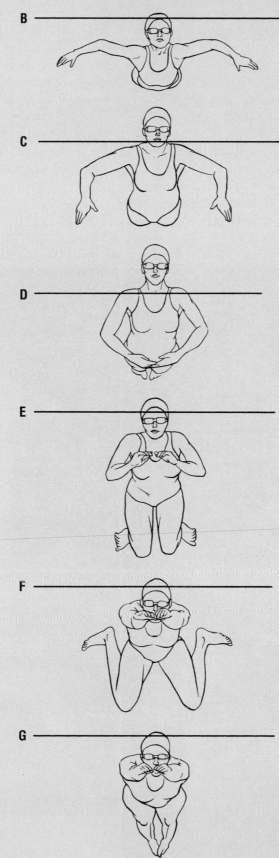

B

C

D

E

F

G

Kick

The breaststroke kick starts from the glide position. Begin to recover by bringing the heels toward the buttocks (Fig. 4-23, *A*). With this action, gradually separate the knees and heels until the knees are hip-width apart and the feet are outside the knees. Keep the heels just under the surface. At the end of the recovery, flex and rotate the ankles so that the toes are pointed outward (Fig. 4-23, *B*) to engage the water with the sides of the feet when propulsive action starts. The strongest propulsion comes from drawing the feet as far forward as possible without upsetting good body position. The ideal distances between the knees and between the heels and buttocks at the end of the recovery vary among swimmers.

With a continuous whipping action, press the feet outward and backward until the feet and ankles touch (Fig. 4-23, *C* and *D*). Extend the ankles and lift the legs and feet slightly. Lift forces on the feet moving outward give some forward propulsion. The pressing action also generates backward thrust. The pressing action starts slowly, then speeds up to the completion of the kick. Propulsion results from the reactive pressure of the water against the soles of the feet and the insides of the feet and lower legs (Fig. 4-24).

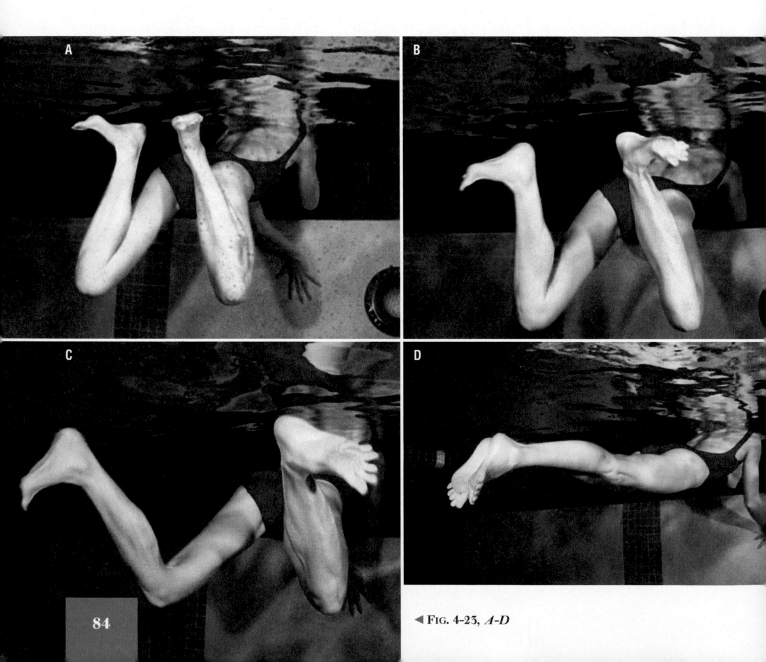

◀ FIG. 4-23, *A-D*

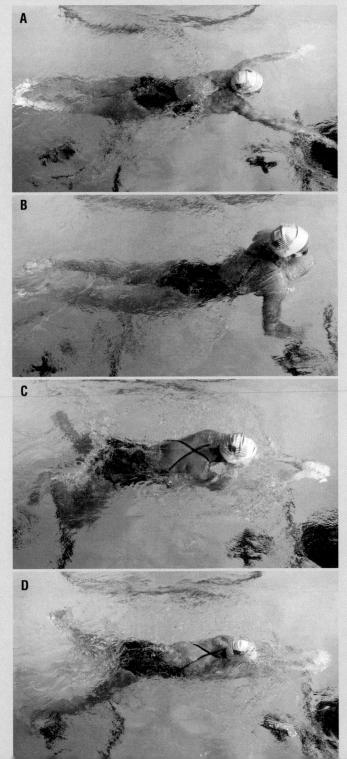

▲ Fig. 4-24

Breathing and Timing

▼ Fig. 4-25, *A-D*

A

B

C

D

As the arms and hands start to pull backward, the head will lift naturally for a breath. Near the end of the arm pull, the mouth just clears the water to allow for an inhale. As the arms start to recover, lower the face into the water. Exhale in a slow, steady manner, mostly through the mouth, from the arm recovery until just before the next breath. At that point, exhale the last of the breath and start lifting the head for the next breath. Breathe during each arm stroke.

From the glide position, start the propulsive phase with the arms (Fig. 4-25, *A*). Near the end of the arm pull, take a breath and start to recover the legs (Fig. 4-25, *B*). Without pause, put the face in the water, start to recover the arms and start the kick (Fig. 4-25, *C*). Once the arms reach about two thirds of their extension forward, start to press backward with the feet. Arms should reach full extension just before the kick ends (Fig. 4-25, *D*). If racing, glide only briefly and start the next stroke before losing forward momentum. Remember the timing of this stroke with the phrase, "Pull and breathe, kick and glide" (Fig. 4-26, *A-D*).

▼ Fig. 4-26, *A-D*

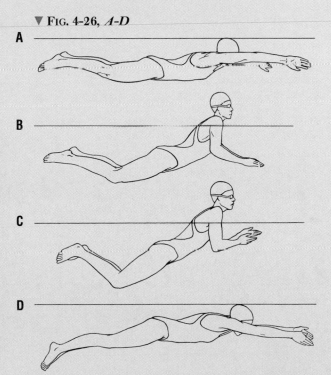

A

B

C

D

Elementary Backstroke

The elementary backstroke is used for recreation, survival swimming and exercising muscle groups not used in other strokes. Swimmers also use this stroke to recover from strenuous effort while still making slow but effective progress through the water. This kick is also used in lifesaving. Breathing is easy because the face stays out of the water.

Hydrodynamic Principles

The most obvious feature of this stroke is the way the arms function as levers in the power phase. The resistance on the whole surface of the arms and hands is overcome by the muscles rotating the arm at the shoulder, using action-reaction propulsion to drive the body forward. Leverage is also used when the knees are extended and when the ankles move from flexed to toes pointed.

Balance, Body Position and Motion

This stroke uses symmetrical and simultaneous movements of the arms and legs. In the glide, the body is in a streamlined position on the back (Fig. 4-27). Most swimmers keep their head submerged to the ears only, with the face always out of the water. The body position is horizontal to the surface of the water. The arms extend along the body with palms against the thighs, and the legs are fully extended and together. The hips stay near the surface at all times in this stroke.

◀ FIG. 4-27

Arm Stroke

A

Recovery

Move the arms continuously and smoothly from the start of the recovery to the completion of the power phase. Keep the arms and hands just below the surface throughout the stroke. From the glide position, recover the arms by bending the elbows so the hands, palms down or in, slide along the sides to near the armpits (Fig. 4-28, *A*).

Power Phase

Point the fingers outward from the shoulders with palms facing back toward the feet. With fingers leading, extend the arms out to the sides until the hands are no farther forward than the top of the head (Fig. 4-28, *B*). Imagine a clock with the head at 12:00 and the feet at 6:00; the hands should extend no farther than 2:00 and 10:00. Without pause, press the palms and the insides of the arms, at the same time and in a broad sweeping motion, back toward the feet (Fig. 4-28, *C*). Keep the arms straight or slightly bent in the propulsive phase. End this motion with the arms and hands in the glide position.

◀ FIG. 4-28, *A-C*

B

C

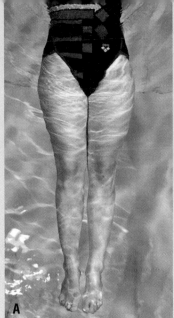
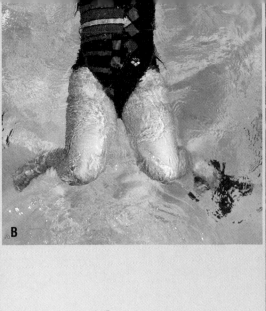
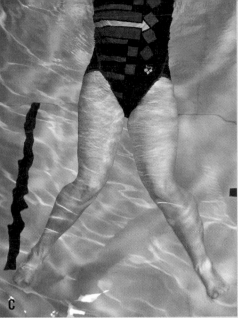

◀ Fig. 4-29, *A-C*

Kick

The kick for this stroke is like the kick used in the breaststroke. Both legs bend at the knee and circle around in a kind of whipping action. The kicking action is continuous and smooth, without a pause between the recovery and the power phase. From the glide position—legs together and straight, toes pointed (Fig. 4-29, *A*)—recover the legs by bending and slightly separating the knees and dropping the heels downward to a point under and outside the knees (Fig. 4-29, *B*). The knees are spread as wide as the hips or slightly wider, with variations among swimmers. Keep the hips and thighs in line. Do not lift the knees by dropping the hips. The recovery uses an easy, rhythmical motion, with back, hips and thighs kept nearly straight. At the end of the recovery, rotate the knees inward slightly while flexing the ankles and rotating the feet outward. Then press the feet backward with a slightly rounded motion (Fig. 4-29, *C*), ending with legs in the glide position. In this action, the feet move into a pointed position. The pressing action of this kick starts slowly and speeds up to completion where the feet touch. The legs remain under water throughout the entire kick. The entire motion of the elementary backstroke kick is illustrated in Figure 4-30.

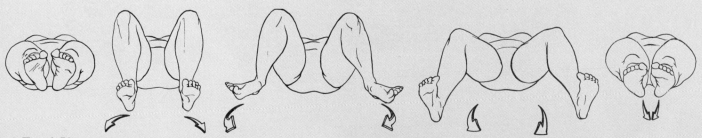

▲ Fig. 4-30

A

B

C

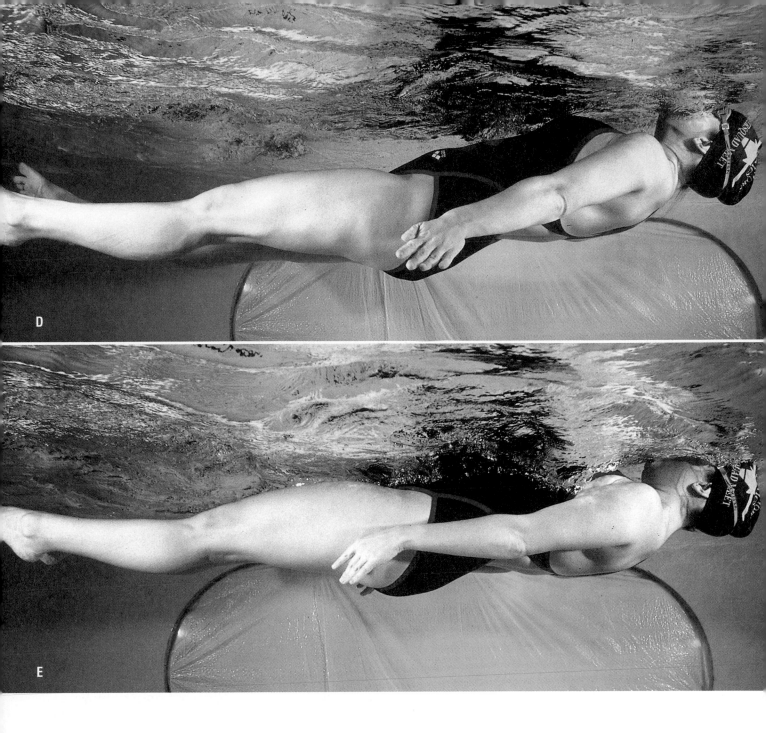

D

E

Breathing and Timing

In this stroke, breathe during each arm stroke. Because the face is always out of the water, breathing is very easy. Inhale as the arms recover up the sides and exhale as the arms press backward during the power phase. Remember to relax and to exhale slowly throughout the arm action.

The arms start their recovery just ahead of the legs.

However, because of their shorter movement and greater strength, the legs finish their thrust at the same time as the arms (Fig. 4-31, *A-E*). After this combined propulsion, glide with the body streamlined. To minimize the drag of the recovery of the arms and legs, glide until most of the momentum is lost.

◀ FIG. 4-31, *A-E*

Inverted Breaststroke

The inverted breaststroke, which evolved from the breast-stroke and elementary backstroke, is a relaxed style of swimming on the back, especially for those with good buoyancy. It has the following characteristics:

▶ The glide position is streamlined, horizontal and on the back, with arms extended beyond the head and legs straight.

▶ The kick is the same as in the elementary backstroke.

The arms, with elbows slightly bent, press outward and back toward the feet until the palms are along the thighs. Without pause, the arms recover along the body to the armpits, where the palms turn up as the hands pass over the shoulders. Fingers first, the hands slide under the ears and extend to glide position.

The swimmer inhales during arm recovery and exhales during the power phase.

The legs recover as the hands move under the ears. The arms are two thirds of the way through the recovery when the propulsive phase of the kick starts, and they reach the thighs just before the kick is finished.

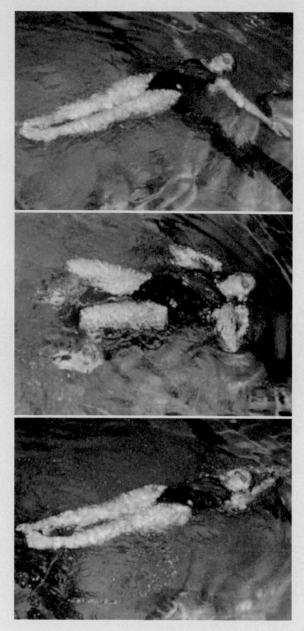

Sidestroke

The sidestroke evolved from the breaststroke because swimmers wanted more speed. The body position reduces frontal resistance and lets the face and one ear stay out of the water. Propulsion comes mainly from the kick. The arms give some propulsion and also stabilize the body in the side-lying position. The sidestroke is easy to learn because the breathing is simple. Because it is a resting stroke, it requires less energy and a swimmer can use it for long distances without tiring easily. The sidestroke is used for both leisure swimming and lifesaving.

Hydrodynamic Principles

A primary principle is important in this stroke, and it has already been mentioned: this stroke was developed from the breaststroke to reduce form drag. Offering a smaller shape while moving through the water, with part of the head and one shoulder out of the water, reduces the water resistance to forward movement.

Body Position and Motion

In the glide, the body is nearly horizontal on its side. Keep the head, back and legs in a straight line, the legs fully extended and together, and the toes pointed (Fig. 4-32). The leading arm (or bottom arm) is extended in front, parallel to the surface, palm down and in line with the body, 6 to 8 inches below the surface of the water. The trailing arm (or top arm) is fully extended toward the feet, hand above the thigh. The lower ear rests in the water close to the shoulder. The face is just high enough to keep the mouth and nose above the water for easy breathing. In general, keep the face looking across the pool, but one can occasionally glance to the front to maintain direction. Keep the head and back aligned throughout the stroke.

◀ Fig. 4-32

Arm Stroke

▶ FIG. 4-33, *A-C*

Leading Arm

The power phase of the leading arm uses a shallow pull. From the glide position, rotate the leading arm slightly to put the palm down and angled slightly outward (the way you are facing). From this catch position, bend the elbow and sweep the hand downward slightly and then back toward the feet, until the hand almost reaches the upper chest (Fig. 4-33, *A*).

Without pausing after the power phase, recover the leading arm by rotating the shoulder and dropping the elbow. Pass the hand under the ear until the fingers point forward (Fig. 4-33, *B*). Thrust the leading arm forward, rotating it so the palm is down for the glide position (Fig. 4-33, *C*).

▼ Fig. 4-34, *A-C*

A

Trailing Arm

During the power phase of the leading arm, recover the trailing arm by drawing the forearm along the body until the hand is nearly in front of the shoulder of the leading arm (Fig. 4-34, *A*). Keep the palm down and angled slightly forward. This creates lift to help keep the face above water. In the power phase, sweep the trailing hand downward slightly and then backward near the body to the glide position (Fig. 4-34, *B* and *C*). Start this phase with the wrist flexed but finish with it extended, so the palm is always toward the feet. The pull pattern for both arms is illustrated in Figure 4-35.

B

C

▼ Fig. 4-35

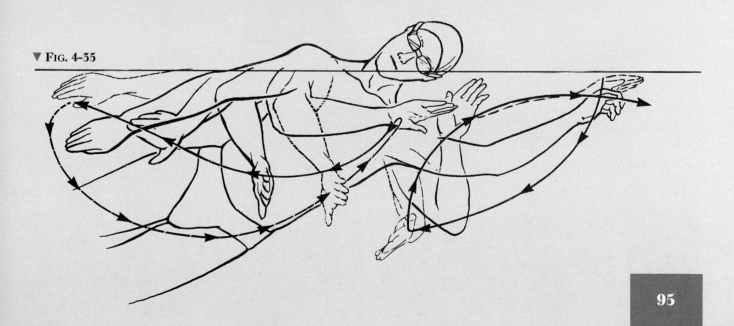

Kick

The sidestroke uses the scissors kick. When done well, this kick is propulsive enough to give a good rest between strokes. In the kick, the legs move smoothly in a plane nearly parallel to the surface. Avoid rolling the hips forward and backward when recovering and kicking. In contrast to the flutter kick, in which the legs move constantly, this kick lets the legs rest during the glide. This kick and its alternate, the inverted scissors kick, are also used for lifesaving carries, treading water, underwater swimming and the trudgen strokes.

From the glide position, recover the legs by flexing the hips and knees and drawing the heels slowly toward the buttocks. Keep the knees close together in this movement (Fig. 4-36, A).

At the end of the recovery (Fig. 4-36, B), to prepare for the kick, flex the top ankle and point the toes of the bottom foot. Move the legs to their catch positions, top leg toward the front of the body, bottom leg toward the back. When extended, the top leg is almost straight (Fig. 4-36, C). The bottom leg extends the thigh slightly to the rear of the trunk, with that knee flexed.

▼ Fɪɢ. 4-36, *A-D*

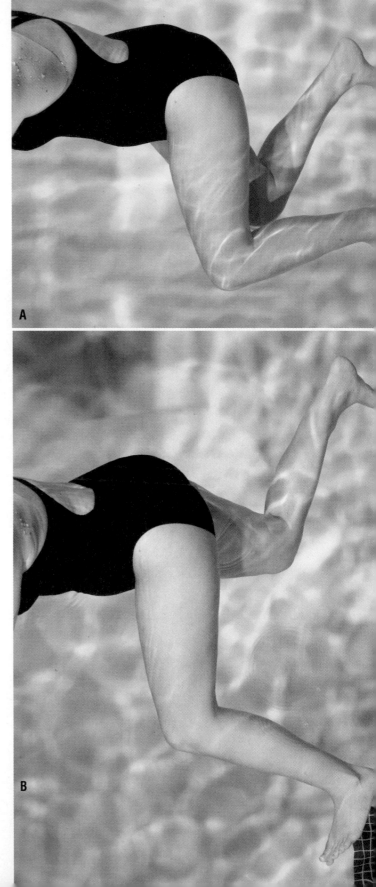

A

B

C

Without pause, press the top leg (which stays straight) backward while extending the bottom leg (like kicking a ball), until both legs are fully extended and together in the glide position (Fig. 4-36, *D*). Push the water with the bottom of the top foot and the top of the bottom foot. While moving the top foot backward, move that ankle from a flexed position to a toes-pointed position to let the sole of the foot press with greatest pressure against the water. Do not let the feet pass each other at the end of the kick. Keep the toes pointed in the glide to reduce drag.

The inverted scissors kick is identical to the scissors kick, except that it reverses the top and bottom leg actions. The top leg (with toes pointed) moves toward the rear of the body, and the bottom leg (with ankle flexed) moves toward the front of the body.

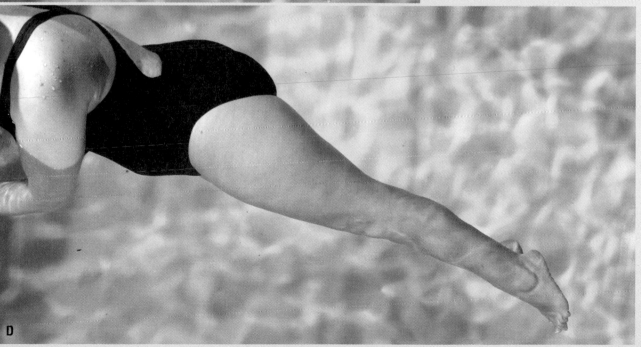

D

Breathing and Timing

A

B

C

With the sidestroke, breathe with each stroke. Inhale through the mouth while recovering the trailing arm and exhale in the power phase of the trailing arm.

From the glide position, start the stroke with the sweep of the leading arm. Then recover the trailing arm and the legs and kick and stroke with the trailing arm as the leading arm recovers (Fig. 4-37, *A* and *B*). The arms and legs are fully extended when the kick and the stroke of the trailing arm is completed (Fig. 4-37, *C*). Glide until the speed slows. Remember not to glide too long, because it takes more energy to start and stop than to keep moving. Figure 4-38 shows the coordination of the arms and legs in the sidestroke.

◀ FIG. 4-37, *A-C*

Overarm Sidestroke

This stroke, which evolved from the sidestroke in 1871, differs from the sidestroke in that the trailing arm recovers out of the water. This reduces the drag of the water on the swimmer. This stroke is sometimes used for leisure swimming. It has the following characteristics:

► Body position, kick, leading arm action and breathing are the same as the sidestroke.
► The trailing arm recovers out of the water with a "high" elbow, and the hand enters just in front of the face, similar to the front crawl.
► The trailing hand enters the water as the leading arm finishes its power phase and the legs recover.
► As the trailing hand starts its power phase, the legs extend and the leading arm recovers.

▼ FIG. 4-38

Summary

We have come a long way since our ancestors found that they could propel themselves safely through the water. New swimming techniques have been invented, improved, adapted and sometimes abandoned. Swimmers, coaches and researchers constantly examine new ways to improve performance. There is no doubt that the continuing study of biomechanics, using the latest technology, will lead to faster and more efficient strokes in the years to come. On the other hand, swimmers a century from now will likely find much in common with today's swimmer.

Starts and Turns

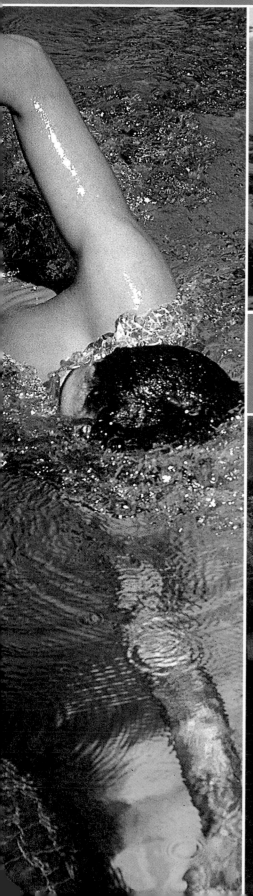

Chapter 5

Starts

Simple starts are used to enter the water and turns are used to turn around in a pool. More advanced starts and turns are used to swim laps more efficiently or in competitive swimming. It is common to see swimmers working out using fast, smooth flip turns to change directions at each end of the pool. These turns take some practice but will help improve swimming efficiency.

Training and supervision are necessary when learning or practicing starting and turning skills. Otherwise, the following problems could result:

▶ Improper use of the starting blocks creates a risk of injuries to the head, neck or back.

▶ Using a starting block that is not anchored securely can lead to injury.

▶ Misjudging the distance from the wall during a turn can cause injury by swimming into the wall or hitting the head in the backstroke.

▶ The heels could hit the wall during a flip turn.

▶ Pushing off at a deep angle is especially dangerous in shallow water.

Readiness

Physical Readiness

To learn to do a head-first entry, some basic swimming skills are required. The swimmer must be able to return to the surface of the water, change directions and swim back to the side of the pool.

Strength also may be a consideration. A swimmer entering the water headfirst must be able to keep the arms overhead during the entry (when the body passes through the surface of the water). The ability to do so can be tested by submerging and pushing forcefully off the side wall of the pool in a streamlined position (arms alongside the head) and gliding. If arm alignment cannot be maintained, postpone learning this skill until upper body strength increases.

Psychological Readiness

Someone about to enter the water headfirst for the first time may feel fear or apprehension. Although caution should be exercised when entering the water in a head-first position, the following progressions can help minimize any fears. This method helps one reach success at each level. If time is taken to master the skills of each step before moving to the next, one will enjoy the experience more and feel more ready to try the next skill. The following are the most common fears of people learning to dive.

Fear of Depth

Some beginners may be afraid that they will not be able to swim back to the surface. In an attempt to stay very near the surface, someone might "belly flop" by lifting the head before entering the water. If a swimmer is not comfortable in deep water, one should improve swimming skills before taking up diving. Surface diving and underwater swimming also will increase self-confidence and skill in moving headfirst.

Fear of Injury

Fear of being injured may cause a person to avoid head-first entries entirely. It is true one may feel a little pain as a result of a poor landing in the water while trying this skill, but safety precautions significantly minimize the chance of injury. Some people may feel fear because they saw someone injured in a dive or may have been hurt themselves. Again, learning the skills for diving in a safe, step-by-step manner prevents injury and helps overcome the fear of injury.

Fear of Height

The view of the distance to the surface from a pool deck may cause anxiety or make some people want to avoid head-first entries altogether. The progressions used in this chapter will help beginners overcome such fears. Start entering the water as close to the surface as possible.

If a swimmer appears to be hesitant at any step in a progression, the previous step should continue to be practiced until one feels confident to proceed. Someone who is very fearful should not try a new skill. If a swimmer cannot concentrate on the skill, one is more likely to be injured while trying it.

Components of a Head-First Entry

Although this skill is referred to as a "head-first" entry, it is important that the arms are always extended above the head so that the fingertips enter the water first, followed by the arms, head, trunk and then the legs. A simple head-first entry has three parts: the stationary starting position; the moment of propulsion, called the takeoff; and the entry into the water. The starting position is often the side of the pool. For competitive swimmers, the starting position is most often starting blocks. The takeoff for a head-first entry is a slight push with the feet. A good entry involves entering the water at a low angle and keeping the body aligned as it enters the water. Also important is the action that occurs once the swimmer enters the water. After entering the water, the swimmer should angle slightly up to return to the surface of the water and then start stroking.

To enter into the water at the desired point of entry, focus on a target (either an imaginary point on the surface or a real or imagined target on the bottom of the pool) until the hands enter the water. It is important to maintain concentration during any head-first entry. Focusing attention on one place is a good way to do this when learning this skill.

Keeping proper body alignment is crucial for a safe entry. Head position is very important because it affects the position of the body in general. Moving the head may cause the body to arch or bend. The beginner who lifts the head too quickly may do a painful belly flop.

Muscular control also is important for proper body alignment and the body tension needed for a safe, effective entry. Try to stay in a streamlined position in flight (the

▼ Fig. 5-1, *A-C*

passage of the body through the air) (Fig. 5-1, *A*). This helps maintain control and helps make entries graceful. Good alignment when entering the water reduces drag and the risk of straining muscles or joints.

A main purpose of the head-first entry is to enter the water to be able to start swimming, whether for recreation, fitness or competition. It is important for swimmers to learn to steer back to the surface once they enter the water (Fig. 5-1, *B* and *C*).

▲ FIG. 5-2

Body Alignment Skills

Body alignment skills are useful for practicing arm and head position in preparation for a head-first entry.

Step 1: Torpedoing

1. Push forcefully from the wall into a glide position in chest-deep water. Keep the eyes open.
2. Maintain straight body alignment: arms straight and overhead, arms covering the ears, thumbs together or interlocked, body tense from arms to feet, toes pointed, legs together.
3. Hold the position until momentum is lost.

Step 2: The Step Dive

The step dive is useful for practicing head and arm position, body alignment and muscle tension. The step dive can be performed from a chair or bench with help from an instructor.

1. Put the chair or bench securely in the water, braced against the side and steadied by an instructor. Stand on the steadied chair or bench. The water should be at least shoulder deep.

2. Extend the arms over the head, bend the knees slightly and lean forward until touching the surface of the water (Fig. 5-2).
3. Push forward into the water with the legs and go just below the surface in a streamlined position. The object is to go out, not down.
4. Once in the water, angle the hands toward the surface of the water to steer the body up.

Step 3: Porpoising

▶ Start as in Step 1, then angle the head and arms down to submerge slightly toward the bottom, move parallel to the surface, angle up and glide to the surface.
▶ As a variation, jump forward and slightly upward from a standing position before angling the head and arms to submerge.
▶ Change body angle in descent and ascent by raising and lowering the head and arms as a single unit.
▶ At all times, cradle the head between arms that are extended in the direction of the motion.

Progression for a Head-First Entry

The steps for learning a head-first entry will give self-confidence and a feeling of success. Swimmers should remember to move through them at their own pace. Some steps might need lots of practice. With good coordination and kinesthetic awareness, one may be able to move more quickly through them. This progression may also be used to learn to enter the water from starting blocks. The hands will break the water at roughly a 45-degree angle, and the head, torso and legs will slide into the water following the safe path. This angle of entry allows one to be parallel to the surface of the water after entry and puts a swimmer in a position to steer up and start stroking.

Sitting Position

1. Sit on the pool edge with feet on the edge of the gutter or against the pool wall.
2. Extend the arms over the head.
3. Focus on a target on the surface that will allow for roughly a 45-degree entry into the water (Fig. 5-3).
4. Lean forward, try to touch the water and push with the legs.
5. On entering the water, straighten the body and extend both legs.
6. Once in the water, angle the hands toward the surface of the water to steer the body up.

▲ FIG. 5-3

Kneeling Position

1. Kneel on one knee while gripping the pool edge with the toes of the other foot. The foot of the kneeling leg should be in a position to help push from the deck.
2. Extend the arms over the head.
3. Focus on a target that will allow for roughly a 45-degree entry into the water (Fig. 5-4).
4. Lean forward, try to touch the water and push with the legs.
5. On entering the water, straighten the body and extend both legs.
6. Once in the water, angle the hands toward the surface of the water to steer the body up.

▲ FIG. 5-4

▼ FIG. 5-5

▼ FIG. 5-6

Compact Position

This dive is quite similar to the dive from the kneeling position.

1. Put one foot forward and one back, with the toes of the leading foot gripping the edge of the deck.
2. Start in the kneeling position.
3. Lift up so that both knees are off the deck and flexed to remain close to the water.
4. Extend the arms above the head.
5. Focus on a target that will allow for roughly a 45-degree entry into the water (Fig. 5-5).
6. Bend forward and try to touch the surface of the water with the hands.
7. Push off toward the water. Bring the legs together on entering the water.
8. Once in the water, angle the hands toward the surface of the water to steer the body up.

Stride Position

After several successful dives from the compact position, one should be ready for a dive from the stride position.

1. Stand upright with one leg forward and one leg back. The toes of the forward foot should grip the edge of the pool.
2. Extend the arms above the head.
3. Focus on a target that will allow for roughly a 45-degree entry into the water. Bend the legs only slightly while bending at the waist toward the water (Fig. 5-6).
4. Try to touch the surface of the water, and lift the back leg until it is in line with the torso. The forward leg should stay as straight as possible.
5. Once in the water, angle the hands toward the surface of the water to steer the body up.

Shallow Dive

The shallow dive is a low-projecting dive done in a streamlined body position. This skill is done by entering the water with great forward momentum at an angle that allows the swimmer to remain near the surface of the water. It is used to enter the water to start swimming, to dive outward away from the side, in rescues when speed is urgent and for racing starts in competition. This entry should only be performed in clear water of known depth. Misjudging the depth or angle of the entry could lead to hitting the bottom and injuring the head, neck or back, risking paralysis or death.

1. Start on the edge of the pool with the feet about shoulder-width apart and the toes gripping the edge (Fig. 5-7, *A*).
2. Flex the hips and knees and bend forward until the upper back is nearly parallel to the pool deck.
3. Focus on your point of entry. To gain momentum for the dive, swing the arms backward and upward, letting the heels rise and the body start to move forward.
4. When the arms reach the farthest point backward, immediately swing the arms forward. Extend the hips, knees, ankles and toes one after another forcibly to drive forward in a line of flight over and nearly parallel to the surface of the water (Fig. 5-7, *B*).
5. Keep the body stretched and the hands interlocked and out in front.
6. During the flight, drop the head slightly between the outstretched arms, which should be angled downward slightly (Fig. 5-7, *C*).
7. Make the entry at roughly a 45-degree angle to the surface of the water. Once under water, steer upward toward the surface with the hands and head.
8. Keep the body fully extended and streamlined while gliding under water. Before losing too much speed, start the leg kick to rise to the surface and start swimming.

Proficiency at this entry leads naturally into competitive racing starts.

▲ Fig. 5-7, *A-C*

▶ Fig. 5-8, *A-F*

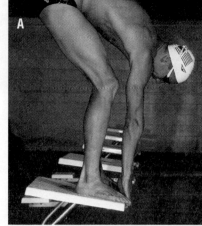

Grab Start

Many swimmers think the grab start is the fastest start for all competitive strokes performed on the front. Before trying the grab start, one must be able to safely perform a shallow dive.

1. To position for the start, curl the toes around the starting block with the feet about shoulder width apart.
2. On the command, "Take your mark," grasp the front edge of the starting block. Put the hands either inside or outside the feet, whichever feels more comfortable. Lower the head and bend the knees slightly (Fig. 5-8, *A*).
3. On the starting signal, pull against the starting block and bend the knees further, so the body starts moving forward. Look forward, release the block and quickly extend the arms forward to lead the body's flight.
4. As the hands release the block, increase the knee bend further and then push off by driving the feet against the block and forcefully extending the hips, knees and ankles (Fig. 5-8, *B*).
5. As the feet leave the block, focus the eyes on and aim the arms and hands at the entry point (Fig. 5-8, *C*).
6. Just before hitting the water, lock the head between the arms and enter smoothly, as if going though a hole in the water (Fig. 5-8, *D* and *E*).
7. Once in the water, angle the hands up toward the surface to decrease the downward motion. Glide in a streamlined position, hands out in front (Fig. 5-8, *F*).
8. Before losing too much speed, start the flutter or dolphin kick, angle slightly toward the surface and follow immediately with the first arm pull. (In the breaststroke, kicking does not start until after the underwater pull.)
9. Take a breath after finishing the first arm cycle.

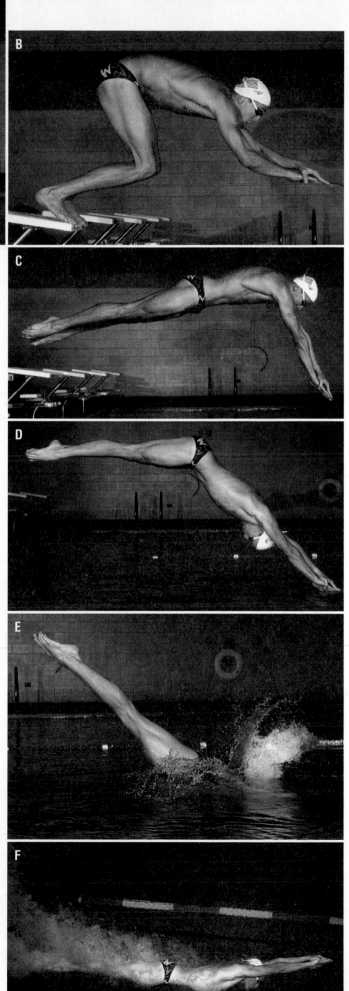

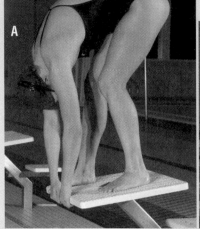

Track Start

The track start is also used in competition for all strokes performed on the front. Before trying the track start, one must be able to do a shallow dive safely.

1. To position for the start, stand with one foot forward and one foot back. Curl the toes of the forward foot around the starting block.
2. On the command, "Take your mark," grasp the front edge of the starting block. Lower the head and bend the knees slightly (Fig. 5-9, *A*).
3. On the starting signal, pull against the starting block and bend the knees further, so the body starts moving forward. Look forward, release the block and quickly extend the arms forward to lead the body's flight.
4. As the hands release the block, increase the knee bend further and then push off by driving the feet against the block and forcefully extending the hips, knees and ankles (Fig. 5-9, *B*).
5. As the feet leave the block, focus the eyes on and aim the arms and hands at the entry point (Fig. 5-9, *C*).
6. Just before hitting the water, lock the head between the arms and enter smoothly, as if going though a hole in the water (Fig. 5-9, *D* and *E*).
7. Once in the water, angle the hands toward the surface to decrease the downward motion. Glide in a streamlined position, hands out in front.
8. Before losing too much speed, start the kick and angle slightly toward the surface and follow immediately with the first arm pull (Fig. 5-9, *F*). (In the breaststroke, kicking does not start until after the underwater pull.)
9. Take a breath after finishing the first arm cycle.

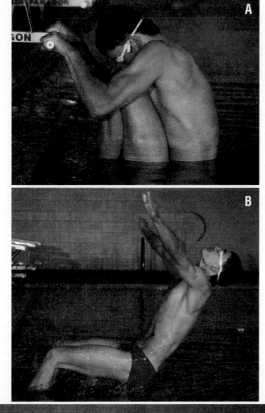

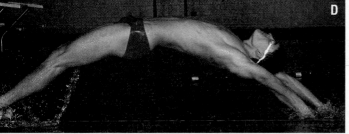

Backstroke Start

1. To get in position for the backstroke start, grasp the starting block with both hands and put the feet parallel on the wall. (National Collegiate Athletic Association [NCAA] and the Federation Internationale de Natation Amateur [FINA] rules currently require the toes to be under the surface.) Move the feet a comfortable distance apart.

2. When the starter says, "Take your mark," bend the arms and pull the body up and out of the water into a crouched position. Bring the head close to the knees and tuck the body as much as possible (Fig. 5-10, *A*).

3. At the starting command, throw the head back and push the arms out and around with palms outward (Fig. 5-10, *B*). Push forcefully with the legs while arching the back and driving the body, hands first, up and out over the water (Fig. 5-10, *C*).

4. Tip the head back and look toward the entry point. The whole body should enter smoothly through a single point in the water (Fig. 5-10, *D* and *E*).

5. Once in the water, adjust the angle of the hands for a streamlined glide (Fig. 5-10, *F*).

6. Before losing too much speed, begin either a flutter or dolphin kick and use the first arm pull to come to the surface with the arm closest to the bottom.

7. Start stroking.

Many swimmers prefer to do several quick dolphin kicks after the start and each turn instead of the flutter kick. Swimmers with a strong dolphin kick may wish to try this. Check with the meet official to see about distances that can be traveled under water before surfacing to start stroking (Fig. 5-11, *A* and *B*).

▼ FIG. 5-11, *A-B*

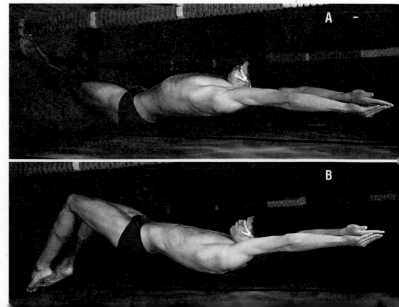

Turns

Swimming for fitness usually takes place in pools, so being able to turn effectively and efficiently at the wall is important. Simple open turns as well as more advanced, competitive turns are described.

Front Crawl Open Turn

1. When approaching the wall, extend the closest arm until it touches the wall.
2. Bend the elbow of the leading arm and drop that shoulder slightly while rotating the body to move the body toward the wall.
3. Tuck the body at the hips and knees; turn and spin away from the leading hand; swing the feet against the wall, one above the other (Fig. 5-12, *A*) (if the right hand is the leading hand, the right foot will be on top); and extend the other arm toward the opposite end.
4. During the spin, lift the face and take a breath.
5. Return the face to the water as the leading hand recovers over the surface (Fig. 5-12, *B*).
6. Extend both arms in front as the legs push off. Keep the body in a streamlined position on one side.
7. Rotate in the glide until face down.
8. Before losing momentum, start flutter kicking to rise to the surface and resume the arm stroke.

▼ FIG. 5-12, *A-B*

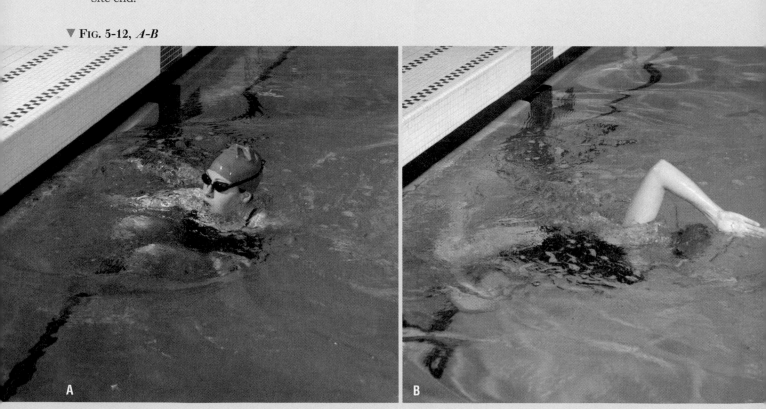

A   B

Sidestroke Open Turn

For a sidestroke open turn, vary the front crawl open turn slightly.

1. To perform the sidestroke open turn, approach with the arm extended and touch the wall with the leading arm.
2. Bend the elbow, drop the shoulder and rotate the back toward the wall.
3. Tuck the body, turn and spin to put the feet on the wall, one above the other.
4. Take a breath and extend both arms while pushing off the wall.
5. Once in the glide position, stay on the side.
6. Pull the trailing arm to the thigh to get ready for the first stroke.

Backstroke Open Turn

With the elementary backstroke or back crawl, gauge the approach to the wall using the backstroke flags, the color change of the lane lines or a glance backward.

1. Fully extend one arm behind the head and take a breath as the palm touches the wall (Fig. 5-13, *A*).
2. Bend the elbow of the leading arm and let the head come near the wall while tucking the body and spinning the hips and legs toward the leading hand (Fig. 5-13, *B*).
3. Sweep the trailing hand toward the head to help the spinning and put both feet on the wall, assuming a sitting position in the water. Submerging the head allows for a smoother, more efficient turn; however, it may be done with the head above water.
4. Push off with the top of the head facing the other end of the pool. Breathe out slowly through the nose during the push-off to keep water from entering the nose.
5. Assume a streamlined position with the arms fully extended over the head (Fig. 5-13, *C*).
6. While pushing off the wall, tuck the chin, angle the hands and arms slightly toward the surface and start kicking.
7. While coming to the surface, start the first arm pull.

▼ Fig. 5-13, *A-C*

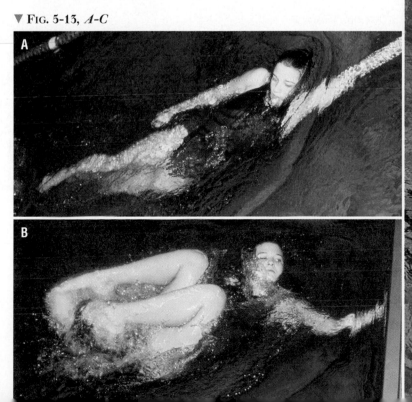

Front Flip Turn

The flip turn is a fast and efficient turn for the front crawl. Watch the bottom markings to help judge the distance from the wall.

1. When one stroke's length (3½ to 4 feet) from the wall, keep the trailing arm at the side while taking the last stroke with the lead arm (Fig. 5-14, *A*). Both hands will end up at the thighs with the palms facing up.

2. Use a dolphin kick to push the hips forward and upward (Fig. 5-14, *B*), and tuck the chin to the chest as the forearms and palms start sweeping toward the head.

3. Leading with the head, do a somersault. During the somersault, the hands will have reached the ears (Fig. 5-14, *C*); this helps complete the forward body roll.

A

B

▲ FIG. 5-14, *A-F*

C

4. Plant the feet on the wall with the toes pointed up or slightly to the side and the knees bent (Fig. 5-14, *D*).
5. Extend the arms into a streamlined position above the head. Push off while facing up or facing to the side; then rotate to a face-down position during the glide (Fig. 5-14, *E* and *F*). The initial speed when pushing off will be faster than the swimming speed.

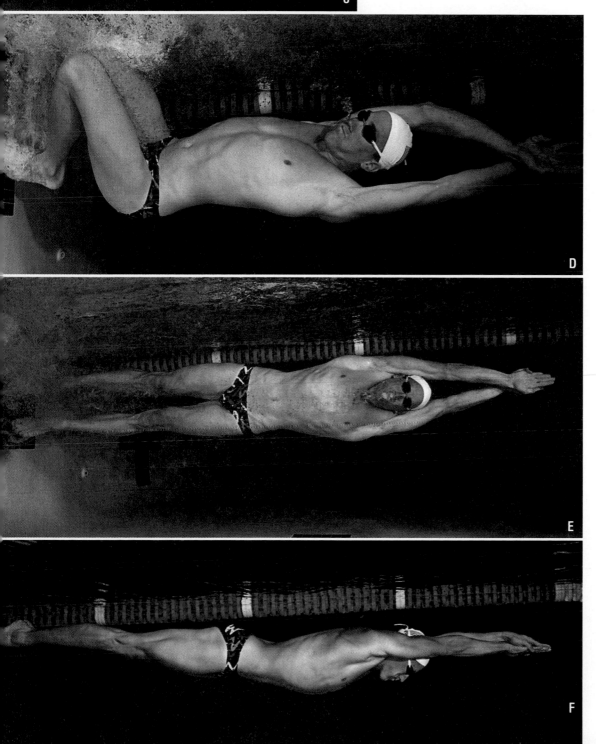

D

E

F

6. Before losing too much speed, start a steady kick and resume the arm stroke with the arm closest to the bottom. Usually, one takes a full arm cycle before taking the first breath. Figure 5-15, *A-F* illustrates the entire sequence of the flip turn.

Some swimmers prefer to rotate into a side-lying position as they plant their feet on the wall, but the push-off on the back is generally considered to be the faster method of turning.

▼ FIG. 5-15, *A-F*

A

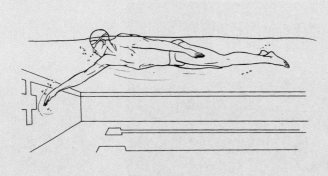

B

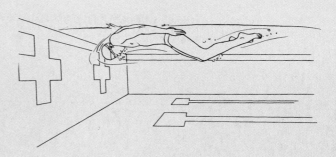

C

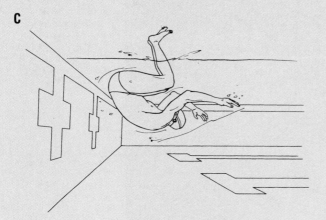

D

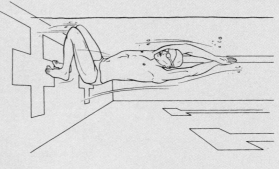

E

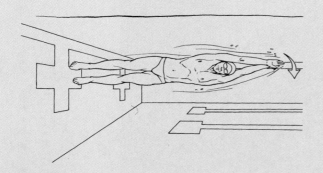

F

Breaststroke Turn

1. Time the last stroke to allow the body to be fully stretched upon reaching the wall (Fig. 5-16, *A*).
2. After both hands touch the wall simultaneously, dip the shoulder on the side to which the turn will occur. The example here starts with dipping the left shoulder to turn left. Tuck the hips and legs tight as they continue to move toward the wall (Fig. 5-16, *B*).
3. As the hands touch the wall, turn the head to the left shoulder. Bend the left elbow and move the left arm backward as close as possible to the body (Fig. 5-16, *C*).
4. When the legs pass under the body, move the right arm over the head, keeping it close to the head. Plant both feet on the wall with toes pointing toward the side, knees bent.
5. Take a deep breath before the head submerges. Extend the arms into a streamlined position while pushing off with the body somewhat on its side (Fig. 5-16, *D*).
6. Rotate to a face-down position while gliding about 1 to 2 feet below the surface.
7. Before losing too much speed, take a complete underwater breaststroke pull to the thighs, glide again and then kick upward as the hands recover close to the body (Fig. 5-16, *E–G*). Surface to resume stroking.

▶ To turn to the right, simply reverse these directions.

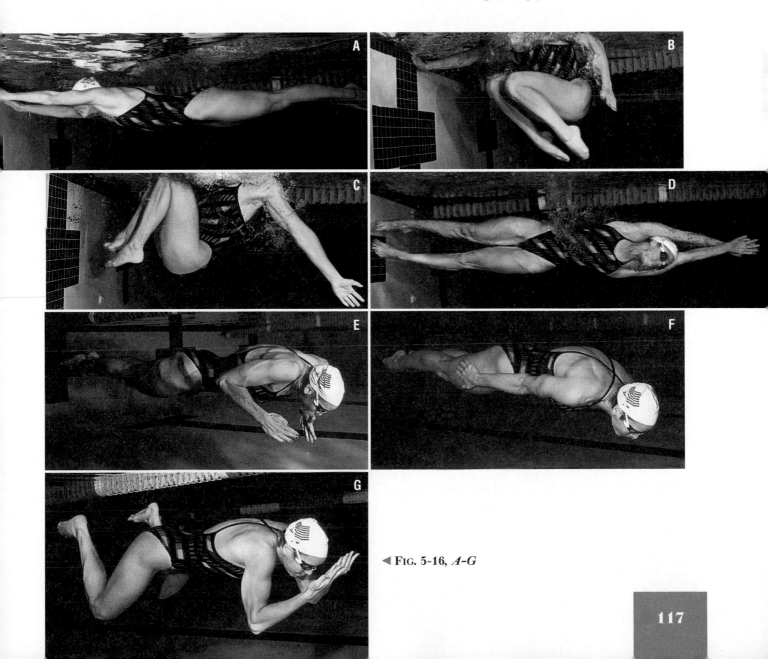

◀ Fig. 5-16, *A-G*

The underwater pull for the breaststroke turn differs from the usual pull because the hands and arms pull all the way past the hips and the hands recover close to the body. This is called a pullout. In competition, one pullout is allowed at the beginning of each length, and then the head must surface. The entire breaststroke turn and underwater pull are illustrated in Figure 5-17, *A-G*.

▼ FIG. 5-17, *A-G*

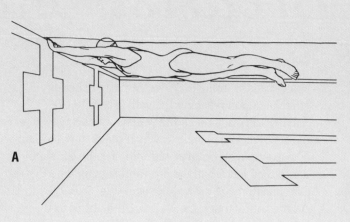

A

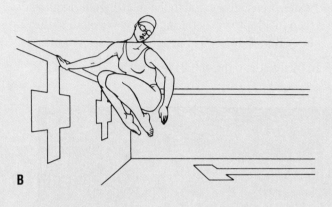

B

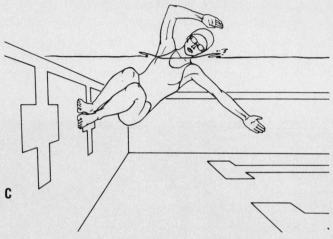

C

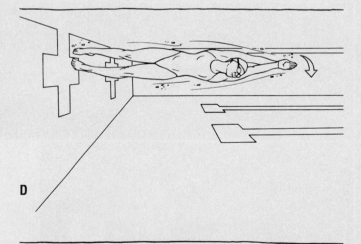

D

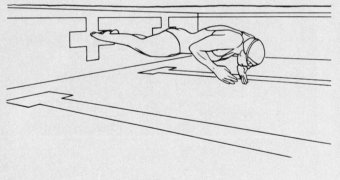

E

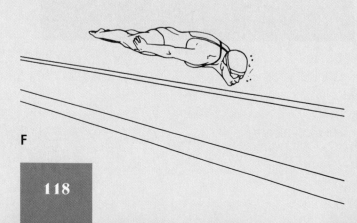

F

G

Butterfly Turn

The turn for the butterfly is similar to the breaststroke turn.

1. Time the last stroke to allow the body to be fully stretched upon reaching the wall (Fig. 5-18, *A*).
2. After both hands touch the wall, dip the shoulder toward the turning side. The example here starts with dipping the left shoulder to turn left. Tuck the hips and legs tight as they continue to move toward the wall (Fig. 5-18, *B*).
3. As the hands touch the wall, turn the head to the left shoulder. Bend the left elbow and move the left arm backward as close as possible to the body (Fig. 5-18, *C*).
4. Plant both feet on the wall with toes pointing toward the side, knees bent. When the legs pass under the body, move the right arm over the head, keeping it close to the head.
5. Take a deep breath before the head submerges. Extend the arms into a streamlined position while pushing off in a side-lying position (Fig. 5-18, *D*).
6. Rotate to a face-down position while gliding about 1 foot below the surface.

▼ FIG. 5-18, *A-D*

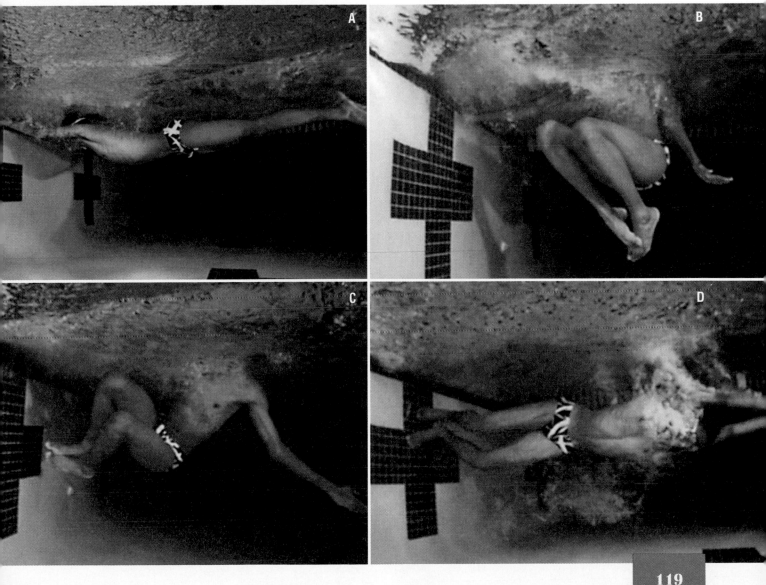

119

7. After the turn, glide a short distance, then dolphin kick to the surface and start stroking. Figure 5-19, *A-D* illustrates the butterfly turn sequence.

▶ To turn to the right, simply reverse these directions.

▶ Fig. 5-19, *A-D*

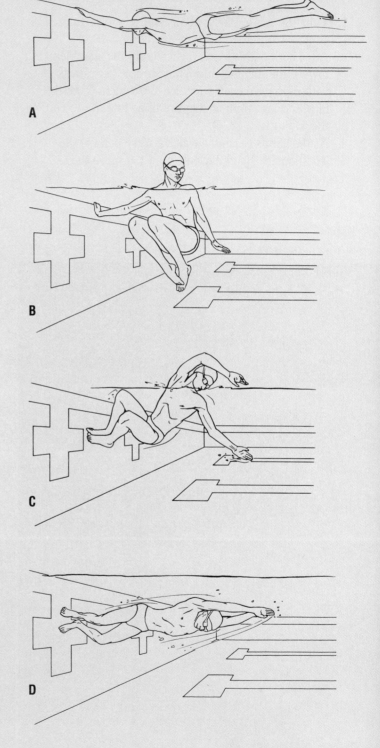

A

B

C

D

Backstroke Flip Turn

Rules for the competitive backstroke turn require the swimmer to touch the wall with any part of the body. During the turn, the shoulders may turn past vertical as long as the motion is part of a continuous turning action. Returning to a position on the back before the feet leave the wall is required.

1. After passing the backstroke flags, accelerate toward the wall.
2. Start the flip one stroke from the wall by turning the head and looking toward the pulling arm as it does the catch (Fig. 5-20, *A*).
3. While pulling, rotate onto the stomach, drive the head downward and stop the pulling hand at the hips. At the same time, the other arm recovers across the body, enters the water in the same position as in the front crawl and pulls to the hips.
4. Drive the head down and start the somersault while tucking the knees tightly to the chest (Fig. 5-20, *B* and *C*). During the somersault, turn both palms up and sweep them toward the head to complete the flip. Keep the legs tucked until the feet contact the wall, toes pointed upward (Fig. 5-20, *D*).
5. While still on the back, push straight off forcefully and go into a streamlined position while leaving the wall (Fig. 5-20, *E*). The entire backstroke flip turn is illustrated in Figure 5-21, *A-F*.

The motion in the turn must be continuous. Any hesitation, dolphin kicks or extra strokes after turning onto the stomach may lead to disqualification in a competition.

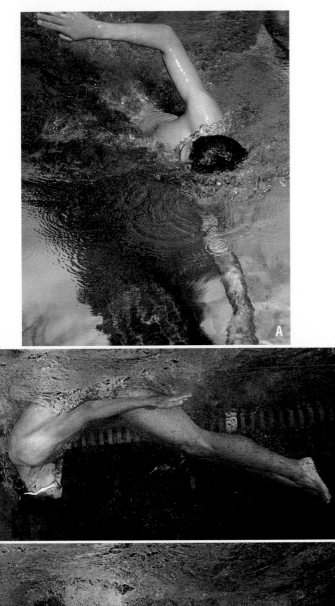

A

B

C

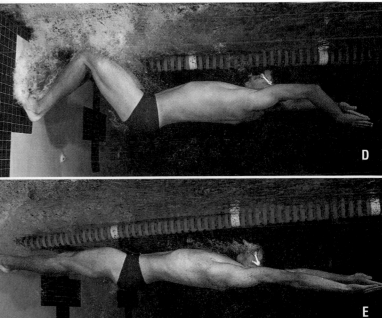

D

E

▲ FIG. 5-20, *A-E*

▼ Fɪɢ. 5-21, *A-F*

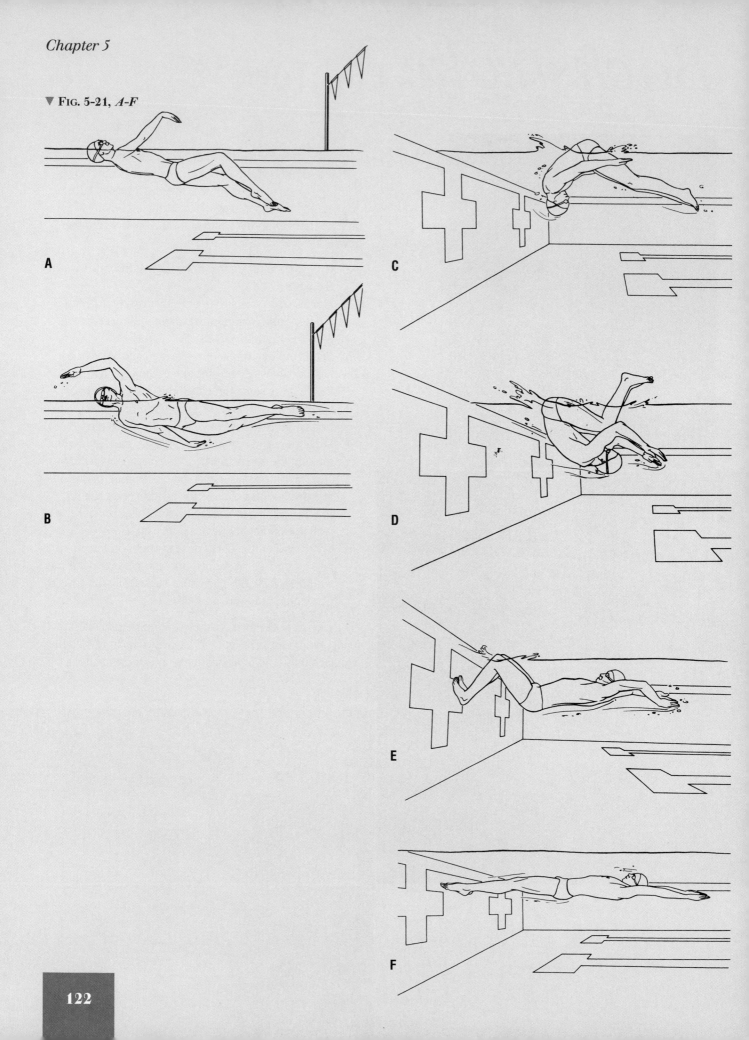

A

B

C

D

E

F

Summary

The skills in this chapter may be learned and practiced over time. A swimmer's goals will change as skills increase. Using more efficient turns for fitness swimming helps make better use of the time in the pool and may make strokes smoother. Effective starts and turns are essential to successful competition. The recreational swimmer can alternate open and speed turns to add variety to any swimming time.

Diving

Chapter 6

At many busy pools on a hot summer day, it is common to see a line of people at the diving board. Many of these children and adults will jump or dive, swim to the side and do it again and again. Some are mastering their dives; others are just having fun.

Thousands of people also enjoy recreational swimming and diving in open water. Think of the adventurers who dive or jump from heights into lakes and rivers or swing from a rope into the old swimming hole. The thrills of height and the fall appeal to the daredevil in many of us. All too often, the thrill-seeker does not think of safety, but when a diving injury happens, it can be very serious. The person who hits his or her head or back against something while diving may suffer permanent catastrophic damage.

Diving can be as safe as most other activities. Knowing how to recognize a safe place for diving, using safe equipment and applying a heavy dose of common sense are the keys to preventing injury. Equipment standards, pool standards, supervision and teaching have come a long way since the early 1900s. Before using a diving board, it is important to have instruction from a competent instructor or coach. All diving should be carefully supervised.

Learning to dive offers many benefits. The practical benefit is being able to enter the water quickly. Diving can help develop muscle tone, flexibility, coordination, balance and visual and kinesthetic awareness. Divers also gain greater self-confidence, courage, determination and motivation.

Whether learning to dive for fun or competition, this chapter is useful. Progressions for learning to dive from the deck and from a diving board are presented. A progression is an ordered set of steps, from the simplest to the most complex, for learning a skill. The progressions in this chapter should help reduce the fears or doubts about diving and help make diving safe. Be sure to get instruction from a qualified instructor or coach before trying any dive.

Risks of Diving

Trauma is a physical injury caused by a violent action. From 1990 to 2000, sports injuries made up 7.2 percent of all spinal cord traumas.* Of these sports-related injuries, more than half were a result of diving into shallow water. Injuries occur from diving into surf, lakes, rivers, quarries and swimming pools. Of the diving injuries, most occurred in water 5 feet deep or less. Very rarely does a head, neck or back injury occur from supervised diving. Only a small percentage of diving injuries occur when divers are using diving boards.

Even an experienced diver can be seriously injured by diving unsafely, diving into water of unknown depth, sliding down a water slide headfirst, falling off a diving board or diving from starting blocks without sufficient training and supervision. It is possible to hit the bottom, an underwater object or another swimmer. Many diving accidents result in paraplegia (paralysis from the waist down) or quadriplegia (total paralysis from the neck down).

Causes of Injuries

Most injuries to the head, neck or back occur in shallow water (Fig. 6-1). Many involve the use of alcohol or other drugs. Diving into open water that is shallow, diving from the deck into the shallow end

*National Spinal Cord Injury Center. Annual Report. May 2001 Fact Sheet: www.spinalcord.uab.edu.

▲ FIG. 6-1

Principles of Diving Safety

The following guidelines are recommended for safe diving:

▶ Learn how to dive safely from a qualified instructor. A self-taught diver is much more likely to be injured.

▶ In a head-first dive, extend the arms with elbows locked alongside the head. Keep the hands together with thumbs touching (or interlocked) and palms facing toward the water. Keeping the arms, wrists and fingers in line with the head helps control the angle of entry. This reduces the impact of the water on the top of the head and helps protect from injury. A diver's body should be tensed and straight from the hands to the pointed toes (Fig. 6-2).

▶ Follow safety rules at all times—never make exceptions.

▶ Do not wear earplugs; pressure changes make them dangerous.

▶ Obey "No Diving" signs. They are there for safety.

▶ Be sure of water depth and ensure that the water is free from obstructions. The first time in the water, ease in or walk in; do not jump or dive.

▶ Never dive into an above-ground pool, the shallow end of any in-ground pool or at a beach.

▶ Never dive into cloudy or murky water.

▶ In open water, always check first for objects under the surface, such as logs, stumps, boulders and pilings.

▶ Check the shape of the pool bottom to be sure the diving area is large enough and deep enough for the intended dive.

of a pool, diving into above-ground pools and unsupervised diving from starting blocks cause most diving accidents. No swimmer can be completely safe in inadequately supervised or improperly maintained swimming areas. Some areas simply are not safe for diving, and experienced divers recognize the dangers and do not dive.

A head, neck or back injury can also happen in the deep end of a pool. Injuries have been associated with dives or falls from diving boards, from jumpboards, from 3-meter stands and from the deck into some in-ground residential pools.

▶ FIG. 6-2

▶ The presence of a diving board does not necessarily mean it is safe to dive. Pools at homes, motels and hotels might not have a safe diving envelope.

▶ When diving from a deck, the area of entry should be free of obstructions (such as lane lines and kickboards) for at least 4 feet on both sides. For dives from a 1-meter diving board, 10 feet of clearance on both sides is necessary.

▶ Dive only off the end of a diving board. Diving off the side of a diving board might result in striking the side of the pool or entering water that is not deep enough.

▶ Do not bounce more than once on the end of a diving board to avoid missing the edge or slipping off the diving board.

▶ Do not run on a diving board or attempt to dive a long way through the air. The water might not be deep enough at the point of entry.

▶ For springboard diving, use equipment that meets the standards set for competition.

▶ Do not dive from a height greater than 1 meter unless trained in elevated entry.

▶ Swim away from the diving board after entering the water. Do not be a hazard for the next diver.

▶ Never use drugs or alcohol when diving.

Pool Safety Guidelines

Records maintained by United States Diving, the national governing body of competitive diving, show that there have been no fatalities or catastrophic injuries during practices or sanctioned competitive diving events. This safety record is mostly a result of careful training and supervision. It is also a result of the construction and maintenance of safe swimming pools and diving boards that meet approved minimum standards, as well as safe locations of diving boards and diving towers.

"No Diving" Signs

Because most head, neck and back injuries occur in shallow water and to people visiting an area for the first time, it is very important to warn everyone of shallow water. Placement of warning signs in key locations

may help prevent injuries. Suggested locations are the deck near the edge of the pool and walls or fences by shallow water. Signs should be visible to anyone entering the pool or approaching shallow water.

Many kinds of warnings signs can be used, such as the following:

▶ "No Diving" painted on the deck in contrasting colors (Fig. 6-3)
▶ Tiled lettering embedded into the deck in contrasting colors (Fig. 6-4)
▶ Universal "No Diving" tiles embedded into the deck
▶ "No Diving" signs mounted on the walls, fences or stands (Figs. 6-5 and 6-6)

Pools with Diving Facilities

Regardless of a pool's location, there may be some diving hazard. Pool owners should ensure that their pools meet minimum standards for safe diving. Standards are often mandated by health department codes or other state regulations. Public and private facilities with 1-meter or 3-meter diving boards and/or towers suitable for competition must meet stringent

▲ Fɪɢ. 6-3

▲ Fig. 6-4

▲ Fig. 6-5

▲ Fig. 6-6

pool design standards. Such standards are set by the National Collegiate Athletic Association (NCAA), the Federation Internationale de Natation Amateur (FINA), United States Diving and other organizations that sponsor diving competition.

All swimming pools with diving boards and towers should display their diving rules near the diving board or tower (Fig. 6-7). These rules should be strictly enforced. Such rules may include the following:

▶ Use the ladder to climb to the diving board or tower. Climbing in any other way is prohibited.
▶ Only one bounce is allowed on the end of the diving board.
▶ Only one person is allowed on the diving board at a time.
▶ No other swimmers are permitted in the diving area when the diving board or tower is in use.

▶ Dive or jump only in a straight line out from the end of the diving board or tower.
▶ Look before diving or jumping to make sure no one is in the diving area.
▶ Swim to the closest ladder or wall immediately after diving or jumping.

▶ Hands must enter the water first when performing a head-first dive.
▶ The tower can be used only with supervision from a qualified instructor or coach.
▶ Learn or practice twisting, somersaulting, and inward and reverse dives only under close supervision of a qualified instructor or coach.

▶ Fig. 6-7

Underwater Ledges

Some swimming pools have underwater ledges (sometimes called safety ledges) that may present a diving hazard (Fig. 6-8). If the ledge is hard to see, it is possible to dive into what seems to be deep water, hit the ledge and injure the head, neck or back. To reduce this risk, use color-contrasting tile or paint to clearly mark both the horizontal and vertical borders of the ledge (Fig. 6-9).

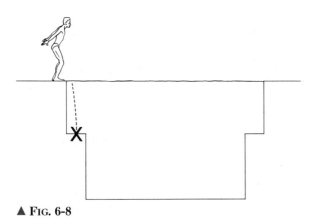

▲ FIG. 6-8

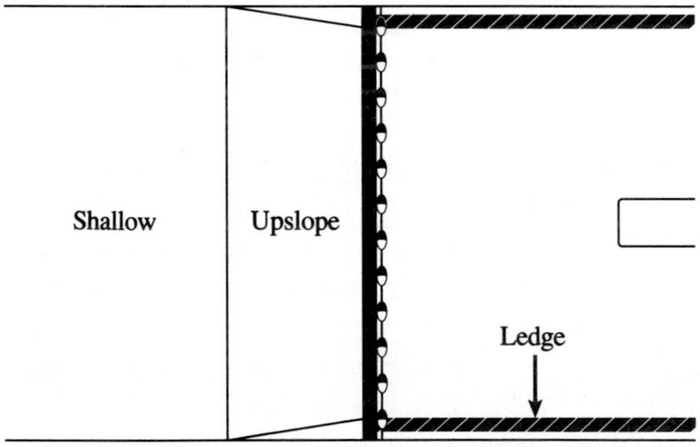

▲ FIG. 6-9

Diving Equipment

Diving equipment varies greatly at different facilities. Years ago, a diving board was just a long wooden plank crudely attached to a stand. It angled upward, making the diver's approach uphill. The stiffness and angle of the board limited the dives that could be done and sometimes made the dives from the board unsafe.

Some diving boards have a wooden core surrounded by a fiberglass outer surface, with a top made of nonslip material. The stand for this kind of diving board generally secures the back end of the board and has a stationary fulcrum (a pivot near the center of a diving board that lets the board bend and spring) (Fig. 6-10). Diving facilities not built to minimum standards may have different board lengths, fulcrum placement, height of the board over the water and board resiliency. These inconsistencies could be dangerous, because a diver cannot tell if the equipment is reliable. One should learn more advanced dives on equipment that meets the standards for competitive diving.

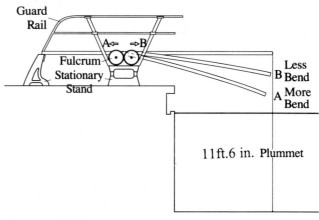

▲ FIG. 6-10

Equipment for competitive diving has evolved into an advanced system of diving board, movable fulcrum and stationary stand. Diving boards used for competition are made of aluminum and coated with an abrasive surface. They are 1 meter or 3 meters in height over the water.

The quality of the stand is important. The stand has a solid base and a movable fulcrum. The movable fulcrum allows adjustments according to strength, weight and timing. Proper adjustment for a diver's abilities is very important for performance. The diving board should stay level when the fulcrum is moved. A level board helps divers reach the proper distance from the board in flight

▲ FIG. 6-11

and entry. A guard rail on each side of the board helps prevent a fall onto the deck. Steps or stairs of nonslip material should give easy access to the diving board from the deck.

Some diving facilities have diving platforms (stationary structures for diving), which are constructed in various ways. Proper construction provides a solid foundation and a nonskid surface. State-of-the-art diving facilities include 1-meter, 3-meter, 5-meter, $7^1/_2$-meter and 10-meter platforms (Fig. 6-11). Use diving platforms only under the direct supervision of a qualified diving coach or instructor.

The depth of the water for springboard diving is an important safety factor. Facilities should ensure that standards set by governing bodies, such as NCAA, FINA and United States Diving, are followed before any diving is permitted.

Residential Pools

In-Ground Pools

In-ground residential pools at homes, apartments and condominiums come in many sizes and shapes. Because most head, neck or back injuries in residential pools come from dives into shallow water, the American Red Cross recommends that pool owners take these precautions:

► Consult the National Spa and Pool Institute, state law and local building codes for pool dimension guidelines to help establish rules for a pool to ensure safe diving activities. For example:
  ● Prohibit all dives into shallow water
  ● Only allow dives from the edge of the pool into deep water
  ● Diving from a diving board should only occur if there is a safe diving envelope (the area of water in front of, below and to the sides of a diving board that is deep enough that a diver will not strike the bottom, regardless of the depth of the water or the design of the pool)
► Clearly mark the location of the breakpoint between shallow and deep water with a buoyed line and mark the deck with signs that indicate depth.
► Place "No Diving" signs on the deck near shallow water and on the fence or wall around the swimming pool or on a stand at the entry to the swimming pool.
► Prohibit elevated entry from any object not specifically designed for diving, such as chairs, fences or balconies.

Even deep water in home pools may be dangerous because of the shape of the bottom and sides of the pool or the placement of the diving board. The average home pool is not long enough or deep enough for safe springboard diving.

Two common designs for in-ground residential pools are the hopper-bottom pool and the spoon-shaped pool. A hopper-bottom pool has a bottom that angles sharply up on all four sides from the deepest point up to the breakpoint (Fig. 6-12, *A* and *B*). Thus, the safe diving envelope is much smaller than it appears. Diving into a hopper-bottom pool may be like diving into a funnel. If the depth markers give only the depth at the deepest point, a diver may think the area for safe diving is larger than it actually is. Diving from either a diving board or the deck, the diver may hit the bottom.

The spoon-shaped pool also may present risks to safe diving because the distance from the end of the diving board to the slope of the bottom is greatly reduced (Fig. 6-13, *A* and *B*). The bottom contour of the spoon-shaped pool may give a false sense of depth and bottom area throughout the deep end.

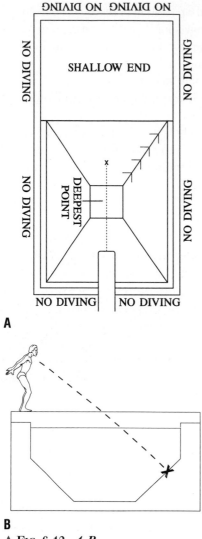

A

▲ Fig. 6-12, *A-B*

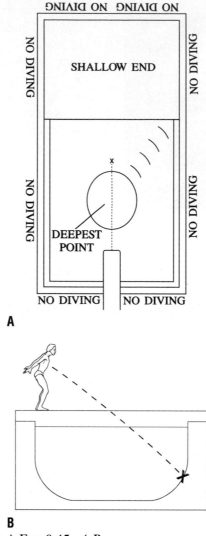

A

▲ Fig. 6-13, *A-B*

Above-Ground Pools

No one should ever dive into an above-ground pool. People have been injured by diving from the deck, the rim or a structure above the edge. Swimmers should use the ladder to enter or ease feetfirst into any above-ground pool to be safe.

Public and Private Pools

Hotel, motel, apartment and public pools may have the same diving hazards found in residential pools. The lack of supervision at many facilities also adds to potential hazards. Before diving, carefully check the pool to make sure it is safe. Check the depth of the water, the length and height of the diving board and the shape of the bottom.

Starting Blocks

Pools designed for competitive swimming are equipped with starting blocks, which can be permanent or removable. Starting blocks at the shallow end of a pool may be a hazard. Competitive swimmers are trained to perform racing starts from blocks. People without training who dive from blocks are at risk. An entry that is too shallow could lead to injury. Starting blocks should be restricted to supervised competitive swimming (Fig. 6-14). At all other times, "No Diving" signs should be posted on each block, the blocks removed or access prevented.

Water Parks and Water Slides

Water parks and water slides have become very popular. Water park pools and slides are built in many sizes and shapes (Fig. 6-15). Slides vary in length, height, angle and direction of descent. With the proper precautions, they can be enjoyable and safe.

To reduce the possibility of injury when using a water slide, follow these guidelines:

▶ Follow all posted instructions.
▶ Always slide feetfirst unless otherwise directed by the ride operator (Fig. 6-16).

▲ Fig. 6-14

▲ Fig. 6-15

▲ Fig. 6-16

Open Water

Oceans and Rivers

Currents and tides can cause the bottom contour of oceans and rivers to change very rapidly. Sunken logs, debris and built-up silt or sand are risks for swimmers who run and dive into the water. Any object under water, even another swimmer, could be a major hazard.

Take care to enter the water safely. Check for "No Diving" signs on the beach or on floats in the water. Never run and dive into an area of moving water. Even when the area seems clear, the current can bring an underwater obstruction into the area within minutes. Wade into the water until

▶ Keep the landing area in front of the slide clear of people.
▶ Do not try deep entries on purpose.
▶ Be sure the slide is anchored securely to the deck.
▶ If the slide has a lip that is higher than the deck or the surface of the water, be sure there is sufficient water depth to keep from striking the bottom.
▶ On speed slides, cross the legs to help prevent injuries.

▲ FIG. 6-17

it is chest-deep. Then plunge out, and not down, using a shallow dive with hands overhead and the head between the arms. Remain near the surface, parallel to the bottom, then steer up to the surface immediately.

Lakes and Quarries

Although lakes and quarries have less water movement than oceans and rivers, the bottom may present hazards. Wind and waves can move submerged debris close to shore. In man-made lakes, submerged tree stumps or logs may be close to shore. In lakes and especially in quarries, boulders may be hidden under water (Fig. 6-17).

Running and diving into a lake or quarry can be very hazardous. In supervised areas, the bottom should be surveyed for obstructions at the beginning of the season and daily thereafter. Any obstruction should be removed or marked with a buoy and a warning sign. Diving should

be prohibited in the area. Unless it is known what safety precautions have been taken in an area, do not assume it is safe. Never run and dive in an unsupervised area. Wade until the water is chest-deep before swimming. Any head-first entry could cause injury.

Never dive from a pier or any other structure into shallow water. If unsure of the depth and bottom con-

tour, do not dive. The water may be shallower than expected. Each time swimming in open water, swimmers should lower themselves into the water feetfirst or wade in from shore the first time they go in the water.

Never dive into a quarry. Often there are underwater obstacles, such as boulders, ledges and equipment from excavation operations. Carefully check the bottom and depth before

Visual and Kinesthetic Awareness

Visual and kinesthetic awareness are very important in learning diving skills. Visual awareness is the ability to stay focused on a reference point to determine a body's position in space, such as during flight from a diving board. Kinesthetic awareness is the ability to perceive what a body is doing at any

given moment, such as being aware of the position of the arms and legs during rotation. Visual and kinesthetic awareness help one maintain control when doing complex dives. Skills can be improved by keeping the eyes open and focused on a fixed reference point. Another person splashing the surface of

the water in front of the diving board can help one focus on the water's surface. This helps maintain awareness of one's body's position in relation to the water and to achieve good body alignment for entry.

entering from any height. Ease in feetfirst to check the bottom and depth. If it is not possible to ease into the water, try another entry point.

Diver Readiness

In the previous chapter, readiness for performing head-first entries was discussed. Factors, such as strength, muscular control and common fears, were presented. These same factors may apply as swimmers learn the simple dive from the pool deck, which has an entry that is more perpendicular to the surface of the water and results in a thrust downward toward the bottom of the pool.

The Red Cross recommends that people first learn to perform head-first entries at a low angle of entry, i.e., enter the water at a slight angle, swim parallel to the surface, steer back to the surface and then begin stroking. After swimmers are skilled in the swimming entry, also known as the shallow dive, they may move on to a basic dive (Fig. 6-18) and then to diving from a board.

While the progressions for learning the basic dive are quite similar to the progressions for learning the shallow dive, it is important to realize that there are differences. The primary differences are in the angle of entry and the resulting underwater swimming path. The following progressions can help minimize fears and can help divers reach success at each level. If time is taken to master the skills of each step before moving to the next, the diver will enjoy the experience more and feel more ready to try the next skill.

▲ Fig. 6-18

Beginning Diving

Components of a Simple Dive

A simple dive has three parts: the stationary starting position; the moment of propulsion, called the takeoff; and the entry into the water. A diver can use different starting positions, as will be discussed later. The takeoff for a simple dive is quite easy, usually a slight push with one or both feet. A good entry involves entering the water at the correct point and keeping the body aligned as it enters the water.

To be sure of diving into the water at the correct point of entry, focus on a target (either an imaginary point on the surface or a real or imagined target on the bottom of the pool) until the hands enter the water.

The diver may close the eyes at that point and open them again after entering the water. For any dive, it is important to maintain concentration. Focusing attention on one place is a good way to do this when learning to dive.

Keeping proper body alignment is crucial for a safe and graceful dive. Head position is very important because it affects the position of the body in general. Moving the head may cause the body to arch or bend. The beginner who lifts the head too quickly may do a painful belly flop.

Muscular control also is important for proper body alignment and the body tension needed for a safe, effective dive. Try to stay in a streamlined position in flight (the passage of the body through the air) (Fig. 6-19). This helps maintain control and helps make dives more graceful. Good alignment when entering the water reduces drag and the risk of straining muscles or joints.

Physical Principles Involved

Form drag is an important principle in diving. Try to keep form drag to a minimum in the entry. Lifting the head before a head-first entry, for example, increases form drag. Not keeping other body parts aligned (such as not straightening the body at the hips) also can cause a part of the body to be stung by the impact with the water. Being out of alignment causes a big splash, and the dive is not as attractive.

Two other physical principles at work in any dive are the law of action and reaction, when the feet push against the deck in the takeoff, and buoyancy, which helps you return to the surface after the dive.

Progression for a Simple Dive

The steps for learning a simple dive from the pool deck will give self-confidence and a feeling of success. Divers should remember to move through them at their own pace. Some steps might need lots of practice. With good coordination and kinesthetic awareness, some divers may be able to move more quickly through them. This progression may also be used to learn to dive from a pier.

Kneeling Position

1. Kneel on one knee while gripping the pool edge with the toes of the other foot (Fig. 6-20). The foot of the kneeling leg should be in a position to help push from the deck.
2. Extend the arms over the head.
3. Focus on a target on the surface of the water 1 to 2 feet from the side. The objective is to dive deep. Focusing on a target helps in entering the water at the right place and at the correct angle, avoiding a belly flop.
4. Lean forward, try to touch the water, and when starting to lose balance, push with the legs.
5. On entering the water, straighten the body and extend both legs.

Practice this skill until it can be done comfortably and without error.

▼ Fig. 6-19

▼ Fig. 6-20

Sparging Systems

Although diving is a noncontact sport, divers do collide with the water without any protective padding. Surprising as this may sound, if a diver lands horizontally on the water from a height of 10 meters, the force of the impact is measured in thousands of pounds. Such an impact, aside from being quite painful, can cause severe injury, including ruptured organs and even detached retinas.

The air sparging system, or "bubble machine," was invented to reduce pain and risk of injury when a diver is learning new dives. Located on the pool bottom, the air sparger shoots air at high velocity into the pool, creating a uniform mixture of air and water in the area where the diver enters the pool. The bubbles form a "mound" of water above the normal surface level of the water to cushion the diver's entry. This protection allows the diver to concentrate on the technique of the dive, rather than on the landing. The beginning diver builds skills and confidence in a more relaxed fashion, thus reducing the risk of injury.

Sparging systems can reduce the force of impact of a diver's body on the water by as much as 80 percent. This means that landing flat from 10 meters on bubbles would have almost the same impact as landing flat from 2 meters on "solid" water. The coach controls the system with a handheld remote that starts and stops the instant air release. The coach can therefore start the sys-

tem before the diver leaves the tower or board and stop it as soon as the diver has entered the water.

Even though the sparging machine can reduce the force of impact, proper alignment is still important. If a diver's body is not "tight" on entry, the force of impact can knock the wind out of the diver and even cause severe tissue injury.

Sparging machines are not a substitute for proper skills and are not to be used as a crutch. They are to be used only to help a diver gain the confidence and

skill needed to perform the dive into "solid" water.

Many uses have been found for sparging systems, aside from reducing the risk of injuries to competitive divers. Surf simulation (wave pools), treadmill swimming, whitewater canoeing and handicap float swims are just a few. When safety precautions are properly taken, as with any activity in or around the water, bubble machines can provide hours of recreational activity for people of any age or circumstance.

Compact Position

Do this dive in much the same manner as the dive from the kneeling position.

1. Put one foot forward and one back, with the toes of the leading foot gripping the edge of the deck.
2. Start in the kneeling position.
3. Lift up so both knees are off the deck and flexed to stay close to the water.
4. Extend the arms above the head.
5. Focus on a target the same distance from the deck as in the dive from a kneeling position (Fig. 6-21).
6. Bend forward and try to touch the surface of the water with the hands.
7. When starting to lose balance, push off toward the water. Bring the legs together when entering the water.

Stride Position

1. After several successful dives from the compact position, one should be ready for a dive from the stride position.
2. Stand upright with one leg forward and one leg back. The toes of the forward foot should grip the edge of the pool.
3. Extend the arms above the head.
4. Focus on a target on the surface 3 to 4 feet from the side. Bend the legs only slightly while bending at the waist toward the water.
5. Try to touch the surface of the water and, while losing balance, lift the back leg until it is in line with the torso (Fig. 6-22). The forward leg should stay as straight as possible.

▲ Fig. 6-22

Standing Dive

The final dive from the deck is the standing dive.

1. Stand with feet about shoulder-width apart with the toes of both feet gripping the edge of the deck.
2. Extend the arms above the head.
3. Focus on a target at the same distance as in a dive from the stride position.
4. Bend at the knees and angle the hands down toward the target (Fig. 6-23, *A*).
5. Push off the deck, lift the hips and extend the legs so they are in line with the torso (Fig. 6-23, *B*).

As divers gain confidence, they may move the feet closer together.

▼ Fig. 6-21

▲ Fig. 6-23, *A-B*

Beginner Progression from Diving Board

Once skilled in diving from the deck, one is ready to learn a standing dive from a diving board. Follow the same progression used to learn to dive from the deck. The surface of the diving board may be rough and scrape the knee in the kneeling position, so consider putting a pad or wet towel over the board. If the diving board has a movable fulcrum, move it all the way forward to make the diving board more stable. Once a diver has learned the same progression to the standing dive, all from a diving

board, he or she is ready to start learning springboard diving skills.

Springboard Diving

Components of a Springboard Dive

A forward springboard dive adds several features to the elements of a simple dive. First, there is a moving start, involving an approach and hurdle. Second, there is the interaction between the diver and the div-

ing board, involving the press and the lift. Third, the diver can execute the dive in many different ways. The propulsive action of the diving board allows time to add twists and somersaults to the trajectory (the curved path of the body through the air). Finally, depending on the dive, the entry may be feetfirst or headfirst.

The approach is the walk toward the end of a diving board before the hurdle (Fig. 6-24, *A*). It consists of at least three steps, taken slowly and

▲ Fig. 6-24, *A*

▲ Fig. 6-24, *B-E*

with good posture. The final step before the hurdle is generally a little longer than the others. The hurdle is the jump to the end of a diving board after the approach (Fig. 6-24, *B* and *C*). These skills determine the diver's trajectory, height and distance in flight.

There are two parts to the interaction between the diver and the diving board. The press is the diver's downward push on the diving board (Fig. 6-24, *D*), and the lift is the force of the diving board pushing the diver into the air (Fig. 6-24, *E*).

Diving from a diving board requires more kinesthetic awareness than diving from a deck. Continuing to use a progression of skills helps develop one's abilities and confidence as a diver. Before starting on a diving board, the diver must be able to do a standing dive from the deck with confidence.

As mentioned earlier, one should learn springboard diving only under the supervision of an instructor or coach. The information that follows is intended for use in Red Cross swimming courses using a 1-meter diving board. If interested in com-

petitive diving, seek instruction from a competent diving instructor or coach.

The three basic positions for executing a dive are the tuck, pike and straight positions. In the tuck position, the body is bent at the hips and knees. Keep the body in a tight ball by grabbing both legs midway between the ankles and knees and pulling the knees to the chest. Draw the heels up to the buttocks (Fig. 6-25, *A*). In the pike position, the body is bent at the hips while the legs are kept straight (Fig. 6-25, *B*). In the straight position, the body is

straight or arched slightly backward with the legs straight and together (Fig. 6-25, *C*). In competition, there is also a free position, which gives the diver an option to use any of the three basic positions, or combinations of the positions, when performing a twisting dive.

Physical Principles Involved

Of the many physical principles that affect a springboard dive, gravity and the law of levers (which affects rotation) are most important. First, the force of gravity affects the diver's upward and downward motion. Lift from the diving board propels the diver upward and

slightly forward, and then gravity slows the upward motion, brings the diver to a stationary position in the air for an instant and pulls him or her down into the water.

Most important here is that the time the diver has in the air for somersaults and turns depends only on the upward lift from the diving board. Adding lateral speed, such as running in the approach, does not increase a diver's time in the air. In fact, expending energy running forward may decrease the height of the hurdle and thus reduce the time in the air. Even with a takeoff that seems vertical, there is enough forward motion to keep a diver clear of the diving board throughout the dive if the hurdle is executed properly.

Another principle involves the rotation of a diver in the air. If the diver exerts the same force for all types of somersaults, the spin will be fastest in the tuck position, slightly slower in the pike position and slowest in the straight position. This is an effect of the law of levers. (See Chapter 2.) Changing body position changes the speed of the rotation. A beginning diver can most easily learn somersaults in the tuck position.

Dry-Land Practice

Approach and Hurdle

The approach and hurdle are important skills for a springboard dive. Practice them repeatedly on land before trying them on a diving board. Be sure the feet and the deck are dry when practicing.

▲ Fig. 6-25, *A-C*

▲ Fɪɢ. 6-26

The hurdle is done by raising the hurdle leg (the leg that is lifted) into a position like that shown in Figure 6-26. The thigh should be at a 90-degree angle to the body and the leg below the knee parallel to or angled slightly back toward the push leg (the leg used to push into the hurdle). Because almost everyone has a dominant side of the body, most divers have a preferred hurdle leg. Because of this, one should at first alternate the legs for the hurdle leg. Once it is determined which leg is preferred, keep using that leg for the hurdle leg.

The first skill to learn is the one-step approach and hurdle. This lets the diver concentrate on the hurdle itself. Put two strips of tape on the deck about 2 feet apart and parallel to each other to mark the distance needed for the hurdle. The first strip is where the toes should be after the last step before the hurdle. The second strip indicates the tip of the diving board.

1. Start with the feet together about 1 foot away from the first strip on the deck.
2. Swing the arms back in preparation for the hurdle.
3. While stepping forward with the push leg to the first strip (Fig. 6-27, *A*), begin to swing the arms backward.
4. Lift the hurdle leg, swing the arms forward and upward into a position above the head and jump upward and forward with the push leg (Fig. 6-27, *B*).
5. The push leg should stay straight during the jump to the second strip (the end of the "diving board"). The distance covered

by the jump depends on a diver's size and strength, but it is usually 1 to 2 feet for adults and less for children.
6. Midway in the hurdle, start to straighten the hurdle leg so that it is in line with the push leg (Fig. 6-27, *C*).
7. Just before landing in front of the second strip of tape, start to swing the arms backward and downward (Fig. 6-27, *D*).
8. Stand on the balls of the feet. (Landing flat-footed on a real diving board will restrict its action and give less lift into the air.)
9. As the feet contact the deck, flex slightly at the hips and knees and swing the arms forward and upward in front of and above the head.
10. In the approach and hurdle, focus on the second strip of tape.
11. Keep the head as erect as possible; the diver should be able to see the second strip of tape during the hurdle.

Once the one-step approach and hurdle is mastered, proceed to the full approach and hurdle in dry-land practice. A full approach involves three or more steps, with the final step being slightly longer. In a three-step approach:

1. Step first with the push leg and start to swing the arms backward while starting the final step of the approach. (If using four steps, start with the hurdle leg.)
2. Focus on the second strip of tape and keep the head erect, as in the one-step approach and hurdle.
3. The arms should be straight during the approach, hurdle and lift.

A 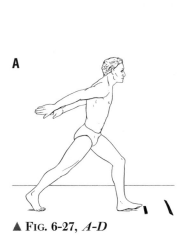 B C D

▲ Fig. 6-27, *A-D*

To estimate the starting point for the full approach, place the heels on the strip that simulates the end of the diving board, facing away from the "water." Do the full approach and hurdle away from the strip of tape. Mark the landing place with a third strip of tape. Now turn around and use this as the starting point for your approach. Practice the full approach and hurdle several times on deck before progressing to the diving board.

Position for Head-First Entry

Body position for the entry from a diving board is even more important than from the deck. The diver must keep good body alignment and rigidity and enter the water vertically. Practice proper body alignment in a standing position before trying head-first dives from the diving board in the following way:

1. Hand position: Place one hand on top of the other and grip the bottom hand with the fingers of the top hand. Interlock the thumbs. Flex both wrists so the palm of the bottom hand hits flat on the surface. This helps keep proper arm position.

2. Arm position: Raise the arms overhead with hands in line with shoulders and hips. Lock the elbows. Press the arms tight against the head (Fig. 6-28, *A*).

3. Head position: Keep the head erect and tilted back slightly. Tilting the head back or forward too far may affect body alignment and rigidity and cause injury.

4. Upper body position: Pull in the stomach and project the rib cage forward (Fig. 6-28, *B*).

5. Hip position: Tilt the top of the pelvis (hips) backward to help reduce sway in the lower back. Such sway can affect body rigidity and lead to injury.

A    B

▲ Fig. 6-28, *A-B*

A

B

C

6. Leg and foot positions: Lock the knees, and keep the legs straight and toes pointed.

Diving Board Skills

After following the progression described earlier from deck to springboard dives, a diver has already learned to do a standing dive from a diving board. The following progressions help one learn other skills for springboard dives.

Forward Dive Fall-In

The forward dive fall-in allows work on correct body alignment and rigidity for the entry without being concerned with the approach, hurdle or flight. Practice correct body position first on dry land, as described earlier.

1. Stand with the toes at the tip of the diving board.
2. Hold the arms straight to the side at a 90-degree angle to the upper body (like the letter T).
3. Bend at the waist so the upper body is at a 90-degree angle to the legs (pike position) and focus on a target on the surface of the water about 4 feet from the tip of the diving board (Fig. 6-29, *A*).
4. Rise up onto the toes and fall forward toward the water, keeping focused on the target.
5. Move the arms laterally to the entry position while falling toward the water (Fig. 6-29, *B*).
6. Extend the body from a pike position to a straight position for the entry (Fig. 6-29, *C*).

Practice this skill thoroughly before moving on.

◀ Fig. 6-29, *A-C*

Takeoffs

The following maneuvers help the diver use the diving board to gain more height for dives. Practice the approach and hurdle on dry land several times before progressing to the diving board. When beginning on the diving board, always start with the fulcrum as far forward as possible for better stability. Once one is comfortable with these dives, the fulcrum can be adjusted.

Standing Jump

The standing jump uses arm action to gain greater height for the flight.

1. Stand at the tip of the diving board with the toes at the edge. Keep arms straight and over the head.
2. Swing the arms backward and downward while flexing at the knees and hips (Fig. 6-30, *A*). Then swing the arms forward and upward while extending, and jump off the diving board and into the water (Fig. 6-30, *B*). Focusing on a point in the middle of the pool helps keep the head in the proper position.
3. Enter feetfirst with head erect, hands at the sides and legs straight (Fig. 6-30, *C*).

▲ Fig. 6-30, *A-C*

One-Step Approach and Hurdle

Do the one-step approach and hurdle on the diving board the same way it was practiced on dry land. At first put a strip of tape across the diving board about 2 feet from the tip to help see where the last step should fall.

When practicing the one-step approach and hurdle, jump to the end of the diving board and spring upward, forward and feetfirst into the water. Do not try to bounce again on the diving board after the hurdle. Beginning divers have a hard time keeping their balance after a jump. Bouncing into the air and trying to land on the diving board can cause an injury.

Full Approach and Hurdle

The final step is to include the approach before the hurdle. Most important, determine the starting point first. Do this the same way as on dry land. Make sure the fulcrum is all the way forward for maximum stability, at least for the first few practice jumps into the water. Continue to enter the water feetfirst.

Entering in Tuck and Pike Positions

Sitting Tuck

A simple dry-land exercise helps one get used to this position.

1. Sit on the deck and pull the knees up to the chest.
2. Grab both legs midway between the ankles and knees, pulling the knees tight to the chest.

Practice this skill also by lying on the back.

Jump Tuck from Deck

After practicing the tuck position sitting or lying on the deck, try the jump tuck from the side of the pool in the following way:

1. Stand at the edge of the pool over deep water. Grip the edge of the pool with the toes. Hold the arms above the head in line with the upper body.
2. Swing the arms backward and downward while flexing the hips and knees.
3. Then swing the arms forward and upward to a position above the head and in front of the shoulders while jumping as high as possible off the edge of the deck.
4. While in flight, pull the legs up to the chest and grab them briefly (Fig. 6-31).
5. Release the legs and straighten them toward the water. Enter feetfirst with head erect, hands at sides and legs straight.

Forward Jump, Tuck Position

The forward jump tuck lets the diver experience the feeling of the tuck position during flight. (The term *position* is sometimes omitted from the names of jumps and dives.) This skill also helps the diver gain body control. Start with a jump from the deck and progress to greater heights to become more comfortable with the tuck position. A gradual progression also helps ensure success with a jump tuck from the 1-meter diving board.

Jump Tuck from Diving Board

The standing jump tuck from a diving board is done in the same manner as from the deck. Practice it until comfortable with this skill before moving on.

► FIG. 6-31

Jump Tuck with One-Step Approach and Hurdle

The next step is to combine the one-step approach and hurdle with the jump tuck. This gives greater height for doing the jump tuck. While in flight, practice the tuck position the same way as in the standing jump tuck.

Jump Tuck with Full Approach and Hurdle

The final step is to do a full approach and hurdle with the jump tuck. Be sure to have mastered the one-step approach and jump tuck before progressing to this step. Do the jump tuck with full approach and hurdle in the same manner as with the one-step approach, but now take three or more steps in the approach. The greatest height is attained in the trajectory with the full approach.

Standing Forward Dive, Tuck Position

Once proper entry technique has been mastered, try a forward dive tuck. The tuck position helps one gain control of the body in flight. It also helps develop timing for the entry. Having already practiced the jump tuck from the deck and diving board, the mechanics of the tuck position should be familiar.

1. Stand at the tip of the diving board with arms overhead.
2. Swing the arms backward and downward and then forward and upward, as in the standing jump tuck.
3. While springing into the air, focus on the entry point. This will help keep the head in the proper position at the start of the dive (Fig. 6-32, *A*).

▲ Fig. 6-32, *A-C*

4. Push the hips up and at the same time let the head go down. Keep focusing on the entry point.
5. Pull the knees up to the chest and grab the legs for a proper tuck position. The body will rotate forward (Fig. 6-32, *B*).
6. Keep focusing on the entry point to tell when to come out of the tuck position to make a vertical entry.
7. While coming out of the tuck, swing the arms out to the side (laterally) to prepare for entry. Swinging the arms out in front can cause the legs to go past vertical.
8. Align the body for the entry (Fig. 6-32, *C*).

Components of a Competitive Dive

Competitive dives have grown in variety and intricacy over the past several decades. New combinations of skills are still being prepared to be used in competition. All dives, however, involve some combination of the following elements, although not all combinations are approved for competition—or are even possible.

Apparatus: A dive may be made from a 1-meter or 3-meter springboard or from a platform that is 1, 3, 5, 7^1/$_2$ or 10 meters high.

Takeoff: A diver may leave the apparatus facing forward (using an approach and hurdle from a springboard or a standing jump from a platform) or facing backward (using a backward press).

Somersaults: Regardless of the takeoff, somersaults may be forward (with a rotation in the direction the diver is facing) or reverse (with the opposite rotation).

Body position: The body may be in tuck, pike or straight position.

Twists: A twist is a rotation along the midline of the body, which is held straight during the twist. Twisting may be combined with somersaults in some dives.

Entry: The entry may be headfirst or feetfirst.

Depending on the combination of elements, each dive is assigned a degree of difficulty. Judges' evaluations are based on the approach, the elevation (whether the dive reaches an appropriate height), the execution and the entry. A diver's score in competition is based on both the degree of difficulty of the dive and the judges' scores.

Rotation in the tuck can be controlled in a number of ways. Rotation is increased if the head is dropped too much before takeoff or by pushing the hips over the head. Practice will help the diver learn to rotate the right amount. If it feels as if the dive is going past vertical, come out of the tuck position and reach for the entry. If it feels as if the dive is short of vertical, stay in the tuck position longer.

One-Step Approach, Forward Dive, Tuck Position

The next step is to combine the one-step approach with the forward dive tuck. Do the one-step approach in the same way as before. This step gives more height than in the standing dive. The timing for entry may be slightly different, but otherwise this dive is like the standing dive.

Full Approach and Hurdle, Forward Dive, Tuck Position

The final step in this progression is to do a full approach and hurdle with a forward dive tuck. Do not take a full spring the first few times trying this. Take a slight spring at first and then progress to a full spring. This will help you become comfortable with the greater height from the spring and the different timing for coming out of the tuck for the entry.

Forward Dive, Pike Position

Do the forward dive in the pike position by pushing the hips up while reaching for the toes (Fig. 6-33, *A* and *B*). Keep the legs straight and bend only at the hips. After touching the toes, extend the arms laterally in preparation for the entry (Fig. 6-33, *C*). Swinging the arms directly forward causes the legs to lift. Practice the forward dive pike using the same steps as the forward dive tuck:

1. Standing forward dive in the pike position
2. One-step approach and hurdle
3. Full approach and hurdle

▼ Fig. 6-33, *A-C*

Summary

Most head, neck or back injuries happen when a person dives into shallow water. Injuries can result from running and diving into open water, diving from docks, diving into quarries and diving from a deck or a diving board into a pool with insufficient diving area or depth. Jumping, falling or being pushed against a solid object also can injure the spine. Most head, neck or back injuries happen at the pool's shallow end, in a corner or where the bottom slopes up toward shallow water.

In open water, such as lakes or rivers, injuries to the head, neck or back can occur in shallow areas and where the water level varies because of tides or currents. Areas with underwater hazards, such as rocks and tree stumps, also cause injuries.

When arriving at any swimming area, look carefully for "No Diving" signs and potential diving hazards. By systematically checking the diving area for any potential hazards, divers can avoid catastrophic injury. By being safety-minded, divers can protect themselves, their families and their friends from severe injury.

With proper instruction, diving can be safe and enjoyable. This chapter described some of the principles involved for learning basic diving skills. Learning these skills in step-by-step progressions is an effective and safe way to develop diving abilities. If interested in competitive diving, competitive programs are available at many public and private schools, at parks and recreation programs and through United States Diving.

Disabilities

and Other Conditions

Chapter 7

The National Council on Disabilities estimates that 54 million Americans have disabilities. Many other people have conditions such as asthma, seizures or a heart ailment that may limit their ability to join in recreational activities. In addition, with aging often comes an increase in chronic disease, especially cardiovascular disease. Many senior citizens with cardiovascular disease and other limiting factors find that aquatics meets their needs for leisure and fitness (Fig. 7-1).

▲ FIG. 7-1

This chapter discusses the benefits of aquatics for people with disabilities or other conditions, gives an overview of various disabilities, lists safety considerations, discusses how facilities should be equipped and surveys program choices.

Regardless of physical condition, it is important to check with a health care provider before starting an aquatics program, especially if one has not exercised in a while. Also, if there is a concern about limitations caused by a physical condition, a health care provider should be consulted before entering a program.

Attitudes and Norms

Disabilities vary in many ways, some slight or not even observable, others more significant. A limitation resulting from impairment is a disability. Impairment is any loss or abnormality of psychological, physiological or anatomical structure or function. It is important that people with disabilities, like anyone else, be able to develop their maximum potential through all possible means.

Society must address its cultural stereotypes. The Americans with Disabilities Act (Public Law [PL] 101-336) has increased awareness that people with disabilities or other conditions are entitled to the benefits of any programs offered in our communities. Many disabled people have shown that they can excel in all walks of life, including sports and recreation, once given the opportunity. Unfortunately, some people still are ignorant and fearful of that which is different or unknown.

During World War II, returning disabled veterans could participate in a Red Cross program called Convalescent Swimming. Red Cross involvement in programs for the disabled continues today. The Red Cross encourages people with disabilities or other conditions to participate in all its aquatics programs. These programs seek not to label the person or restrict the activities but to meet everyone's individual needs and to focus on their ability, not disability. All people are encouraged to join in these programs based on their own performance standards. A program's focus on similarities in people's needs and behaviors, rather than differ-

▲ FIG. 7-2

ences, has a positive effect for everyone. The goal should always be for the person with a disability to be included in regular, mainstream aquatics activities before being placed in a separate program.

Benefits of Participation in Aquatics

Several activities in or on the water offer opportunities for those with disabilities or other conditions to fulfill their potential. Aquatics programs help such individuals meet their desire for challenge, success, recognition, accomplishment and social activity. Swimming in particular has great value, regardless of one's age or physical condition. Swimming and aquatic exercise have proved useful in rehabilitation. This chapter focuses on activities conducted in a pool. However, aquatics encompasses much more than that.

National organizations for many water sports have addressed the needs of the disabled. Canoeing, kayaking, rowing, sailing, scuba diving and even water skiing are open to a wide range of participants. A person who becomes comfortable in a pool setting should be encouraged to explore additional aquatics programs. Overall, aquatics offers physiological, psychological and social benefits.

Physiological Benefits

Swimming can enhance one's overall physical fitness. Swimming improves and maintains cardiovascular endurance (the ability of the heart, lungs and circulatory system to sustain vigorous activity), muscular strength and endurance and flexibility. It can also help with weight management.

Swimming may also help to improve motor function (the brain's ability to direct reflexive and voluntary movement activities). Motor function includes the following components:

► Speed—The ability to act or move with different velocities
► Agility—The ability to change direction during locomotion
► Perceptual motor function—The ability to integrate what one is perceiving with what one is doing; to develop balance, control and visual and auditory discrimination; and to improve spatial orientation (the understanding of one's location in space and position with reference to other objects)

Although anyone who exercises regularly in the water may gain physiological benefits, these benefits may be particularly important to a person with a disability or other condition. Water may be the only environment where some people can move freely and improve their physical fitness (Fig. 7-2).

Psychological Benefits

Everyone has a need for psychological growth and for improving one's sense of well-being and one's confidence. The psychological benefits of swimming for people with disabilities or other conditions include:

▶ Experiencing success. The opportunity to do something well and to feel successful is very important. In a society traditionally structured for nondisabled people, success is often denied people with disabilities. However, aquatic activities can give everyone the opportunity to reach their goals successfully (Fig. 7-3).

▶ Enhancing self-confidence. Being successful makes people feel better about themselves. When others, especially peers, see a person as successful, self-confidence improves. This increased self-esteem can lessen the emotional impact of the disability.

▶ Having fun. Many people enjoy swimming. People with disabilities or other conditions are no exception. One can have great fun jumping in and moving through or under the water (Fig. 7-4).

▶ Independent mobility. The ability to move more freely in water can be a tremendous psychological boost, especially for those with few

▲ Fig. 7-4

chances to move on their own. Many movements that are difficult or even impossible on land can be done in water. People with disabling conditions can do many things in the water similar to the nondisabled.

Social Benefits

A person's sense of limitation is affected by the reactions of others. In the past, negative reactions often made small disabilities feel like great barriers. Society is trying to change these conditions by helping people be included in society through different activities. Aquatic activities have many social benefits, such as:

▶ Peer-group interaction. Activities in the water can provide opportu-

▼ Fig. 7-3

Needs of People with Disabilities

People differ in many ways, some of which may affect participation in aquatics. The following sections describe some categories of differences.

Sensory Function

The sensory functions are sight, touch, taste, smell and hearing. While differences in taste and smell seldom matter for aquatics, differences in hearing, sight and touch can affect one's safety in the water. These differences also affect how people learn, how they perform in and around water and what teaching techniques are effective for them.

Hearing Impairment

Many people with a hearing impairment (partial or total loss of hearing) were born with it. Hearing problems can also result from childhood disease or advancing age. Some people with hearing impairment may have trouble with balance and/or coordination. This can affect their adjustment to the water.

A person with hearing impairment must focus more on communication when learning to swim. Because they usually cannot wear hearing aids in the water, people with moderate hearing loss have the same need for clear communication as someone with profound loss. Thus, communication is done visually by demonstration, gesture, lip reading and

nities for acceptance by peers and for learning acceptable social behavior, such as sharing and waiting one's turn.
► Normalization or inclusion. Categories and labels for disabilities often focus on the impairment rather than the person. All people should have opportunities to function in the mainstream of society. Aquatics is no exception. People with disabilities or other conditions should participate fully in aquatics programs with nondisabled peers. Swimming in groups also helps one make friends (Fig. 7-5).
► Safety. As one gains more aquatic skills, personal and family safety in, on or near the water improves. This benefit is a primary goal of the Red Cross aquatics program.

▲ Fig. 7-5

▲ Fig. 7-6

signing (Fig. 7-6). People with hearing impairment should wear goggles and keep their eyes open while swimming.

Vision Impairment

Vision impairment (a partial or total loss of sight) may be present from birth or caused by infection, injury or advancing age. It may also be caused by health conditions, such as diabetes or macular degeneration.

For people with vision impairment, learning to swim requires speech, touch and audible signals, such as whistles. Such people should keep their ears above the water and learn strokes that keep the ears out of the water. Other techniques include placing their hands on the limbs of another swimmer when strokes are demonstrated and measuring distances in steps or strokes.

People with partial vision should use as much functional vision as possible. They can wear glasses while swimming. Encouraging such swimmers to wear an old pair is best, because pool chemicals can corrode frames. An elastic strap or a swimming cap will keep them in place. Diving should not be permitted when glasses are worn. Individuals with contact lenses should wear goggles or a face mask and should avoid diving, surface diving and swimming under water. Masks may also be fitted with prescription lenses.

Someone who is totally blind may need a seeing partner. When moving on land, the blind person grasps the partner's elbow and follows the partner's body movement, along with the lead of the elbow, to help learn and to feel secure. The guide should not grasp the nonsighted person.

Tactile Impairment

Tactile impairment is the partial or total loss of the sense of touch. Someone with a spinal injury might not feel anything in areas of the body below the injury. A person with spina bifida also usually lacks both sensation and motor function in the lower part of the body.

Lack of sensation should not keep anyone out of the water. Because people with tactile impairment would not feel scratches, abrasions, burns or the rubbing that causes blisters, they must take care to avoid scratching or scraping the skin in the pool. Healing of such an injury is often slow. They must also take care to avoid temperature extremes, wear protective foot covering and check frequently for red skin (which may indicate a reaction to water pressure). Check the shower temperature before it is used before and after swimming.

Kinesthetic awareness is the conscious sense of where the body or its parts are positioned or how they are moving at any given moment. If this function is impaired, the person may not sense his or her body's position in relation to space and other objects (Fig. 7-7). There may be problems with balance in the water, swimming in a straight line and learning to float and recover.

Mental Function

Mental function includes intelligence and the capacity to reason, process and store information. The degree of such an impairment determines how successful the person may be in a regular aquatics program. Most people with this impairment can participate successfully in regular aquatics programs.

Impairment in Intelligence

The most common form of intellectual impairment is cognitive disability. Cognitive disability can be present at birth or as a result of a medical condition, such as stroke. Individuals with cognitive disabilities can have difficulty with understanding, knowing, judgment and decision-making skills. They are below average in intellectual functioning and slow in intellectual development and aca-

demic progress. However, abilities vary greatly within this population. Many can experience success in regular aquatics programs, whereas others may need a more specialized setting.

Developmental delay is common in people with cognitive disability. Learning and development may take place at a slower rate, and as a result, developmental and mental ages lag behind chronological age. In motor skills, however, many people with cognitive disability are more like than unlike their nondisabled peers.

Down syndrome is a congenital disorder that usually causes delays in physical and intellectual development. People with Down syndrome vary widely in mental abilities, behavior and physical development. Many people with Down syndrome can be included in regular aquatics programs.

A small number of people with Down syndrome may also have atlantoaxial instability. This is a weakness in the ligaments between the first two vertebrae. A swimmer with this condition must not dive, and a health care profes-

▼ Fɪɢ. 7-7

159

sional should be consulted about other possible limitations. The National Down Syndrome Congress recommends cervical X-rays to determine whether this condition exists.

Impairment in Information Processing

There are several forms of this impairment, such as learning disabilities, autism and behavioral or emotional disturbances. Many people with this impairment do well in regular aquatics programs. However, a specialized program should be considered if this impairment affects the person's ability to follow directions, follow safety procedures, behave well in the group or function with relative independence.

People with autism (a mental disorder characterized by extreme withdrawal and inability to relate to people) may have severely limited communication skills. Very few people with extreme autism can interact well enough to participate successfully in regular aquatics programs.

Behavior or emotional disturbances vary widely. Some behavior differences cannot be seen in most settings. Others may inhibit an individual's functional behavior, so that the person requires extra care. Behaviorally or emotionally disturbed individuals who can relate positively to the aquatic experience and control their behavior in the group can participate successfully in a regular aquatics program. If the behavior is not appropriate, particularly in terms of safety, specialized aquatics programming should be considered.

A calm class environment, clear expectations about behavior and consistency in enforcing safety procedures and rules help provide a positive swimming experience.

Motor Function

Motor function refers to the brain's ability to direct both reflexive and voluntary movements. The brain and nervous system control the muscular and skeletal systems. Impairment in any of these systems can result in decreased physical capability. If the person cannot use a body part because of impaired or lost function, motor activity can be limited. Orthopedic impairments are disorders of bones, joints and tendons. Neurologic impairments are disorders of the nervous system, including the spinal cord, nerves and brain. Such impairments may impede locomotor function and can be caused by trauma (such as amputation, spinal lesions, peripheral nerve injury, head injury or stroke), a congenital condition (such as spina bifida) or an infection (such as poliomyelitis or tuberculosis). Impairment may also be caused by dislocated hips, joint replacements and osteomyelitis (an inflammation of bone and bone marrow that is usually caused by bacterial infection).

Loss of Motor Function

Complete loss of use of a body part can result from congenital or traumatic amputation. A prosthesis such as an artificial limb may be used for land activities. Often the person can function quite normally on land, and the absence of a limb may not even be noticeable. However, a prosthesis must usually be removed before the person enters the water. The person may need a larger locker or a special place to keep the prosthesis while swimming. A private dressing area is desirable. Someone with a single leg can usually get from the locker room to the pool by another method such as seat scooting on the deck. Most people with amputations can participate successfully in regular swimming programs.

Complete or partial loss of the use of a body part can also result from spinal cord injury, stroke or damage to nerves controlling those body parts. Whatever the cause, nerve impulses from the brain do not reach the muscles to move the body part. Paralysis (the loss of sensation, voluntary motion or both) or paresis (partial loss of sensation, voluntary motion or both) may affect the legs (as in paraplegia), one side of the body (as in hemiplegia) or both arms and legs (as in quadriplegia).

A person with paralysis may have other body dysfunction. People lacking bowel and bladder control usually are on a bowel training program or wear a collection bag. People who have had a stroke may have varying degrees of paralysis and sometimes aphasia. Aphasia is the absence or impairment of the ability to communicate through speech, writing or other nonverbal methods. Special considerations for people with paralysis include the following:

► Programs should be conducted in uniform, warm temperatures. Avoid sudden temperature changes.

▶ Weight-bearing activities should be limited, unless directed by a physician.

▶ If sensation is reduced, especially in the hands and feet, the person should be careful to avoid cuts or abrasions caused by scraping.

▶ Poor circulation increases a tendency toward chilling and fatigue, which should be prevented.

▶ Individuals with bowel or bladder control problems should empty collection bags before swimming and be sure the bags are secured to the body. If the person does not have a collection bag, a cloth diaper and tight-fitting rubber pants should be worn.

▶ People lacking the function of a body part can participate successfully in regular aquatics programs (Fig. 7-8). They may need

assistance in the locker room, moving to the pool and entering the water. Paralysis of multiple body parts may limit motor function so severely that a specialized aquatics program is needed until the person adjusts to and becomes mobile in the water.

Impairment of Motor Function

Motor function can also be temporarily impaired because of illness or trauma, a permanent but stable condition or a progressively degenerative condition, such as muscular dystrophy or amyotrophic lateral sclerosis (ALS), also called Lou Gehrig's disease. Other temporary conditions that impair motor function include recovery from orthopedic surgery, broken bones, and mus-

cle strains and sprains. For such people, aquatics can play an important part in rehabilitation.

Rehabilitation is also important for someone with permanent motor impairment, such as cerebral palsy. Cerebral palsy is a central nervous system dysfunction in which the person has limited or no control of the muscles. The degree of impairment varies greatly from mild to severe. Cerebral palsy is caused by damage to the brain before, during or after birth. It is not degenerative, which means that it does not get worse over time, though the exact symptoms can change over a person's lifetime. The extent to which the effects of cerebral palsy are visible depends on the degree of damage. A person with cerebral palsy might have any of these characteristics:

▶ Limited range of movement in affected joint areas

▶ Limited control over voluntary movement of affected limbs or joints

▶ Random or involuntary movements

▶ Absence of normal muscle tone or an overabundance of muscle tone

▶ Abnormal muscle reflex patterns

▶ Impaired speech

▶ Possible seizures

These characteristics may lead to limited mobility. People with cerebral palsy may walk unaided, walk with crutches, wear braces, use a manual wheelchair or use an electric wheelchair. They may speak well or

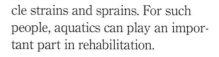

◀ Fig. 7-8

use a conversation board or mechanical communication device. They may have poor breath control and difficulty keeping the mouth closed. Some people mildly affected with cerebral palsy can participate quite successfully in regular aquatics programs. Swimming is very good for increasing and maintaining range of motion in joints and muscle flexibility. With greater impairment, specialized aquatics instruction may be needed.

Degenerative conditions may affect a person's participation in aquatics over time. Multiple sclerosis, ALS and various forms of muscular dystrophy lead to decreasing motor function. Most people can join regular aquatics programs in early phases of these diseases. As the condition progresses, the following changes are likely:

▶ Decreased control over voluntary motor activity
▶ Weakened muscles
▶ Increased susceptibility to other illnesses
▶ Impaired balance
▶ Increased difficulty with locomotion
▶ Decreased thresholds for fatigue
▶ Impairment of other body functions
▶ Development of sensory symptoms, such as numbness, tingling and sensations of pain

People who swam before the onset or progression of the disease can stay functional in the water long after motor function on land is severely impaired. With help in the locker room and transfers to and from the pool, they may stay with their peers and family members in a regular program as long as they wish. Someone who joins a program after the disease is progressing or who is experiencing problems in breathing, maintaining head control, recovering balance or staying in a safe position in the water may need specialized instruction and assistance.

Other Physical Conditions

Other physical conditions may require extra attention when the person joins an aquatics program. These conditions should not prevent the person from participating in aquatics. In fact, people who have any of the following conditions can benefit greatly from aquatic exercise.

Aging

With aging often comes an increase in chronic disease, especially cardiovascular disease. For many people, however, much of the reduced function that occurs with aging is related to physical inactivity. Exercise is a key element for good health and independent living for the elderly.

Elders who want to learn to swim or resume swimming again but have not gotten much exercise recently should talk to a health care provider before starting any exercise program. They should also begin gradually. The primary goal is usually to reach and maintain a level of fitness, improve one's physical condition or delay the onset of chronic disease. Most aquatics programs for the elderly are very similar to other programs (Fig. 7-9). The water should be slightly warmer, at least 83° F (28° C), and the aquatic activity should be less intense than that for a younger group. For those with a chronic disease, the intensity may have to be reduced even more.

◀ FIG. 7-9

Arthritis

The major goal of an aquatics program for arthritics is to decrease pain and increase the range of motion in the affected joints (Fig. 7-10). Aerobic exercise of moderate intensity is effective and also improves cardiovascular endurance. People with arthritis are generally more comfortable in warmer water (86° to 95° F or 30° to 35° C), although water at the high end of this range may be too warm for an aerobic workout. Aquatic activities should not worsen the pain. If pain results and does not subside within 2 hours after the workout, the person should shorten future workouts or modify the painful activity.

Asthma or Allergies

Someone with asthma or allergies can enjoy aquatics. Indeed, the breath control learned with aquatic skills often helps relieve the symptoms of asthma and allergies. Those who are allergic to pool chemicals should seek out a pool with a different chemical composition. A person using an asthma medication inhaler should keep the inhaler at poolside. If respiratory distress occurs, breathing can be improved by moving the person to a calm, quiet environment; keeping him or her warm; allowing the person to rest; and helping focus his or her attention on something other than breathing.

Cardiac and Blood Conditions

Persons with a blood disorder (such as sickle cell anemia) or a cardiac condition can join in aquatic activities that are paced to their level of endurance and involve minimal physical stress. Comfort is important. When the person gets cold or tired, experiences discomfort or otherwise becomes stressed, activity should be terminated for the day. Overexertion is to be avoided.

Aerobic exercise is good for people recovering from some cardiovascular or respiratory conditions. Walking and swimming are the most popular activities for cardiac rehabilitation, but aquatic exercise is also popular because it is easily tolerated, is low impact and has a low risk of injury.

▼ FIG. 7-10

In most cases, the body's response to exercise in the water is like that on land, provided that the water is a proper temperature. Cold water slows the heart rate and is a stress on the cardiovascular system. Water that is too warm may cause heat stress.

Cardiac patients should exercise at a lower intensity, depending on their physical abilities, but aquatic exercise is safe for most cardiac patients. An exception is the post-operative patient requiring continuous monitoring for variations in heart rate. Patients should follow guidelines set by their health care providers.

Cystic Fibrosis

Cystic fibrosis is an inherited disorder of the glands that causes abnormalities in respiration, perspiration and digestion, as well as hyperactivity of the autonomic nervous system. A person with cystic fibrosis can join an aquatics program during the early stages of the disease. Breathing exercises learned in aquatics can enhance air exchange in the lungs and help maintain health and fitness. The person may need to cough and spit phlegm often. Having an individual towel poolside for each person to spit into is a good idea. When the person becomes tired or cold, the activity should stop for the day. As the disease progresses, aquatic activity will become too physically stressful for the body and will eventually have to stop. Physical comfort and the person's desire to continue are the key factors in deciding how long to stay in a program.

Diabetes

Persons with diabetes should never exercise alone because of the risk of a diabetic emergency. Increased activity may upset one's insulin balance. Dizziness, drowsiness and confusion can be serious problems in the water and may lead to a dangerous situation. A diabetic emergency can result in unconsciousness. Individuals with diabetes should have snacks on hand.

Fragile Bones

People with osteogenesis imperfecta (fragile bones) find swimming an excellent form of exercise, because swimming helps build muscle mass, stimulate bone growth and maintain flexibility. They must be careful to avoid

physical trauma, which could occur from such things as manipulating a body part, swimming in turbulent water or colliding with another person. They should always wear a life jacket for safety and use strokes that are not strenuous, such as the sidestroke or elementary backstroke. They should not dive or jump into the water.

Obesity

People who are overweight should exercise at a moderate level for the first few weeks. After that, they may extend the workout because the duration of the exercise is more important for weight management than intensity. Because this group is extremely buoyant, it is important that the limbs move with sufficient speed to make the exercise beneficial.

The overweight person is at some risk for coronary heart disease and may have other risk factors, such as high blood pressure, high blood sugar and high cholesterol. Aerobic exercise provides benefits that counteract all these risk factors. Changes in body composition occur slowly unless the diet is modified as well. Weight management programs that combine diet with exercise produce better results than diet or exercise alone (Fig. 7-11). The key to successful weight management is to follow the program consistently. Obese people may find it easier to stay with an aquatic exercise program because the environment is cool, comfortable and relaxing, as well as beneficial.

Seizures

Seizures may be a symptom of other medical conditions. In general, a person who has seizures that are medically controlled can join an aquatics program, as long as it is closely supervised. If a seizure occurs while the person is in the water, the person should not return to the water that day. A seizure that occurs in the water is an emergency and should be treated as such. Usually a person with active seizures should not join an aquatics program until the seizures are under control.

Swimmers with conditions that can cause seizures usually do not need a special program, but more careful observation may be needed. Because the condition cannot be seen, one should notify the instructor or lifeguard of any condition that could lead to a seizure or loss of consciousness.

▲ Fig. 7-11

Safety

Hazards exist in any aquatics program but are a greater risk for some people with disabilities or other conditions. The person's vision, balance, sense of direction, concept of space, depth perception and muscular control should all be considered. For instance, a wet pool deck that a nondisabled person can safely cross can be a real hazard to someone with limited mobility.

Both the participant and the instructor of the program should be aware of the following special considerations:

▶ People with impaired mobility, balance or motor control may need help moving on wet decks and ramps. A person using crutches or a walker or who has a prosthesis also may need help.
▶ If an individual uses a wheelchair, it should be used between the locker room and pool. Showering should be omitted and the chair should be covered with towels after the swim. Brakes must be locked when the person is entering and leaving the chair. Children, too, should use their wheelchairs, as it is unsafe to carry anyone, even small children, on wet, slippery decks.
▶ People with limited control of their legs should not enter the water feetfirst from a diving board or from a height; twisting and injury to muscles are possible. Simple entries from the deck should be learned.
▶ In outdoor settings, temperature fluctuations and sun exposure should be closely monitored.

Safety precautions for specific medical conditions should be followed carefully. When in doubt, check the doctor's recommendation.

To ensure safety for the visually impaired, decks should be kept free of clutter, doors should be kept either completely closed or wide open rather than ajar, possible hazards should be explained verbally, life lines should be used to mark depth variance, and people with visual disabilities should be instructed to alert the instructor or lifeguard when they need help.

Safety education is a vital part of every aquatics program. Safety skills can be learned in an enjoyable way by all who use the swimming area. Everyone should learn personal safety skills, such as how to wear a life jacket, and should take basic water safety courses. Everyone should learn nonswimming rescue skills consistent with their abilities.

Facilities

Relatively few swimming facilities in the United States were built exclusively for people with disabilities. However, with little or no adaptation, swimming facilities can be used by most people with disabilities (Fig. 7-12). The Education for Handicapped Children Act (PL 94-142) has helped ensure accessible education facilities. Many com-

▲ Fig. 7-12

- ▶ Directional signs for people with impaired hearing
- ▶ Doorways wide enough for wheelchairs (32-inch minimum width)

Locker Rooms

- ▶ Accessible bathroom facilities for people with impaired mobility
- ▶ Directional signs for people with impaired hearing
- ▶ Private dressing rooms for people who wear a prosthesis or urinary device or who have other privacy needs
- ▶ Uncomplicated traffic pattern to pool area to ease access for people with visual impairment
- ▶ Handheld or low-level shower heads for people who shower seated in a chair or on the floor
- ▶ A shower chair for use by people with impaired balance or mobility
- ▶ Shower temperatures set to prevent scalding
- ▶ Grab bars in toilets and in shower areas for people with impaired mobility
- ▶ A dressing table or area of floor specially covered and designated for people who need to dress or be helped to dress lying down
- ▶ Hair dryers mounted at various heights

munity pools are attached to schools and recreation departments and, under this law, must be accessible to people with disabilities. The Americans with Disabilities Act requires that people with disabilities have access to all community recreation programs.

People with disabilities and those who assist in their care should consider several factors when choosing a

facility. The specific disability determines which factors to consider.

Building Structure

- ▶ Parking for people with motor impairment near the entrance to the facility
- ▶ Absence of stairs between entry and locker rooms
- ▶ Easily understood hallway access for people with vision impairment

Pool

- ▶ Decks free of clutter
- ▶ Clearly understandable safety signs and depth markings; signs with pictures and words, a tape recording of pool rules and a textured contour line along a wall; clear indication of depth, exits and location of emergency equipment
- ▶ Life lines marking changes of depth

- Chair lifts, ramp and/or walk-in steps (may be portable)
- Handholds at or slightly above water level; if it is hard to hold on to the edge of the pool, a rope or railing can be added
- Devices to assist a person with a disability in and out of the water; several types of lifts are available for pool use, most of which are portable and can be removed from the deck when not in use

Programming

People with disabilities or other conditions have many different opportunities to participate in aquatics programs. On one end of the continuum are regular programs in which people with disabilities are included in the same lessons and activities as the nondisabled (Fig. 7-13). This is called mainstreaming. On the other extreme is one-to-one instruction in an adapted aquatics program provided by a Water Safety instructor specially trained to teach people with disabilities. Between these extremes are a variety of possibilities.

The selection of the right program is an important decision. People with disabilities or other conditions should participate in whatever program best meets their needs. They should also be able to move from program to program when their needs change. Everyone should have access to Red Cross aquatics programs. However, program administrators also have a responsibility to others in the class or program. At times, it is necessary to set up special programs for people with disabilities or other conditions so that everyone can benefit from the classes they take.

People with disabilities or other conditions have the following rights and responsibilities when they are applying for an aquatics program:

- The right to general information about the aquatics program, so they can determine if it suits their needs
- The right to apply for entry into the program
- The right to a specific explanation if the instructor believes the program is not suitable for the person
- The responsibility to give the instructor any pertinent information concerning their condition
- The responsibility to comply with an instructor's request for a pretest or trial lesson if needed
- The responsibility to provide one's own assistance, if needed, for dressing and for pool entry and exit

People with disabilities or other conditions also must choose between mainstream programming and special programming. For those who can join a mainstream program, aquatics is a rich, rewarding experience. However, not all people can or will ever be ready for mainstream programs. The decision must be made on an individual basis, considering both the needs of the person and the benefits and structure of the program. Both mainstream and non-mainstream programs have advantages and disadvantages, as shown in the following chart.

▼ **Fig. 7-13**

Mainstreaming

Advantages

Increased opportunity for participation

Possibility for family or social group to participate together

Stronger self-concept as a result of success

Development of skills transferable to any aquatic environment

Opportunity to enjoy peer and community contact

Disadvantages

Lack of instructors trained in mainstreaming

Lack of accessible facilities

Program might not adapt to meet individual needs

Larger class sizes might not give enough support

Possible lack of peer sensitivity

Nonmainstreaming

Advantages

Instruction given by specially trained instructors

Class size is small

Peers may be more sensitive and considerate

Adapted programs are often held in specially designed facilities, making accessibility easier

Disadvantages

Environment is not average mix of people

Interaction with larger groups of people is not usually possible

Opportunities might not be available for families to participate together

Participants might not learn to participate in nonadapted facilities

Expanding Opportunities in Aquatics

Competition

People with disabilities or other conditions have opportunities in two types of competitive programs. The first is with nondisabled peers. Regular swim teams and swim clubs should be open to any person who makes the qualifying standards, despite any impairment. A disability should not be a barrier to successful competition against nondisabled peers.

Competition is also available through organizations geared to those with specific disabilities (Fig 7-14). Organizations such as Special Olympics offer athletes at all levels of ability the opportunity to train and compete in basic aquatics skills. Competition is also available at the elite level for athletes with disabilities, including the Paralympics, which are held in the same year and at the same venues as the Olympic Games, and the FINA World Swimming Championships.

Recreation

Recreational activity is important for everyone. Recreational activities include skin diving, scuba diving (Fig. 7-15), boating, adventure recreation, water sports and water park activities. All these are opportunities to develop additional aquatic skills. People with disabilities or other conditions who are interested

Phil Cole/ALLSPORT

◀ Fig. 7-14

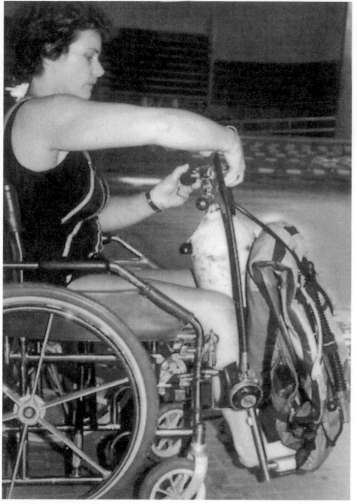

▲ Fig. 7-15

in any of these activities should do the following:

► Determine what swim skills are needed to begin the activity and learn those skills first.
► Get a medical recommendation before starting a new, active leisure pursuit, especially those involving adventure or risk.
► Take any needed lessons from a qualified or certified instructor.
► Advise the instructor, program director and lifeguard of any limitations. This knowledge will help them provide a safe environment.

► Participate with a nondisabled buddy. This can make learning more fun and ensures a person is there to help if needed.

People with disabilities are river rafting, arctic kayaking, solo sailing, exploring the ocean bottom, sliding down flumes, photographing coral reefs, channel swimming, slalom water skiing (Fig. 7-16) and generally doing everything that nondisabled people are doing.

► Fig. 7-16

169

Summary

People with disabilities or other conditions can participate successfully in aquatic activities. Whether their goal is fitness, competition or recreation, aquatics programs are a way to meet their needs and individual differences.

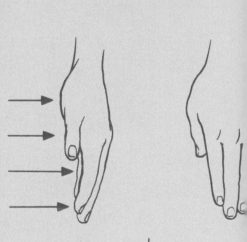

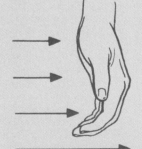

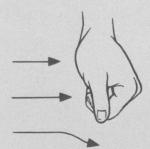

Lifetime Fitness

Chapter 8

Because of modern technology, most people use less physical effort in our daily living than did previous generations. People do not exert themselves enough to maintain good physical health and fitness in most job-related activities. People with inactive lifestyles are more prone to various serious health problems, including cardiovascular disease (disease of the heart and blood vessels), obesity, hypertension (high blood pressure), diabetes (from inadequate insulin in the body) and muscle and joint problems. If people exercised more, far fewer would die from cardiovascular disease. Now more than ever, people need physical activity in their daily lives. On an encouraging note: starting or continuing an exercise program will help lead to a longer, healthier life.

Physical fitness is a vital component of good health. It was once defined as the capacity to carry out everyday activities without excessive fatigue and still having enough energy in reserve for emergencies. However, our present everyday activities are far less strenuous than in the past. Physical fitness is no longer viewed as just the absence of disease. Fitness is a means to reach optimum health.

Health

This chapter presents information on two basic types of aquatic fitness programs: fitness swimming and aquatic exercise. Fitness swimming is a program in which the workouts use swimming strokes to reach a specified level of intensity sustained for a set time (Fig. 8-1). Fitness swimming is an excellent way to improve overall physical fitness and especially the health of the cardiovascular system (the heart and blood vessels, which bring oxygen and nutrients to the body through the circulation of blood).

▲ Fig. 8-1

▲ FIG. 8-2

Aquatic exercise is an in-water fitness activity generally performed in a vertical position with the face out of the water (Fig. 8-2). In aquatic exercise, one walks, jogs, jumps and bounces in shallow water or runs in deeper water, sometimes using a flotation device (Fig. 8-3). Limbs are pushed or pulled to cause resistance in the water. One example is standing in neck-deep water and flexing the elbows to bring the palms toward the shoulder (biceps curl). Some aquatic exercise programs focus on cardiovascular fitness; others emphasize muscular strength and flexibility.

Before beginning any physical activity or fitness program, a participant should see a health care provider for a thorough examination. This is especially true if the individual has not exercised for a long time.

Training refers to a physical improvement program designed to prepare a person for competition in a sport. It is characterized by exercise of higher intensity than that used to improve health-related fitness. A person who undertakes a training program should already have a good level of fitness before the training begins.

▼ FIG. 8-3

To include aquatics in a fitness program, the information in this chapter will be helpful. To train for greater levels of fitness or for swimming competition, Chapter 9 provides guidance for a more strenuous approach to aquatic workouts.

Benefits of Aerobic Exercise

Aerobic exercise is sustained, rhythmic, physical exercise that requires additional effort by the heart and lungs to meet the increased demand by the skeletal muscles for oxygen. Such exercise, when it is frequent enough, changes the body in ways that improve health. The benefits of aerobic exercise are known as the training effect. The body improves in the following ways:

▶ Cardiovascular endurance
▶ Muscular strength and endurance
▶ Flexibility
▶ Weight management

▲ FIG. 8-5

Cardiovascular Endurance

The cardiovascular, or circulatory, system supplies oxygen and nutrients to the body through the blood. Cardiovascular diseases cause more than half the deaths in the United States. The most common type is coronary artery disease. This results from the narrowing and hardening of the coronary arteries, which carry needed oxygen-rich blood to the heart (Fig. 8-4, *A* and *B*). Risk factors that contribute to coronary artery disease include:

▶ Smoking
▶ High blood pressure
▶ Obesity
▶ High cholesterol in the blood
▶ Diabetes
▶ Lack of exercise

▶ FIG. 8-4, *A-B*

Coronary arteries

A

B

Unblocked   Partially blocked   Completely blocked

With the right exercise, cardiovascular efficiency (also known as aerobic capacity) improves (Fig. 8-5). The heart becomes stronger and can pump more blood with each beat. Circulation improves and the blood vessels stay healthy. Other benefits include:

▶ Lower heart rate at rest and in moderate exercise
▶ Shorter recovery time (the time it takes for the heart to resume its regular rate after exercise)

▶ Improved blood circulation to heart muscle
▶ Increased capacity of the blood to carry oxygen
▶ Increased ability of muscles to use oxygen
▶ Decreased lactic acid, a byproduct of exercise that may cause muscle soreness and fatigue
▶ Lower resting blood pressure (especially in people with high blood pressure)
▶ Lower cholesterol levels

Muscular Strength and Endurance

Muscular performance involves both strength and endurance. Muscular strength is the ability of muscle to exert force. Strength leads to endurance, power and resistance to fatigue. Muscular strength protects against joint injury and helps maintain good posture.

Weakness in some muscles causes an imbalance that can impair normal movement and cause pain. For instance, weak abdominal muscles combined with poor flexibility in the lower back and hamstring muscles (at the back of the thigh) can lead to lower back pain. Lower back pain is a major problem in the United States, costing millions of dollars a year in lost productivity. Muscular imbalances cause up to 80 percent of all lower back problems. Muscular strength is an important factor for staying healthy, and aquatic activity is a popular, effective way to develop this strength.

Muscular endurance is the ability of muscle to contract repeatedly with the same force over an extended period. Greater muscular strength often improves muscular endurance. For many people and activities, muscular endurance, which helps to resist fatigue, is more important than strength for athletic activity.

Muscular strength and endurance generally decrease as a person gets older or becomes less active. This may reduce one's ability to do everyday chores and enjoy recreation. For this reason, the American College of Sports Medicine recommends that muscular development exercises be performed two or three times per week.

Aerobic exercise has the following benefits, especially when strength and flexibility exercises are included:

▶ Improved range of motion and function
▶ Increased strength and endurance
▶ Increased strength of tendons and ligaments
▶ Improved muscle tone
▶ Improved posture
▶ Reduction of lower back pain and other disorders caused by inactivity

Measuring Body Composition

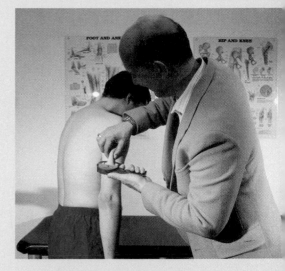

Body composition can be tested to see the effect of a diet and training program on muscle and fat composition. The test breaks down body weight into the total lean weight and the total fat weight. When exercising and watching the diet, muscle strength and capacity increase and percentage of body fat declines. The body composition test allows monitoring of any changes.

There are many ways to measure body composition. Anthropometric tests measure the circumference of different body parts and then calculate body composition. Skinfold tests use a caliper to measure fat under the skin at different places, then make similar calculations. Bioimpedance tests measure electric currents through the body. Because the electrical properties of fat differ from those of muscle, the measurements can be used to calculate body composition.

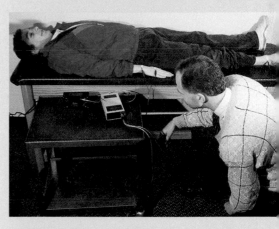

A more accurate technique is underwater weighing, also known as hydrostatic weighing. This technique is based on the principle discovered by Archimedes, a mathematician and inventor who lived in ancient Greece. According to legend, Archimedes was looking for a way to determine the purity of the gold in King Hiero's crown when he discovered the physical principle of buoyancy. This is the basis for hydrostatic weighing. (For more details on buoyancy, see Chapter 2.)

Weighing a person in water provides the total body density (weight/volume). Because fat is less dense than bone and muscle, a person with a higher percentage of body fat will have a lower density. Thus, hydrostatic weighing can be used to determine the amount of body fat.

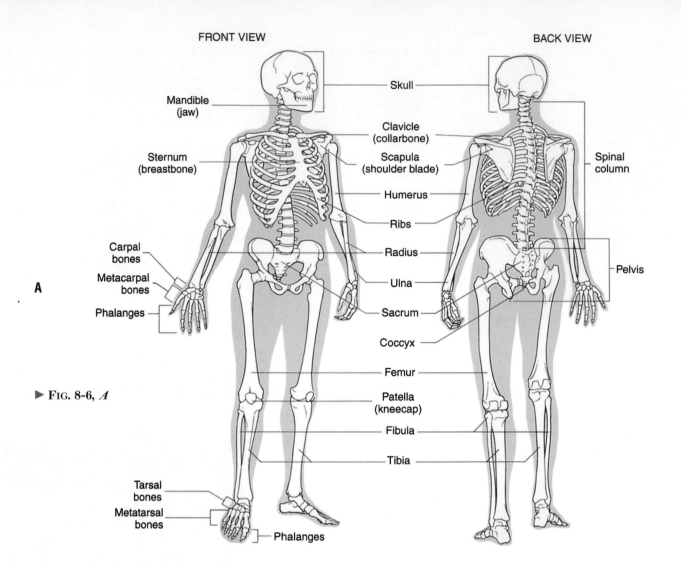

FRONT VIEW · BACK VIEW

- Skull
- Mandible (jaw)
- Clavicle (collarbone)
- Sternum (breastbone)
- Scapula (shoulder blade)
- Spinal column
- Humerus
- Ribs
- Carpal bones
- Radius
- Metacarpal bones
- Ulna
- Pelvis
- Phalanges
- Sacrum
- Coccyx
- Femur
- Patella (kneecap)
- Fibula
- Tibia
- Tarsal bones
- Metatarsal bones
- Phalanges

A

▶ FIG. 8-6, *A*

Flexibility

Flexibility is the range of motion of a joint or group of joints. Flexibility varies from joint to joint in the same person. Flexibility in some joints does not translate to overall body flexibility. Sufficient flexibility helps prevent injuries to the bones, muscles, tendons and ligaments (Fig. 8-6, *A* and *B*). Ligaments are the strong elastic tissues that hold bones in place at joints (Fig. 8-7). Tendons attach muscles to bones. Flexibility is partly determined by heredity but can be improved by stretching. Stretching is an important part of the warm-up for any exercise. If a workout includes a muscular development set, be sure to stretch the exercised muscles at the beginning and end of the session.

Weight Management

Up to half the adults in the United States are thought to be overfat. That means the percentage of fat in their bodies is higher than recommended. This is not the same as being overweight. A person is overweight if the weight is more than the average based on sex, height and frame size. These standards are published in tables with a weight range for males and females of different heights and frame sizes. However, most of these tables do not account for body composition. Because muscle is heavier than fat, a person with large muscles may be classified as overweight while having a normal percentage of body fat. It is important to consider actual body fat, as well as weight. For information on how to have body fat measured, ask a doctor or other health care specialist.

Overfat individuals are at greater risk for many chronic health problems, such as diabetes, high blood pressure, coronary artery disease, stroke and some types of cancer. A person is considered obese if body fat exceeds 25 percent of total body weight for males or 30 percent for females. Obese people are 2.5 times more likely to

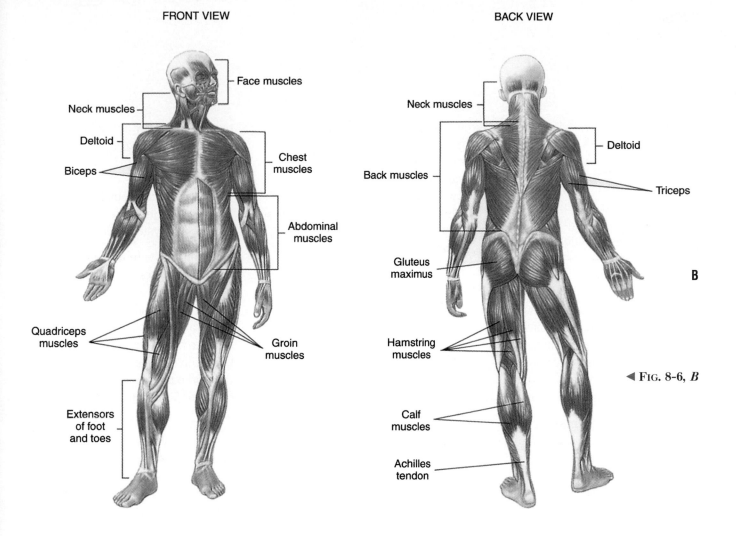

FRONT VIEW

- Face muscles
- Neck muscles
- Deltoid
- Biceps
- Chest muscles
- Abdominal muscles
- Quadriceps muscles
- Groin muscles
- Extensors of foot and toes

BACK VIEW

- Neck muscles
- Deltoid
- Back muscles
- Triceps
- Gluteus maximus
- Hamstring muscles
- Calf muscles
- Achilles tendon

B

◀ FIG. 8-6, *B*

die of cardiovascular disease than people with normal body fat. For these reasons, proper body weight and percentage of body fat have become a national health priority.

Regular exercise is important for successful long-term weight control. Exercise increases the basal metabolic rate (the amount of calories the body burns at rest). Moderately intense exercise also depresses appetite and improves mood. A person who exercises can eat more than an inactive person and still not gain weight.

Aerobic exercise helps control body weight in the following ways:

▶ Increases the rate at which the body burns calories
▶ Decreases body fat
▶ Maintains lean muscle tissue when losing weight or dieting
▶ Increases the body's ability to use fat as fuel

▶ FIG. 8-7

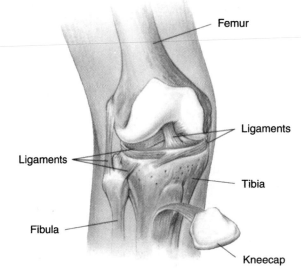

- Femur
- Ligaments
- Ligaments
- Tibia
- Fibula
- Kneecap

Specific Benefits of Exercising in Water

Whether engaging in aquatic exercise or fitness swimming, exercise in water has unique benefits. Buoyancy decreases the impact on the joints and thus the risk of injury. Because water helps cool the body during exercise, workouts in cool water are refreshing, a benefit for those prone to heat stress. On the other hand, exercise in warm water increases blood circulation and promotes healing of injured tissues. Warm water eases muscle spasms, relaxes tight muscles and increases joint motion.

Aquatic exercise is a popular form of aerobic exercise. Water resistance also helps improve muscular strength and endurance. Moving in and through the water helps maintain and improve flexibility. Because water resistance can be controlled or adjusted by the participant's speed or motions, workouts can be designed to meet the needs of everyone regardless of their age or fitness level.

Adjusting Exercise Levels

The body is affected by any exertion. Pulse and breathing rates speed up, sweat starts and additional calories are burned. Physical fitness comes from exerting the body beyond certain limits. To reach or maintain a level of fitness, exercise must put sufficient stress on the cardiovascular system to cause it to adapt beyond its current state, without too much or too little work, and

it must be of sufficient duration. To become more fit, one must work harder than normal so that the capacities of the muscular and cardiovascular systems increase. This is called *overload*. Exercise sessions should occur at least three times a week to maintain the same level of fitness.

Setting Up an Exercise Program

To reach and stay at a healthy level of fitness, an exercise program needs to be established and followed. A sound fitness program depends on the frequency, intensity and duration of the workouts. If a person is striving for improvement in a specific area, the exercise program must include the particular exercise, activity or skill he or she wants to improve.

Frequency means how often the exercise is done. Exercise 3 to 5 days a week. Exercising more than 5 days a week usually does not lead to additional improvement and may lead to increased injury and fatigue. Frequency of exercise depends on individual fitness goals. For example, to lose fat, it is better to exercise 5 days a week rather than 3.

Intensity is how hard a person works out when he or she exercises. This is the most difficult of the three factors to assess. Results are best if the intensity of the workout stays within an optimum range. If exercising below this level, cardiovascular improvement is slower. Very-low-intensity exercise does have some benefits, but the benefits to the cardiovascular system are greatly

reduced. Intensity above the target range can cause excessive fatigue and can lead to injuries. High-intensity exercise is difficult to sustain, so workouts usually are shorter and the resulting benefit to the cardiovascular system is limited.

Duration, or the time spent during each exercise session, also affects the benefits. Spend at least 30 minutes at the recommended level of intensity. Warm up should last 5 to 10 minutes before the aerobic activity. Gradually decrease the intensity of the workout, then stretch to cooldown for 5 to 10 minutes.

Type refers to the kind of exercise performed. When choosing the type, one should consider the principle of specificity. For example, to improve one's level of cardiovascular fitness, one should engage in cardiovascular types of exercises. The basic rule is that to improve performance, one must practice the particular exercise, activity or skill one wants to improve.

Target Heart Rate Range

One way to determine if one is exercising at the proper intensity is to measure heart rate, because this measures physiological stress. The more intense the exercise, the higher the heart rate. The ideal heart rate range for an individual to maintain during exercise for greatest cardiovascular benefit is called the *target heart rate range* (Fig. 8-8). It is calculated in several ways. The best way is to calculate a percentage of the predicted maximum heart rate (MHR), which depends on age and resting heart rate (RHR). The best

▶ **Fig. 8-8**

% of Maximum	20	30	40	50	60	70	80	90
10	83/14	84/14	83/14	83/14	81/13	80/13	79/13	78/13
20	98/16	98/16	94/16	98/16	90/15	88/15	86/14	84/14
30	110/18	107/18	104/17	101/17	98/16	96/15	92/15	89/15
40	123/20	119/20	115/19	111/19	107/18	103/17	99/17	93/16
50	136/23	131/22	126/21	121/20	116/19	111/19	106/18	101/17
60	148/25	143/24	137/23	131/22	125/21	119/20	113/19	107/18
70	162/27	155/26	148/25	141/23	134/22	127/21	120/20	113/19
80	174/29	166/28	158/26	150/25	142/24	134/22	126/21	118/20
90	182/31	178/30	169/28	160/27	151/25	142/24	133/22	124/21

Age (years)

time to take a resting heart rate measurement is upon waking in the morning. Alternatively, one can lie quietly for at least 10 minutes and then take a pulse for a full minute.

In general, a workout should raise the heart rate to between 60 and 90 percent of the predicted maximum heart rate. This determines an individual's approximate target heart rate range. Once the resting heart rate is known, the target heart rate range can be calculated more accurately in a few easy steps. First, find the predicted maximum heart rate by subtracting age from 220 (Step A in Table 8-1). Then subtract the resting heart rate from that number (Step B). Multiply this by 60 percent (the lower limit of the recommended intensity) and add back the resting heart rate (Step C). Also multiply the number in Step B by 90 percent (the upper limit of the recommended intensity) and add back the resting heart rate (Step D). The target heart rate range (in beats per minute) is between the lower and the upper intensity limits (Step E). Divide the numbers in Step C and D by 6 (Steps F and G) for the target heart rate range in beats per 10 seconds (Step H). When taking the pulse during exercise, compare the actual heart rate for 10 seconds against the target heart rate range for the same amount of time. Table 8-1 shows how

TABLE 8-1 Calculating the Target Heart Rate Range for Land-Based Exercise for a Person Age 30 with a Resting Heart Rate of 78

A. 220 − 30 (age)	= 190 (MHR)
B. 190 − 78 (RHR)	= 112
C. (112 × .60) + 78	= 145 (60% intensity)
D. (112 × .90) + 78	= 179 (90% intensity)
E. Target heart range	= 145–179 beats per minute
F. 145 ÷ 6	= 24
G. 179 ÷ 6	= 30
H. Target heart rate range	= 24–30 beats per 10 seconds

to use the formula to find the target heart rate range for a person age 30 with a resulting heart rate of 78. Consult a physician to determine one's ideal heart rate.

The target heart rate range with swimming should be 10 to 13 beats below that for similar exercise on land. A swimmer's horizontal position and the water pressure

TABLE 8-2 Calculating the Target Heart Rate Range for Swimming for a Person Age 30 with a Resting Heart Rate of 78

A. 220 − 30 (age)	= 190 (MHR)
B. 190 − 78 (RHR)	= 112
C. (112 × .60) + 78–13	= 132 (60% intensity)
D. (112 × .90) + 78–13	= 166 (90% intensity)
E. Target heart range	= 132–166 beats per minute
F. 145 ÷ 6	= 22
G. 166 ÷ 6	= 28
H. Target heart rate range	= 22–28 beats per 10 seconds

▲ FIG. 8-9

on the body in swimming prevent the heart rate from increasing as much as in vertical, dry-land exercise of the same intensity. Remember to lower the target heart rate range by this much for fitness swimming (Table 8-2).

Although target heart rates for swimming are 10 to 13 beats lower than for similar dry-land exercise, the issue is less clear for aquatic exercise. Some research shows that heart rates from vertical aquatic exercise are lower than rates on dry land. Other studies report that heart rates are the same as rates in dry land programs with similar intensity. By subtracting 10 to 13 beats from the target heart rate range when doing aquatic exercise, it is possible to underestimate the intensity and target heart rate range needed to reach goals.

Keep the heart rate within the target range for the type of exercise to achieve safe and consistent progress toward fitness goals. The 60- to 90-percent range is appropriate for most people. The cardiovascular health of a sedentary person may begin to improve with an intensity level as low as 40 to 50 percent. Very fit athletes might not reach their training goals until they reach 90-percent intensity. Consult a physician to determine appropriate intensity.

As suggested earlier, the heart rate can be measured during exercise with a pulse check (Fig. 8-9). Feel the pulse at the radial artery in the wrist or the carotid artery in the neck (Fig. 8-10, *A* and *B*). The heart rate will drop fast

▶ FIG. 8-10, *A–B*

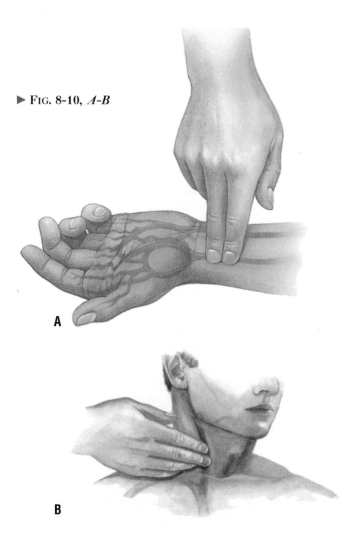

A

B

during this pause, so find the pulse quickly. Count the beats for 10 seconds and compare the results with the target heart rate range in beats per 10 seconds. (Or multiply by 6 to calculate the target heart rate range in beats per minute). To check the pulse, start timing on the first beat and count "0." Count "1" on the second beat, and so on.

If the heart rate is below the target range, increase the intensity of the workout. Move faster or, in aquatic exercise, make larger arm and leg motions or increase water resistance. If the heart rate is above the target intensity range, decrease the intensity. Make smaller movements, slow down or take rest breaks more often. If one is often above or below the target intensity range but it still feels as if it is the right intensity, this formula might not work as well for that individual. In that case, consider using the method of rating perceived exertion as an alternative means of evaluating exercise intensity.

Rate of Perceived Exertion

Many factors, such as stress, illness and fatigue, can affect heart rates. In addition, because obtaining accurate exercise heart rates can be difficult while continuing vigorous exercise, an alternative method of monitoring intensity has been developed. This method is called the rating of perceived exertion (RPE). RPE is a valid and reliable method for determining the intensity of a workout and is based on how hard an individual feels he or she is working. Studies have shown that RPE correlates highly with other intensity indicators, such as heart rate and breathing rate (Fig. 8-11).

In the initial phase of an exercise program, RPE often is used with the heart rate to monitor intensity. To do this, identify a number on the RPE scale that corresponds with the perceived intensity, then check the heart rate to see how the two numbers relate. Once the relationship between heart rate and RPE is understood, rely less on heart rate and more on the how it feels.

Safety Considerations for a Fitness Program

For most people, a fitness program is not risky. Some people, however, cannot start a program at 60-percent intensity and continue for 30 minutes. If a person has not exercised in a long while, this intensity could even be dangerous. Always obtain a general health assessment

Perceived Exertion	% Workload
20	100%
19-Very, Very Hard	90%
18	
17-Very Hard	80%
16	
15 Hard	70%
14	
13-Somewhat Hard	60%
12	
11-Fairly Light	50%
10	
9-Very Light	40%
8	
7-Very, Very light	
6	

▲ Fig. 8-11

from a health care provider to measure level of fitness whenever beginning an exercise program.

A health assessment can be a physical examination or an exercise stress test (Fig. 8-12) with blood testing. Consult a health care provider. Once the initial level of fitness is determined, the exercise intensity that is safe for beginning a program can be determined.

Knowledge of current swimming skill level also is very important. At lower skill levels, one may use more energy, even at slow speeds, because one is less efficient. Swimming even one length of the pool can be exhausting for novices. Rest as often as needed and use resting strokes, like the sidestroke and the elementary backstroke, when starting a program. Check heart rate or monitor RPE at each break to make sure it is within the appropriate target range. The goal is to gradually increase the time spent continuously swimming while decreasing the rest breaks to increase intensity levels slowly.

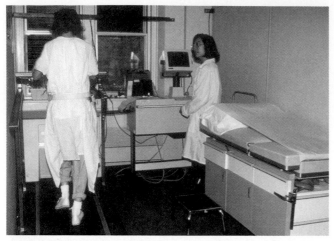

▲ Fig. 8-12

▲ Fig. 8-13

Always watch for exercise warning signals. They may mean immediate medical attention is needed. The following signals indicate the workout should be stopped:

▶ An abnormal heart action (such as a heart rate that stays high for some time after completing the exercise session)
▶ Pain or pressure in the chest, arm or throat
▶ Dizziness, lightheadedness or confusion during or immediately following the workout
▶ Breathlessness or wheezing

If any of these signals are present, tell the instructor or lifeguard. If conditions persist, see a health care provider.

Components of a Workout

A workout should be designed to meet individual fitness goals. A typical safe and effective workout includes a warm-up, stretching, an aerobic set (the main part of the workout) and a cool-down. A muscular development set may occur in addition to the aerobic activity.

Warm-Up

The warm-up prepares the body for the increased work. The warm-up increases blood flow and helps adjust to the workout environment. Because pool water is often 15° to 20° F (8° to 11° C) cooler than skin temperature, spend some time warming up at poolside before entering the

water. The warm-up should last 5 to 10 minutes and may consist of slow walking, jogging or low-intensity swimming (Fig. 8-13).

Stretching

Stretching makes joints more flexible and improves range of motion (Fig. 8-14). Stretch during the warm-up or right after it. Stretching can prevent soreness and can improve performance. It can also reduce the risk of injury to muscles and joints.

▲ Fig. 8-14

Safe stretching requires slow, gentle movements, holding the stretch for 10 to 30 seconds. Do not force a joint beyond the normal range of motion or use a bouncing motion. There should be no pain or discomfort during the stretch.

Aerobic Set

To benefit from an aerobic workout, keep the heart rate in the target range for at least 30 minutes. At a lower level of intensity, fitness level will likely not increase much. The aerobic set should make up 50 to 70 percent of the workout time and distance. Much of the following sections on fitness swimming and aquatic exercise apply to the aerobic sets for those exercise programs.

Muscular Development Set

The American College of Sports Medicine recommends that a fitness program include some exercise for muscular development. Probably the most popular form of exercise for muscular development is resistance training (weight lifting). The muscles are progressively overloaded by using barbells, dumbbells or weight machines (Fig. 8-15). Strength development for fitness should be general in nature. That is, try to overload muscles from each major muscle group rather than focusing on a few muscle groups. It is best to use one or two exercises for each muscle group.

A person needs to warm up thoroughly and be instructed in the proper way of executing each exercise. The next step is to identify the appropriate weight for each exercise for the individual's current level of strength. It is recommended that a beginner use a weight that can be lifted 12 to 15 times in one set. If it is not possible to lift the weight at least 12 times without a break in the set, the weight is too heavy for that exercise.

Once the amount of weight to be used for each exercise is selected, begin the weight training program. A standard program for beginners is to lift the selected weight 10 times (repetitions) for 2 to 3 sets. The more often you do resistance training, the easier the selected weight will be to lift. As improvement occurs, try each exercise with the next heavier weight to maintain an overload on the muscle group. Strength training should be performed two or three times per week as part of a regular fitness program.

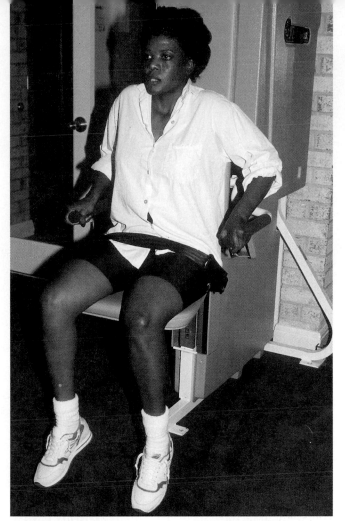

▲ Fig. 8-15

For more information on safe weight-training techniques, consult a coach or a trainer at a health club.

Strength training with aquatic exercise is another way for fitness swimmers to improve muscular strength and endurance. In aquatic exercise, because it is hard to calculate the resistance of the water, performing only three sets might not provide the overload needed to increase strength and endurance. The overload for strength improvement may depend solely on increasing the speed of movement, number of sets or number of repetitions per set. One should rely on perception of overload to determine if one is working hard enough.

Cool-Down

The last part of the workout is a cool-down period. This is a tapering off to let the heart rate, blood pressure and metabolic rate return to their resting levels. A proper cool-down helps return the blood from the working muscles to the brain, lungs and internal organs. The cool-down helps the body recover from fatigue and may reduce muscle soreness later.

Cool-down activities are like warm-up activities. Change to a resting stroke to slow down the workout gradually and keep blood from collecting in the muscles (Fig. 8-16). Stretch in a stationary position toward the end of the cool-down, but not immediately after strenuous activity in the aerobic set or the muscular development set. A typical cool-down lasts 5 to 10 minutes.

Phases of a Fitness Program

Fitness improves when the exertion of the workout gradually increases. As the body adapts to a workload, the work level gradually should increase. This is referred to as progression. Increase the workload by increasing the frequency, intensity or duration (time) of the workouts. In general, increase the duration first, then the intensity or frequency. Remember, fitness level will not improve unless the stress of the exercise on the body is increased.

How fast one's condition improves depends on the fitness level at the beginning of the program and other individual factors. For safe and effective exercise, increase the overload gradually in three phases: the initial phase, the improvement phase and the maintenance phase. It is possible for one's condition to decline if the workload decreases or stops.

Initial Phase

This phase should include exercise of a low intensity. If you have not exercised in a long time, this phase helps increase the workload slowly and comfortably. Move on to the improvement phase when able to comfortably maintain 60-percent intensity for at least 30 minutes. Be patient. Up to 10 weeks may be necessary before going to the improvement phase.

Improvement Phase

The improvement phase begins upon reaching the minimum level to attain cardiovascular fitness, namely, exercising three times per week for at least 20 minutes at a level of at least 60-percent intensity. Fitness will improve by increasing frequency, intensity or duration. For example, exercising five times a week leads to improvements sooner than only three times a week, if all else is the same. Improvement comes more rapidly in this phase than in the initial phase, but be sure to stay well within the target heart rate range. Remember to increase the session duration before increasing intensity or frequency.

Maintenance Phase

The maintenance phase begins when fitness goals have been achieved. The goal here is to sustain the fitness level rather than increase the workload. Exercise at a comfortable level and set different goals. For example, if the cardiovascular system is more fit, consider working on learning a new stroke or exploring other activities to vary the program. This will help keep workouts interesting.

Reversibility of Training

The physical fitness gained from exercise can be lost. By stopping regular exercise, one's fitness level will decrease and gradually return to pre-exercise program shape. It is better to maintain a current level of fitness than to let it decline and try to regain it. Having once been physically fit does not make it any easier to get back into shape, except that it may not be necessary to learn specific workout skills again. Fitness declines quickly but can be maintained with as few as two workouts a week. The key is to develop fitness habits to use for a lifetime.

Fitness Swimming

Design a fitness swimming program carefully. This means starting at the right level and following an effective progression in the exercise plan. This section aids in designing a program to progress from an inactive lifestyle to a desired fitness level. Depending on current fitness level, moving through the initial phase quickly or even skipping it may be an option. Remember, the success of a program depends on a comfortable, practical plan that can be sustained through the future.

Always use a warm-up, stretching, an aerobic set and a cool-down in each workout. Include a muscular development set in two or three workouts each week.

Remember that the target heart rate range with swimming should be 10 to 13 beats below that for similar exercise on land. Remember to lower the target heart rate range by this much for fitness swimming.

Check the heart rate before, during and after workouts to ensure the right intensity. Also, check the resting heart rate every few weeks because exercise gradually lowers it. Then recalculate the target heart rate range to make sure the body is still overloaded without exceeding the target range.

Initial Phase

The following are examples of specific exercises for designing a program. These assumptions have been made:

1. The pool is 25 yards long (a common length for pools in the United States). If the pool is longer or shorter, make adjustments.
2. The swimmer can swim one length of the pool using any stroke.
3. Workouts occur on 3 nonconsecutive days per week.
4. A gradual warm-up is completed, including stretching exercises, before the aerobic set.

Between lengths, rest or walk or jog in the water for 15 to 30 seconds (Fig. 8-17). Try to keep a continuous effort without becoming too tired. To find a safe level to start, swim one length and check the heart rate. If it is above the target range, start with Step 1. If the heart rate is well within the target range, start with Step 3. If the water is too deep for walking or jogging, use a life jacket or stay in water no deeper than the shoulders. Remember that using a life jacket does not substitute for knowing how to swim.

▲ FIG. 8-17

In this phase of the program, reaching the target heart rate range of 60-percent intensity is not necessary. Individuals who have not exercised in a long while should begin at 50 percent for the progression.

Proceed with each step of the workout until it can be done easily, keeping the heart rate close to the lower limit of the target range. The initial phase can take as long as 10 weeks, so do not try to rush through it at an uncomfortable pace.

Step 1   In chest-deep water, walk 5 minutes and exercise the upper body with an underwater arm stroke, such as the breaststroke. Check the heart rate after each length. If, after walking 5 minutes, the heart rate does not rise above the target heart rate range, rest 15 to 30 seconds and do the 5-minute walk two more times. Gradually decrease the rest period until it is possible to do it for 15 minutes continuously. Be sure the heart rate does not go past the upper limit of the target range.

Step 2   In chest-deep water, walk one length using the arm stroke as is in Step 1, then jog one length. Rest 15 to 20 seconds after the jogging length.

Continue for 15 minutes. Check the heart rate at each break. Gradually decrease the rest breaks until it is possible to walk or jog 15 minutes continuously. Check the heart rate every 5 minutes in the workout.

Step 3   Swim one length at a pace that takes more effort than jogging and then rest by walking or jogging one length. Continue for 5 minutes. Check the heart rate to be sure the heart rate is not too high. If it is, rest another minute. If the heart rate is within the target range, continue alternating swimming lengths with walking or jogging lengths. Check the heart rate every 5 minutes. Gradually decrease the rest breaks until it is possible to swim or jog continuously for 15 minutes.

Step 4   Swim one length with effort, rest 15 to 30 seconds, and swim another length. Use a resting stroke on the second length or just swim more slowly. Check the heart rate. Continue this sequence for 15 minutes. Gradually decrease the rest break to 10 seconds.

Step 5   When it is possible to swim 15 minutes continuously or with minimum rest as in Step 4, recalculate the target heart rate range at 60 percent and repeat Step 4. When it is possible to swim continuously for 15 minutes at an intensity of 60 percent, the initial phase is complete. Move on to the improvement phase.

There are several ways to check one's progress. One way is to check the resting heart rate every 3 to 4 weeks. As fitness level improves, the resting heart rate will drop. As it drops, be sure to recalculate the target range with the new resting heart rate to continue to overload the system properly. Another indication of progress is that the heart rate returns to normal more quickly as fitness improves.

Improvement Phase

People have very different improvement phases. If starting out with a low level of fitness, expect to progress more slowly than someone who is more fit. There are two options here. Level 1 is for someone progressing from the previous phase. Level 2 offers other training methods to add variety to the program. Both options use the assumptions listed for the initial phase.

Level 1

These steps move in 2-week increments. Do not move to a more difficult step until it is possible to do the prior step easily. The full 2 weeks may not be necessary for some steps.

Weeks 1–2   Swim two lengths. Rest 15 to 30 seconds. Repeat for 15 minutes. Check the heart rate during the breaks.

Weeks 3–4   Swim three lengths followed by a slow length or resting stroke. Rest 15 to 30 seconds. Continue for 20 minutes. Through this period, gradually shorten the rest breaks to 10 seconds.

Weeks 5–6   Swim five lengths followed by a slow length or resting stroke. Rest 15 to 30 seconds. Check the heart rate. Continue for 20 minutes. With each successive workout, gradually decrease the rest breaks to 10 seconds.

Weeks 7–8   Swim continuously for 20 minutes. Rest only when needed but not longer than 10 seconds. If possible, use resting strokes instead of breaks. Check the heart rate every 10 minutes in the workout.

Weeks 9–10   Swim continuously for 20 minutes. With each successive workout, add one or two lengths until it is possible to swim continuously for 30 minutes.

Weeks 11–12   Swim 30 minutes continuously without rest. In the last week of this progression, test the progress by swimming a timed 12-minute swim.

After reaching the 30-minute goal, continue to increase the overload by raising the intensity or lengthening the workout. When doing this, be sure to change only one variable (frequency, intensity or time) at a time. Keep the progression gradual.

Level 2

Whatever the level of fitness, design the workout with various training methods. When planning the workout, remember the principles of frequency, intensity, duration and type, and do not try to progress too fast.

Cooper 12-Minute Swimming Test

The 12-minute swimming test, devised by Kenneth Cooper, M.D., is an easy, inexpensive way for men and women of all ages to test their aerobic capacity (oxygen consumption) and to chart their fitness program (Table 8-3).

The test encourages the swimmer to cover the greatest distance possible in 12 minutes, using whatever stroke is preferred, resting as necessary, but going as far as he or she can.

For instance, a woman between the ages of 30 and 39 is in excellent condition if she can swim 550 yards or more in the 12 minutes allowed for the test. However, a woman of the same age would be considered in very poor condition if she could not swim at least 250 yards in the same time.

The easiest way to take the test is to swim in a pool with known dimensions, and it helps to have someone there to record the number of laps and the time, preferably with a sweep second hand.

Care must be taken with the 12-minute test, however. It is not recommended for anyone older than 35 years of age, unless he or she has already developed good aerobic capacity. The best way to determine this, of course, is to see a physician.

Chapter 9 describes many training techniques that can be incorporated into the workout. These help develop specific aspects of fitness or swimming skills. Use each technique alone or combine them.

TABLE 8-3   Cooper 12-Minute Swimming Test
Distance (Yards) Swum in 12 Minutes

FITNESS CATEGORY		AGE (YEARS)					
		13–19	20–29	30–39	40–49	50–59	>60*
I. Very poor	(men)	<500*	<400	<350	<300	<250	<250
	(women)	<400	<300	<250	<200	<150	<150
II. Poor	(men)	500–599	400–499	350–449	300–399	250–349	250–299
	(women)	400–499	300–399	250–349	200–299	150–249	150–199
III. Fair	(men)	600–699	500–599	450–549	400–499	350–449	300–399
	(women)	500–599	400–499	350–449	300–399	250–349	200–299
IV. Good	(men)	700–799	600–699	550–649	500–599	450–549	400–499
	(women)	600–699	500–599	450–549	400–499	350–449	300–399
V. Excellent	(men)	>800	>700	>650	>600	>550	>500
	(women)	>700	>600	>550	>500	>450	>400

*< Means "less than"; > means "more than."

From Cooper K. H.: *The Aerobics Program for Total Well-Being,* New York: Bantam Books, 1982.

Maintenance Phase

Once fitness goals are achieved, there may not be a desire to increase the workload any more. Consider the original goals and either set new ones or maintain the current fitness level by staying with the present workout. What is most important is that at least the minimum level of fitness is maintained. If the goal is to train for competition, take a look at the methods described in Chapter 9.

Swimming Etiquette

It may be frustrating during a swimming workout to have to share the pool with other swimmers. Cyclists do not have to share their bikes, and runners can usually find a quiet road, but fitness swimmers rarely get a lane to themselves. Proper swimming etiquette helps ease this problem.

To share a lane, all swimmers should be organized and cooperative and know their swimming levels. First figure out the exercise speed. The workout will be better in a lane where other swimmers are doing a similar type of workout (pulls, kicks, repeat short distances, long continuous swims) at a speed similar to the individual's workout plan. Many pools have lanes for fast, medium and slow swimmers, but the speed within a lane will still vary a great deal.

Once the best lane is selected, circle swimming should be done so that all swimmers can enjoy the workout (Fig. 8-18). Circle swimming is swimming in a counterclockwise pattern around the line on the pool bottom in the lane's center. With the correct etiquette, a faster swimmer overtaking a slower swimmer in the lane signals to pass by tapping the lead swimmer's foot. The lead swimmer should stop at the wall or pull over to the right to let the faster swimmer pass. It is common courtesy to allow the new lead swimmer at least a 5-second lead before following. Although this may seem to disrupt the workout, such short breaks will not affect the intensity.

Aquatic Exercise

Aquatic exercise has grown in part from athletics. Coaches wanted to rehabilitate injured athletes in a way that was safe but also good for cardiovascular conditioning. Water exercise was the perfect activity. Aquatic exercise programs are now a physical fitness avenue for health-

▲ FIG. 8-18

conscious people, in addition to being a rehabilitation method.

Aquatic exercise programs vary in many ways. The water temperature and depth, the style of aerobic exercises and the specific range of motions all vary from program to program (Fig. 8-19). People engage in aquatic exercise to manage weight, relieve stress, feel better and generally become more fit. An advantage of aquatic exercise is that in many programs one does not have to know how to swim.

People with disabilities may get a special benefit from aquatic exercise. As discussed in Chapter 7, these individuals can improve their level of fitness, range of motion and muscu-

lar strength and endurance with aquatic activity.

Factors That Affect the Workout

In aquatic exercise, maintain the proper intensity by adjusting the body position and by moving in the water. The following factors affect the intensity the most:

► Buoyancy, as it relates to proper water depth and body position
► Resistance the working muscles must overcome, affected by how much surface area the body presents as it moves through the water
► Speed of movement
► Type of movement

▼ FIG. 8-19

Buoyancy and Water Depth

Buoyancy reduces the apparent pull of gravity on the limbs and trunk. The closer the depth is to the standing person's height, the more support it gives. Exercise in water that is only ankle or knee deep does little to reduce the impact of the feet landing when jogging or jumping. In deeper water, the body has more buoyancy, but in neck-deep water it is hard to keep balance and control. Increased buoyancy also reduces the workload, so it could be difficult to get the heart rate into the target range.

Exercise in chest-deep water may be best because the arms stay submerged. Using the arms also helps maintain balance and proper body alignment. The effort of pushing the water improves upper body strength and endurance and helps make the exercise aerobic. Arm work under water improves the muscles that stabilize the trunk. These muscles, particularly the abdominal muscles, gain strength and help reduce stress in the lower back.

Obese people may need to adjust their workouts if their hips and thighs cause the center of buoyancy to be lower. The legs then tend to rise toward the surface, making it hard to keep balance. Obese people may want to exercise in shallower water, but it should still be deep enough to support and protect the body from hard landings.

The manner of exercise also affects the intensity of the workout. With bouncing and bounding movements (such as those commonly associated with aerobic exercise done out of the water), the heart rate might not reach the target range because the body has a short rest while it drifts back to the bottom. However, movements involving walking, jogging or bouncing in the water can be of value as progress toward workouts of higher intensity is made. Aquatic exercise helps avoid problems that are associated with the impact of landing.

Resistance

Exercise intensity is greater when the surface area of the body is larger, creating greater drag. By choosing which limbs to maneuver in which ways, adjust the resistance the body encounters when it pushes against the water. For example, a biceps curl uses more effort with an open hand than with a fist (Fig. 8-20). Moving a longer body segment, such as the whole arm kept straight from the shoulder, uses more effort than a shorter body segment, such as the forearm during a biceps curl. Adjust resistance by using equipment designed for aquatic exercise.

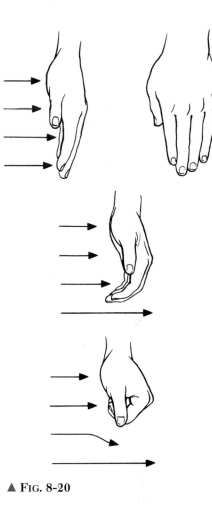

▲ Fig. 8-20

Speed of Movement

The speed of movement in the exercise also affects the intensity of the workout. Faster movements result in greater resistance and use more effort. In aquatic exercise, this principle applies both to the speed of moving individual limbs and the speed of moving the whole body from one point in the pool to another.

Type of Movement

Some types of movement require more effort than others. When limbs move through the water in aquatic exercise, the water is set in motion and stays in motion. If you continue moving with the water, there will be less resistance. Maintain resistance by accelerating the limb (moving it faster and faster) or changing direction to move out of or against the flow of water.

Arm movements can be used in combination with leg movements to create a wide variety of exercise techniques. Bouncing, leaping, running and walking forward, backward and sideways are variations of lower body movements. Scooping, lifting, punching and squeezing water are

▲ Fig. 8-21

variations of upper body movements. Resistance is adjusted by using a cupped hand or slicing the hand through the water. For instance, while jogging in shallow water, bursts of quick, short arm movements can increase cardiovascular fitness.

Workout Design

An aquatic exercise workout should have the same components as a fitness swimming workout. The warm-up lasts 5 to 10 minutes and consists of walking, slow jogging and slow aerobic activities, in the water or at poolside if the water is not warm enough. Stretching may be added after the warm-up. If there is a chill early in the workout, try stretching after the aerobic set.

The aerobic set should be rhythmic and continuous and use both arms and legs (Fig. 8-21). Monitor the heart rate several times during this set to be sure it stays in the target range.

Two or three times each week, the workout should include a muscular development set. This promotes flexibility, range of motion, strength and muscular endurance.

The cool-down in an aquatic workout should consist of slow, rhythmic activities. A good format for the cooldown is simply to reverse the warm-up activities.

Aquatic Exercise for Muscular Development

The intensity of resistance training increases directly with the size of the surface area and the speed of movement. One is effectively lifting more weight if movements are faster and the surface area meeting resistance is larger.

Equipment

Several products are designed to provide greater overload during resistance training (Fig. 8-22). Some use the principle of buoyancy to increase exercise intensity. Wearing buoyant cuffs on wrists or ankles means that greater force must be used to move limbs deeper. Other devices increase the surface area of the limbs to provide resistance. Devices for aquatic resistance training are not recommended for the beginner. For most people, the water alone provides an adequate overload for improvements in strength and muscular endurance. However, the more advanced exerciser may need such equipment to help maintain the proper intensity for his or her workout. Check with a physician before using equipment if there is any history of joint problems.

Safety Precautions

Follow these guidelines to keep the aquatic exercise safe:

► Never exercise alone in a pool.
► Use the right equipment. It is important to use equipment specifically designed for aquatic exercise. Improvised equipment may cause injury. Always use equipment that can be controlled. Once a piece of equipment is put in motion, it may continue to move, striking the body. Without enough strength to stop and reverse the motion or to stabilize the body during the movement, safety may be jeopardized.
► Keep the body centered. Body alignment is especially important when you are using equipment for resistance training. Choose exercises in which the movement is toward and away from the center of the body.

Movements with limbs fully extended, such as leg or arm circles, may cause injury.

▶ Stabilize the trunk when lifting limbs and any equipment through the water. The larger surface area of such devices requires a greater degree of trunk stability for safe lifting technique. Stability throughout the lift is affected by the inertia of the equipment and, to a limited degree, by buoyancy. When performing lifting motions, the back should be flat, with the abdominal muscles tight, knees slightly bent and feet flat on the pool bottom.

▶ Isolate and work one muscle group at a time. This focuses the attention and gives the best improvement for individual muscle groups. Be sure to exercise opposing muscle groups equally.

▶ Work major muscle groups first. If smaller, assisting muscle groups are worked first, they will fatigue early and limit the work possible with major muscle groups.

▶ Plan movements. First imagine where the piece of equipment will be at the end of the movement, then perform the action. Use exercises that involve a full range of motion and be sure to return fully to the starting position. Be sure the equipment stays in the water. Shock to joints and muscles when equipment passes into or out of the water can cause injury.

▶ Use correct breathing. Do not hold the breath. This increases blood pressure and may increase feelings of stress. Instead, adjust the breathing to the rhythm of the exercise. Exhale during the work phase and inhale during the recovery phase.

▶ Stop any exercise that causes sharp pain. Sharp pain can be a signal of a serious health problem. Seek immediate help for persistent pain in the chest or arm (pain that does not go away within 10 minutes and is not relieved by resting or changing position). Report any recurring pain to a health care provider.

▲ Fig. 8-22

Progressions for Aquatic Exercise

Progress can be easy in aquatic exercise because there are three factors (resistance due to surface area, speed of movement and type of movement) used to reach the necessary level of intensity. If one is less fit, start with low-level exercises, such as walking in chest-deep water or slow jogging in waist-deep water. Use slow, rhythmic movements with small surface areas. If one is generally fit, exercise with larger surface areas, faster speeds and angular motion to reach the right intensity. Once able to adjust the intensity, it is possible to exercise in the same class with others who are exercising at different intensities.

The key to progressively overloading the system and maintaining target heart rates is to control how surface area, speed and type of movement interact (Fig. 8-23). It is possible to stay at the same intensity with a smaller surface area (for example, moving from chest-deep water to waist-deep water) by increasing the speed of movement (such as walking or jogging faster). Change from angular motion to curved motion without losing intensity by increasing the surface area or the speed.

Courtesy of Terri Lees

Progression Continuum

- Maintain speed
- Incorporate periods of longer levers and more angular motion

- Greater speed
- Short levers
- Curvilinear motion

- Maintain medium speed
- Incorporate periods of longer levers and more angular motion

- Medium speed movement
- Short levers
- Curvilinear motion

- Maintain slow speed of movement
- Incorporate periods with longer levers (more surface area) and alternate curvilinear and angular motion

- Slow speed of movement
- Small surface area (short levers)
- Curvilinear

▲ Fɪɢ. 8-23

Summary

Regular aerobic exercise is beneficial in many ways. Water is a good vehicle for reaching one's fitness goals with a low risk of injury. A fitness program can be designed to meet individual needs, whether a novice or a star athlete. A program should be supervised, monitored often and evaluated for its success. If the current program is not producing desired results, reevaluate it and adjust it to reach the goals more effectively. If the program gives the desired results, a person is more likely to keep exercising and enjoying the benefits of greater health. When enrolling in any water fitness exercise program, be sure that the instructors are trained or certified to teach water exercise programs.

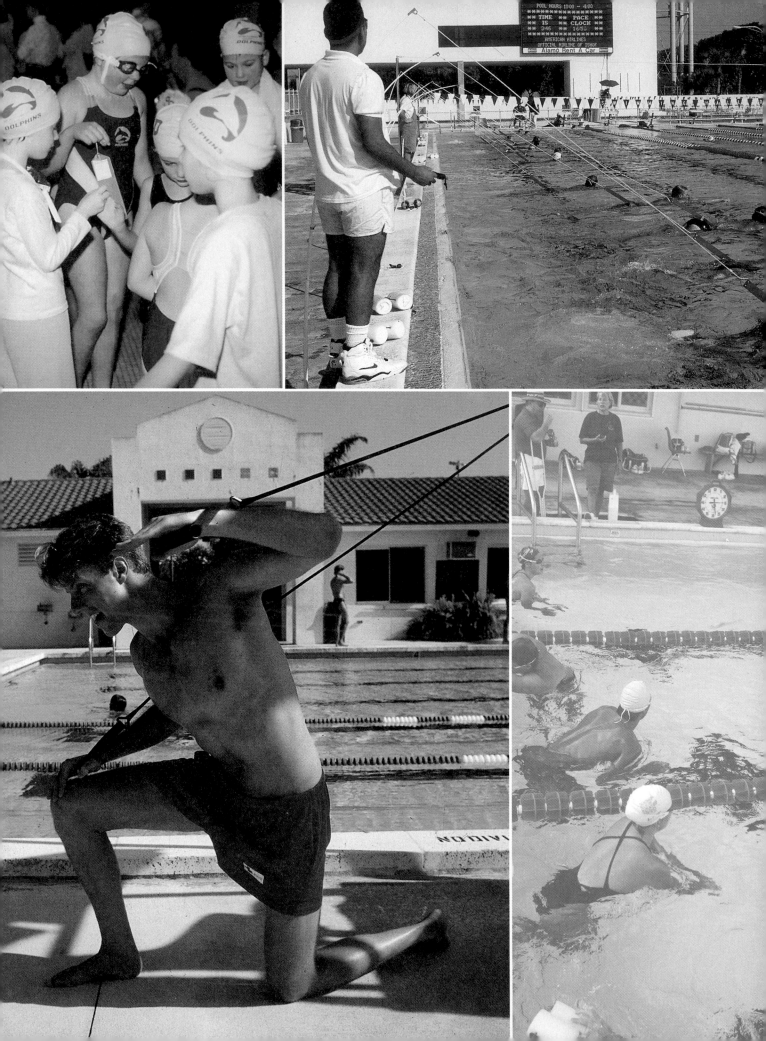

Training

Chapter 9

Some people define training as any organized program of exercise designed to reach a certain level of fitness or performance. Because the preceding chapter focused on helping individuals meet fitness goals, this chapter focuses on expanding the range of options. Learning how to train to increase the strength or endurance of specific muscle groups or to learn or improve skills helps prepare one for competition.

Training differs from fitness exercise in several ways. The first difference is the intensity of workouts. The goal of fitness exercise is to stay within the target heart rate range, usually at the lower end if just starting a fitness program. When training, one is often at the upper end of the target rate range and, for brief periods, above it. The second difference is in the amount of time spent in muscular development. The American College of Sports Medicine recommends that muscular development exercises be performed two or three times per week, whether the objective is fitness or training. In a training program, improved strength and endurance is a critical goal. Thus, muscular development sets are usually more frequent and more extensive in a training program. Competitive swimmers train nearly every day and do more than one session per day.

Principles of Training

A training program should follow certain principles to help achieve goals. The following sections provide guidelines for any type of aerobic exercise, including aquatic exercise and fitness swimming.

Specificity

The principle of specificity states that the benefits of exercise relate directly to the activity performed. Put another way, beyond the general benefits of exercise, there is very little transfer of effects from one kind of activity to another. For example, a runner who trains on the track will not have much improvement in swimming performance. Specific arm muscles do most of the work in swimming, whereas specific leg muscles are used in running. Still, both activities improve one's aerobic capacity.

The principle of specificity is important in two areas: the energy system used and the nerves and muscles exercised in a given activity. The following sections explain the importance for any training program.

Energy Systems

Two major energy systems supply energy to the muscles. The anaerobic (without oxygen) energy system uses the most rapidly available source of energy—sugars and carbohydrates stored in the body—for muscular activity. The anaerobic energy system is the primary source of energy for anaerobic exercise (exercise at an intensity such that oxygen demand by the skeletal muscles is not consistently met). A person who is fit is usually exercising anaerobically if the heart rate is above the 85-percent level of intensity. For someone who is unfit or underfit, exercise may be anaerobic at an intensity much less than 85 percent. (For more information on target heart rate range as an indicator of intensity, see Chapter 8.)

For longer-lasting exercise, the aerobic (oxygen-using) energy system gives the muscles energy. This system breaks down carbohydrates, fats and proteins for energy. The body uses this system for aerobic exercise (sustained, rhythmic, physical exercise that requires additional effort by the heart and lungs to meet the increased demand by the skeletal muscles for oxygen).

The specific energy system the body uses in an activity depends on how long and intense the activity is. The benefits of training depend on which energy system is being used. Improvements in the aerobic energy system need continuous, low- to moderate-intensity training. Improvements in the anaerobic energy system need high-intensity, short-duration training. For example, if you are training to improve your sprint performance, swimming workouts that only focus on repeated distances at low intensities are not effective (Fig. 9-1). Types of cxercise can be located along a continuum such as below.

▲ Fig. 9-1

Mostly Aerobic (Low to Moderate Intensity, Long Duration)

Swimming
Aerobics or aquatic exercise
Distance running or walking
Distance cycling
Cross-country skiing
Rowing
Workouts on exercise equipment, such as bikes and treadmills

Mixture of Aerobic and Anaerobic Exercise

Water polo
Recreational basketball
Racquetball
Weight training
Baseball or softball
Football

Mostly Anaerobic (High Intensity, Short Duration)

Sprints of any kind (running, swimming, cycling, etc.)
Field events in track competition

Overload

The principle of overload states that a body system improves only if the system is regularly worked at loads greater than normal. For example, muscular strength is increased by lifting weights, but the amount of weight must gradually increase if the goal is to continue increasing strength. Muscular endurance, on the other hand, is improved by increasing the number of repetitions rather than the load—for example, lifting the same weight more times.

Chapter 8 explained how to adjust three factors to overload the whole body or specific muscle groups or systems. These are frequency, intensity and duration. It also explained ways to monitor exercise intensity, including keeping track of heart rate or using the rating of perceived exertion (RPE), both of which indicate how hard one is working. The perception of how hard one is working can be a reliable indicator of exercise intensity, especially for experienced swimmers.

Progression

As the body adapts to any workload, gradually increase that level. Improvement will not occur unless the load is raised above the original overload. This principle of progression is shown in the phases of a fitness program in Chapter 8. This principle also affects how an athlete designs the training season.

Stroke Length and Stroke Frequency

An obvious training goal for competitive swimmers is to improve speed. To do this, two concepts are involved. Stroke length is the distance traveled in one complete cycle of the arms: from the time the hand enters the water, through the pull phase, to exit and reentry. To determine stroke length, count the cycles it takes to swim a known distance, then divide that distance by the number of strokes. Stroke frequency is the number of complete arm cycles in a specified length of time. To determine stroke frequency, count the cycles swum in a known amount of time, then divide the number of cycles by the number of seconds. For example, a swimmer covers 50 meters in 25 seconds with 25 arm strokes:

$$\textbf{Stroke Length} =$$
$$\textbf{distance stroked/number of cycles} =$$
$$\textbf{50 meters/25 cycles} = \textbf{2.0 meters/cycle}$$

$$\textbf{Stroke Frequency} = \textbf{number of cycles/time} =$$
$$\textbf{25 cycles/25 seconds} = \textbf{1 cycle/second}$$

Speed is the product of stroke length and stroke frequency. Using the above example, speed would be:

$$\textbf{Speed} = \textbf{stroke length} \times \textbf{stroke frequency} =$$
$$\textbf{2 meters/cycle} \times \textbf{1 cycle/second} =$$
$$\textbf{2 meters/second}$$

To increase speed, a corresponding increase in stroke length or stroke frequency is needed. Increase speed efficiently by improving the stroke to get greater distance from each stroke without increasing the number of cycles per second.

Training Techniques

The following are several training techniques that can be used in workouts to meet specific fitness and training goals. Use them alone or in combination. The distances and speed swum and the duration of rest periods depend on various factors, such as the time set aside for training, training goals and the observations of a coach or trainer, if present. Using different techniques also adds variety to workouts.

Over Distance

The over-distance method involves swimming long distances with moderate exertion with short or no rest periods (Fig. 9-2). Over-distance training is used to improve endurance. The heart rate stays in the low to middle level of the target range for the whole swim. This is also an effective warm-up activity.

Fartlek

The fartlek method gets its name from the Swedish word that means "speed play" and was popularized by runners. It breaks swims into slow and fast lengths of the pool, using the same stroke. It can make long swims more interesting and is good for developing speed and endurance at the same time.

Interval Sets

Interval sets are one of the most common swimming training methods. Intervals are a series of repeat swims of

▲ FIG. 9-2

the same distance and time interval (Fig. 9-3). They give a specific rest period between the time spent swimming. The entire swim series is a set.

An example of an interval set is "8 × 100 on 1:30." The first number represents the number of times to repeat the distance. The second number (100 in this case) is the distance of each swim in yards or meters, and the 1 minute and 30 seconds is the total amount of time for the swim and rest. If swimming the 100 in 1:15, 15 seconds are available for rest. This short rest period keeps the heart rate within the target range without dropping back to a resting rate. Used primarily in the main set of a workout, interval swimming is the best all-around method to develop both speed and endurance.

Repetition

Repetition is a technique that uses swim sets of the same distance, done at close to maximum effort (up to 90 percent of maximum), but with rest periods as long as or longer than the swim time. Repetition sets develop speed and anaerobic capacity. This training method is used after a good aerobic base is developed. It is usually done after the aerobic set as a muscular development set.

Sprints

Sprints are short, fast swims (100-percent effort) to simulate race conditions. The rest between sprints is usually long enough to let the heart return to its resting rate. Like repetition swims, sprints improve anaerobic capacity.

Straight Sets

With the straight-set method, a steady speed is maintained throughout the set. Monitoring time helps keep an even pace. This method is often used by distance swimmers.

Negative Split Sets

Negative splitting involves swimming the second half of each swim period faster than the first half. For example, if swimming 200 yards four times, the second 100 should be faster than the first 100 in each repetition.

Descending Sets

Often confused with negative splitting, *descending sets* refers to decreasing the time on successive swims. To swim 200 yards four times in a descending set, each 200 would be faster than the 200 preceding it.

► FIG. 9-3

▲ Fig. 9-4, *A-B*

Ladders

Ladders are several swims with regular increases or decreases in distance. For example, swim a 25, then a 50 and finally a 75.

Pyramids

A pyramid is a swim of regular increases and decreases in distance. For example, swim a 25, then a 50, then a 75, then a 50 and finally a 25. A variation of both pyramids and ladders is to increase the number of times the distance is repeated as the distances get shorter, for example, 1×500, 2×400, 3×300, 4×200 and 5×100.

Broken Swims

Broken swims divide a target distance into shorter intervals with a short rest (for example, 10 seconds) between. The goal is to swim each segment at a faster pace than could be maintained over the entire distance. Each segment is timed. On completing the entire swim, subtract the total time of rest from the total time to determine swimming pace. Broken swims are a highly motivating method of training because they simulate stress conditions of competition while yielding a swimming time that may be faster than racing time for an actual event. Broken swims are often combined with other variations, such as negative splits and descending swims.

Dry-Land Training

Dry-land training uses out-of-the-water training techniques to improve swimming skills. These techniques fall into two areas: flexibility and strength training. Done properly, resistance training builds both strength and flexibility (Fig. 9-4, *A* and *B*). A half hour of resistance training 3 days a week, combined with 15 minutes of stretching, can produce favorable results. If there is time, consider doing dry-land strength training after water training so that training in the pool is not affected by fatigue from the dry-land training.

The Training Season

In general, there are two competitive swimming seasons. The short-course season for 25-yard pools usually runs from September to May; the long-course season for 50-meter pools usually runs from June to August.

For either season, training should follow three phases to culminate at the competitive event. These phases are individually set, based on personal goals. The phase of training determines the type of workouts. The following is a description of each training phase of the swimming season, along with suggested workouts to assist effective training.

Early Season Phase

About 6 to 8 weeks long, the early season phase focuses on general conditioning to build a foundation for the whole season. Long, easy swims using various strokes help build endurance. Swim at a slower rate and make needed changes to stroke technique, flip turns and breathing patterns. Supplement swimming with dry-land exercise to help improve strength, flexibility and cardio-vascular conditioning.

Mid-Season Phase

In the mid-season phase, which is about 8 to 12 weeks long, start to tailor individual training to specific goals. Workouts increase in distance, so pay more attention to fine tuning strokes (Fig. 9-5). Quality is the emphasis of the workout. Use dry-land training at maintenance level during this time.

Taper Phase

The taper phase is the last and shortest part of training, usually lasting 1 to 3 weeks. As the set date for peak performance draws near, decrease the distances to swim but raise the intensity almost to racing speed. Do this by resting more between sets and by using broken swims and descending sets. Practice starts and turns to improve technique. The specifics of the taper phase depend on the individual and the length and time of training in the earlier phases. For example, sprinters usually taper longer than distance swimmers and older athletes taper longer than younger athletes.

Sample Training Workouts

The following workouts are divided into the three phases. They include samples of over distance, fartlek, interval and sprints.

Early Season

Warm-up	4 × 200 swim/pull/kick/swim
Main set	800 maintain even pace at 100s
	1,650 broken swim with 15 seconds rest after each interval
	1 × 500
	1 × 400
	1 × 300
	1 × 200
	1 × 100
	1 × 75
	1 × 50
	1 × 25
Cool-down	200 easy swim

▼ FIG. 9-5

Mid-Season

Warm-up	8 × 100 alternating between swimming and kicking
Main set	5 × 200 broken swims on 4:00 with 10 seconds rest at each break
	1 × 100
	2 × 50
	5 × 300, swim first 200, kick last 100; rest 15 seconds between swims
Cool-down	12 × 50 on 1:00

Taper Phase

Warm-up	300 easy swim
	6 × 50 descending set on 2:00
Main set	4 × 100 broken swims on 3:00 with 20 seconds rest at each break
	2 × 50
Cool-down	200 easy swim
	starts and turns

Tips for the First Meet

To find out about local meets, contact the local pool or swim team or get in touch with one of the organizations discussed in Chapter 1 (Fig. 9-6). They can help find a local organization that sponsors meets. Work with them to get a meet information sheet with lists of events, deadlines and other information, such as club membership.

Look over information about the meet carefully. Complete the entry form, and do not forget any entry fees or deadlines. For a club or team, the coach may send in all the registrations together. Swimmers should choose which events they feel comfortable entering and check that they are spaced far enough apart for rest in between. Make a list of entered events and when they occur in the meet. There will probably be enough anxiety without having to remember an exact schedule. During the meet, if more rest is needed, it is okay to change plans even after entering. Just let the officials know of the change in plans. This is called a *scratch*.

At the first meet, there may be feelings of uncertainty. Almost everyone feels the jitters, so do not be surprised if there are a few "butterflies in the stomach" or if sleeping the night before is difficult. Refer to the "Items to Bring to a Swim Meet" list for what to bring.

Items to Bring to a Swim Meet

▶ *Swim suits.* Because it is no fun sitting around in a wet suit, bring more than one. Change into a dry suit after warm-ups and your events.

▼ Fɪɢ. 9-6

- *Swim cap* (if you wear one). An extra one is handy in case of rips.
- *Goggles.* A spare pair or strap is a good idea.
- *Towels.* Bring at least two, the larger the better.
- *Warm clothes.* To keep from getting chilled between events, wear a sweat suit, t-shirt, and socks and shoes. If outdoors, bring a hat, sunglasses or umbrella for protection from the sun.
- *Toiletries.* Remember the shampoo, soap and lotions for cleaning up after the meet. For safety, use plastic bottles only.
- *Lock.* Keep belongings safe in a locker.
- *Water.*
- *Snacks.*

Other items to have along are a pencil and paper to keep notes and records, a stopwatch, a beach chair, a cooler, pain relief medication, cash and a camera.

A lot of time is spent training the body for competition, but it is also important to prepare the mind. Think positively. Meets are a way to evaluate training and performance that will help set new goals for the next season. Moreover, help the body perform by "rehearsing" the event mentally again and again. To build self-confidence, think about the things done well.

When arriving at the pool, check in with the meet organizers to verify the events entered. This information should be listed on the heat sheet, usually posted in a window, on a bulletin board or on a table.

Some events are divided into heats. This is done when there are more competitors than there are lanes in the pool. At such times, entrants are organized into several groupings (for example, eight competitors at a time if the pool has eight lanes). Depending on the organization of the meet, the winner may be the person who swims the fastest time in his or her heat or the fastest swimmers from several heats may match each other in a final heat.

Now it is time to warm up. Look for published warm-up rules and safety procedures. Find a lane with people swimming about the same speed as you. Do not dive into the warm-up pool; ease into the pool from the edge or jump feetfirst. Pay attention to others in the lane. While swimming a few laps, loosen up. Practice the strokes to be swum. The warm-up should raise the pulse rate. While warming up, orient to the pool. Get used to the targets on

the wall and find out if the wall is slippery. If swimming the backstroke, check to see if the flags are the same number of strokes from the wall. If not used to the starting blocks, get up on one to judge the distance to the water. It may be more comfortable to start from the deck or in the water.

During the race, swim at a constant pace. Use the first few strokes to establish a pace and stroke rhythm. Stay mentally alert during the race by focusing on whatever actions—such as turns—that required hard work to get right. Try to get someone to time splits (segments of a race) during the race. This will help analyze race performance. The data collected are now a standard for setting future goals.

After the race, keep moving until the body cools down and the pulse returns to normal. If there is a warm-down area, stay in the water and do some easy laps, bob, scull or float. If there is no warm-down area, walk around the pool area until the body recovers. Review the race. If the time was not as good as hoped, remember there will be another chance. Feel proud if the time improved even slightly. The important thing is to have fun while improving health.

Training for Open-Water Competition

Triathlons and cross-training techniques have led more and more people to open-water competitions (Fig. 9-7). Open-water swimmers need to consider the psychological and physical differences of open water. A swimmer may be apprehensive of being disoriented, of hazards in open water (rocks, sandbars, bites and stings from marine life) or of being overpowered by the water. The uncertainty is probably more threatening than the actual situation. Staying calm, knowing personal limits and using the techniques discussed next will help in coping with tense moments.

Whenever swimming in open water, there may be a risk of hypothermia. This life-threatening situation happens when the body loses so much heat that the core temperature drops below normal. Be alert to the possibility of hypothermia if the water temperature is below 70° F (21° C). Temperatures below 60° F (15° C)

▲ FIG. 9-7

▼ FIG. 9-8

pose an immediate threat of hypothermia. Constant shivering is an important warning signal. An even more critical signal is loss of judgment, which can quickly worsen the effects of the cold.

Following certain precautions helps prevent hypothermia. First, practice in cold water. Repeated exposure to cold water acclimates the body. Second, wear insulation. Most heat is lost through the head. Wearing multiple swim caps or a neoprene swim cap helps hold the heat in (Fig. 9-8). Also wear a racing wet suit or vest to insulate the body (Fig. 9-9).

Open-water swimmers need to study the various courses they race. They need to have an understanding of the open-water environment in which they will be swimming. They need to practice spotting marker buoys and work transitions, starts and finishes. They should also check to see that race organizers have taken steps to ensure safety. Rescue personnel in small boats should accompany the swimmers. A system should be in place to ensure that everyone who enters the water is known to have exited.

Training in the Pool

Training for open water is much like training for a long-distance swim. Train in the longest pool available or swim around the perimeter of the pool. The fewer turns taken, the more carryover there will be for the long-distance event.

Practice taking the goggles off and putting them on in the deep end without the support of the pool bottom or sides. Also practice the proper methods for releasing a cramp in deep water. (See Chapter 10.) This should be practiced in the pool. It is safer to plan ahead.

Training in Open Water

For better or for worse, the best way to train for open-water swimming is by doing it. Never swim alone; swim with a partner or notify the lifeguard of plans. Be aware of certain characteristics of open water. Open water is rarely as calm

as the roughest, most crowded pool. To combat roughness, recover elbows higher and roll the shoulders more to keep from catching them on the waves.

Getting off course can be a problem in open water. To swim in a straight line, look. Lift the head after breathing and before putting the face back in the water. Practice this in the pool before venturing out into open water. Alternating breathing (breathing on each side) or having a friend paddle alongside in a boat also will help with swimming in a straight line.

The Event Itself

The start of any open-water event is usually chaotic (Fig. 9-10). Races with a lot of swimmers often use staggered starts, so swimmers will be asked to position themselves. Be honest and smart. If unsure of time, start among swimmers of moderate ability. Avoid being an obstacle for better swimmers to climb over and go around. Staying to the side of the pack may mean swimming slightly farther to get on course, but one will avoid the jumble of swimmers in a mass start. In most events, wearing a provided swimming cap may be required. For safety, many meets use color-coded caps based on age or ability. If unsure of your ability, request a cap color to alert the lifeguards. If dropping out of an open-water event, immediately notify the course officials so that everyone is accounted for at the end of the race.

▲ FIG. 9-10

Cross-Training– Triathlon

For today's fitness expert, cross-training means combining several fitness components to maintain optimum health. This includes stretching to warm-up and cool-down the musculoskeletal system to reduce the risk of injury; resistance and weight training to increase strength; and aerobic endurance activities to improve cardiovascular fitness. Also included is a diet rich in nutrients to meet daily requirements.

Sports enthusiasts bring an additional meaning to the definition of cross-training. Cross-training is a method of exercising so that the effects of training in one sport enhance the effects in another. Simply put, it combines two or more aerobic endurance sports into one training program.

The benefits of such a program are clear. The stress on the bones, muscles and tendons used primarily in one sport is markedly reduced because the person uses different muscle groups in the other sports. In addition to strengthening the different muscle groups, the cross-trainer diminishes the risk of injury. An added benefit of cross-training, of course, is the fun involved in multiple sports.

Triathlons are increasingly popular cross-training competitions. In general, a triathlon could be a race combining any three sports done consecutively, such as kayaking, cycling and running. However, the most common configuration is swimming, bicycling and running, in that order. The best-known triathlon is the Ironman Triathlon World Championship held in Kona, Hawaii. It is a 2.4-mile swim, a 112-mile bike ride and a 26.2-mile run. Worldwide, it is considered the premier endurance event. Each contestant completes each event individually.

A triathlon can also be a relay competition. Three teammates compete, each doing one leg of the race. It can also be organized as a stage-event triathlon, in which each sport has a set start and finish time, possibly on different days.

Competing in the three events of any triathlon is an example of what can be achieved through cross-training: total body fitness. This requires full development of motor skills, muscular strength and cardiovascular fitness. It also involves all the ingredients of maintaining optimum health.

Courtesy Getty Images

Summary

Training takes more time, effort and planning than fitness swimming or aquatic exercise, but the rewards are great. Health benefits include cardiovascular endurance, muscular strength, flexibility and weight management. The guidelines in this chapter can help in developing a training program to meet individual needs.

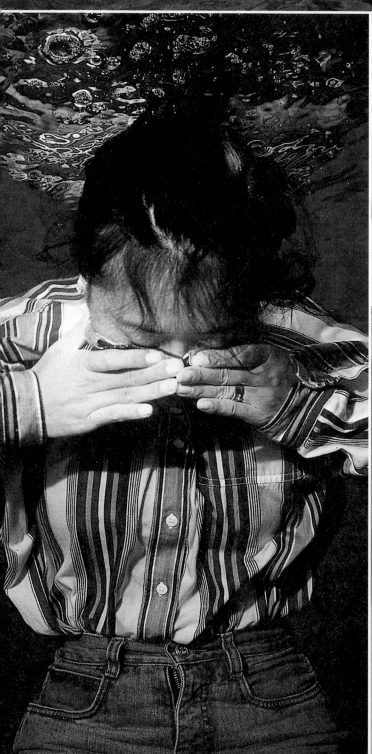

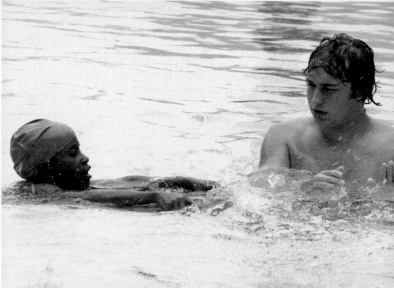

Water Safety

Chapter 10

Water provides people with some of the most enjoyable recreational activities, but water can be dangerous. Drowning is death by suffocation in water. Most people do not realize that many who drown never intended to go in the water in the first place. It is tragic that many of these deaths could have been prevented if the victim had followed basic rules of safety. Do not become one of these victims. Learn and follow the rules to enjoy aquatic activities safely.

Everyone should learn to swim well. Everyone should know basic water rescue methods to help themselves or someone else in an emergency. Everyone should also know about the emergency medical services (EMS) system and how to activate it. Contact a local Red Cross chapter to learn about and enroll in courses that provide instruction in water safety, as well as first aid and cardiopulmonary resuscitation (CPR).

This chapter addresses safety issues for swimming and similar activities around water and ice. This chapter also describes safe, simple rescue techniques for water emergencies and basic first aid for heat- and cold-related emergencies and other conditions. Much of the safety information in this chapter also applies to boating, but specific boating safety issues are not covered. Before participating in boating activities, seek instruction in boat handling and safety.

Planning for Safety

General Water Safety Tips

The best thing anyone can do to stay safe in, on and around the water is to learn to swim. The Red Cross has swimming courses for people of any age and swimming ability. To enroll in a swimming course, contact a local Red Cross chapter.

Follow these general water safety tips whenever swimming in any body of water (pools, lakes, ponds, quarries, canals, rivers or oceans):

▶ Always swim with a buddy; never swim alone.
▶ Read and obey all rules and posted signs (Fig. 10-1).
▶ Swim in areas supervised by a lifeguard.
▶ Children or inexperienced swimmers should take extra precautions, such as wearing a U.S. Coast Guard–approved life jacket when around the water.

▼ Fig. 10-1

Too Much of a Good Thing

Although brief exposure to the sun stimulates the skin to produce the vitamin D necessary for the healthy formation of bones, prolonged exposure can cause problems such as skin cancer and premature aging—a classic case of too much of a good thing being bad.

There are two kinds of ultraviolet (UV) light rays to be concerned about. Ultraviolet beta rays (UVB) are the burn-producing rays that more commonly cause skin cancer. These are the rays that damage the skin's surface and cause blistering and perhaps peeling. The other rays, ultraviolet alpha rays (UVA), have been heralded by tanning salons as "safe rays." Tanning salons claim to use lights that only emit UVA rays. Although UVA rays may not appear as harmful as UVB rays to the skin's surface, they more readily penetrate the deeper layers of the skin. This increases the risk of skin cancer, skin aging, eye damage and genetic changes that may alter the skin's ability to fight disease.

To avoid getting too much sun, avoid exposure to the sun between 10:00 A.M. and 4:00 P.M. UV rays are most harmful during this period. Wear proper clothing to prevent overexposure. Also, take care to protect the skin and eyes whenever exposure to the sun is expected.

Commercial sunscreens come in various strengths. The American Academy of Dermatology recommends year-round sun protection, including use of a high sun protection factor (SPF) sunscreen, for all individuals, but particularly for those who are fair-skinned and sunburn easily. The Food and Drug Administration (FDA) has evaluated SPF readings and recognizes values between 2 and 15. The American Cancer Society recommends an SPF containing a rating of 15 or higher. To get a sense of the effectiveness of SPF, an SPF 4 blocks out 75 percent of the sun's burning UV rays, an SPF 15 blocks out 93 percent and an SPF 30 blocks out 97 percent of the burning UV rays.

For maximum effect, sunscreen should be applied 20 to 30 minutes before exposure to the sun and reapplied frequently. Swimmers should use sunscreens labeled as water resistant and reapply them as described in the labeling. Remember also to use lip balm with an SPF of 15 or higher.

Choose sunscreen that claims to be broad spectrum—protecting against both UVB and UVA rays. Carefully check the label to determine the protection a product offers. Some products only offer protection against UVB rays.

It is equally important to protect the eyes from sun damage. Wear polarized sunglasses that absorb at least 90 percent of UV sunlight. Polarized sunglasses are like sunscreen for the eyes and protect against damage that can occur from UV rays.

► Watch out for the "dangerous too's"—too tired, too cold, too far from safety, too much sun, too much strenuous activity.

► Set water safety rules for the whole family based on swimming abilities (for example, inexperienced swimmers should stay in water less than chest deep).

► Swimmers should be knowledgeable of the water environment they are in and its potential hazards, such as deep and shallow areas, currents, depth changes, obstructions and where the entry and exit points are located. The more informed people are, the more aware they will be of hazards and safe practices.

► Know how to prevent, recognize and respond to emergencies.

► Use a feet-first entry when entering the water.

► Enter headfirst only when the area is clearly marked for diving and has no obstructions.

► Do not mix alcohol with swimming, diving or boating. Alcohol impairs judgment, balance and coordination; affects swimming and diving skills; and reduces the body's ability to stay warm.

▲ FIG. 10-2

Additional Water Safety Tips

Watching Children Around Water

► Maintain constant supervision. Watch children around any water (such as pools, rivers, lakes, bathtubs, toilets and even buckets of water), no matter how well the child can swim and no matter how shallow the water.
► Stay within an arm's reach of an inexperienced swimmer while he or she is in the water.
► Do not rely on substitutes. The use of flotation devices and inflatable toys cannot replace parental supervision. Such devices could suddenly shift position, lose air or slip out from underneath, leaving the child in a dangerous situation.
► Prevent access to water features, such as small ponds and waterfalls.
► Empty kiddie pools immediately after use. Do not leave water in an unattended pool of any kind.
► Use safety locks on toilets and keep bathroom doors closed and toilet bowl covers down if there are small children in the home.
► Empty cleaning buckets immediately after use.

► When visiting another home, check the site for potential water hazards and always supervise children.
► Teach children to swim by enrolling them in a Red Cross Learn-to-Swim course. The decision to provide a child with early aquatic experiences is a gift that will have lifelong rewards (Fig. 10-2).
► Family members should participate in a Red Cross water safety course. A water safety course encourages safe practices and provides lifelong safety skills.
► Learn CPR and first aid. Parents and other caregivers, such as grandparents, older siblings and babysitters, should take a CPR and first aid course. Knowing these skills can be important around the water, and this will expand one's capabilities in providing care for a child.

► Contact a local Red Cross chapter for further information on enrolling in Learn-to-Swim program, water safety and infant, child and adult CPR courses.

Participation in a Learn-to-Swim program does not "drownproof" anyone. It is only the first step in developing water safety and swimming skills. Year-round practice, regular exposure to water and positive encouragement are the tools needed for improving swimming skills or developing a comfort level in water.

Tips to Prevent Swimmer's Ear

► After swimming, get the water out of the ears. Tilt the head and jump energetically several times, or use a towel to gently wipe the outer ear. Do not rub. One can also aim a hair dryer on a low set-

Swimmer's Ear

Moisture that remains in the S-shaped ear canal after swimming promotes the growth of organisms that cause infection. Chronic irritation of this sort is called "swimmer's ear." Pool water with or without chlorine and fresh water can lead to infection. Swimmer's ear may also depend on how long and how deep the swimmer or diver is in the water. If the ear is painful or swollen, or if feeling of "fullness" in the ear or even mild hearing loss develops, see a doctor. These annoying signals could lead to a more serious inner ear infection and even long-term damage to the ear.

ting toward the ear. Gently pull down the ear lobe and blow warm air into the ear from several inches away.

▶ Over-the-counter eardrops contain one or more agents to evaporate the water, kill the organisms and moisturize the ear canal. Ask a doctor to recommend a brand.

▶ Wear a swim cap or wet suit hood, especially for surfing or sailboarding. This can help slow or prevent the formation of bony growths in the ear canal, which are thought to be caused by prolonged exposure to wind and cold water. These protrusions cause the ear canal's outer surface to become thin and inflamed. A properly fitted cap or hood keeps the ears warm and protects them from the wind.

▶ Do not use wax-type ear plugs. They may damage the ear canal and make infection more likely. Silicone earplugs provide better protection. Do not use any ear plugs when surface diving.

▶ Ask a doctor how to flush out the ears using warm water and an ear syringe.

▶ Do not scratch, touch or put anything into the ears, because this may bring bacteria into the ear canal and remove protective ear wax.

▶ If young children have ear tubes, only allow swimming activities approved by their physician.

Weather Conditions

Whether in a pool or in open water, do not swim in storms, fog or high winds. One also should not swim if bad weather is expected. Leave the water when rain starts or at the first sound of thunder or sight of lightning. Because water conducts electricity, being in the water during an electrical storm is dangerous. Get to an enclosed area, if possible. Do not stay in an open area, under a tree or near anything metal. The National Weather Service recommends waiting at least 30 minutes from the last observance of thunder or lightning before resuming activity in the water.

Do not swim after a storm if the water seems to be rising or there is flooding, because currents may become very strong. The clarity and depth of the water may change, and new unseen obstacles may become hazards.

Always try to stay aware of bad weather that may be coming. Television and radio stations broadcast weather reports all day. Weather radios, CB radios and scanners also can keep one informed. Many areas have 24-hour telephone service for weather reports. Watch the sky. Rolling, dark clouds or large clouds with cauliflower-like tops announce an approaching storm.

Life Jackets

Anyone who cannot swim well should wear or have a life jacket if they are going to be in, on or around the water. Even good swimmers should wear a life jacket when boating or water skiing or if there is any chance of falling or being thrown into the water. It is more important to wear a life jacket when the water is cold. There are several types and many styles of life jackets, and they are rated for their buoyancy and purposes. Swimming ability, activity and water conditions help determine which type to use. For any type, be sure it is U.S. Coast Guard approved and in good condition. Local laws may require wearing one. Be sure that the life jacket fits correctly and is worn properly. Practice putting it on and swimming with it in shallow water. The life jacket must be easily accessible in an emergency or it has no value.

Certain types of life jackets are made to turn an unconscious person in the water from a face-down position to a vertical or slightly tipped-back position. Other flotation devices, such as buoyant cushions and ring buoys, do not take the place of life jackets, but they may be good throwing aids in an emergency (Fig. 10-3). They should also be U.S. Coast Guard approved.

▼ **FIG. 10-3**

Conditions to Look for Before Swimming

Safety around the water also means knowing what one is getting into before doing it. When first arriving at the water, take a minute to look around at the conditions before entering the water. Check with others, such as lifeguards or park rangers, about water conditions. The following table shows what conditions to watch for in different aquatic environments.

	SWIMMING POOLS	WATER PARKS	PONDS, RIVERS OR LAKES	OCEAN BEACHES
Lifeguards on duty	X	X	X	X
Rules clearly posted and easy to read	X	X	X	X
Clean water that is tested regularly	X	X	X	X
Able to see the bottom of the pool or drain	X	X		
Clean, well-maintained beaches and deck areas	X	X	X	X
Nonslip surfaces	X	X	X	X
Free of electrical equipment or power lines	X	X	X	X
Emergency communication to get help	X	X	X	X
Safety equipment	X	X	X	X
Clearly marked water depths	X	X		
Buoyed lines to separate shallow and deep water	X	X	X	
Firm and gently sloping bottom			X	X
No sudden drop-offs, large logs, rocks, submerged objects	X	X	X	X
Well-constructed rafts, piers, docks			X	X
Free of dangerous currents		X	X	X
Free of dangerous aquatic life			X	X
Signals for wave conditions		X	X*	X
Boats and surfboards prohibited from swimming area			X	X

*For very large lakes.

Wear a life jacket or have one available when in, on or around the water. The U.S. Coast Guard has categorized personal flotation devices into five types. The four wearable types may have permanent flotation or may be inflatable.

▶ Type I (offshore life jackets): Designed for boating or sailing on the open ocean, rough seas or on remote waters where a rescue could be delayed. They turn most unconscious wearers in the water from a face-down position to a vertical or slightly tipped-back position.

▶ Type II (near shore): Designed for recreational canoeing or sailing in inland waters where a rescue would likely occur quickly. They may help turn an unconscious person in the water from a face-down position to a vertical or slightly tipped-back position. Type II life jackets have less buoyancy than type I life jackets but are more comfortable to wear.

▶ Type III (flotation aids): Often used for general boating in calm inland waters or for the specialized activity that is marked on the device, such as skiing, hunting, fishing, canoeing or kayaking. These "float coats" or vests may keep a conscious person in a vertical or slightly tipped-back position. Type III is more comfortable for active water sports than types I and II.

▶ Type IV (throwable devices): Flotation devices, such as a buoyant cushion or the ring buoy, are not worn but can be thrown to a victim in an emergency. A buoyant cushion may be used as a seat cushion. These devices do not take the place of wearing a life jacket.

▶ Type V (restricted-use life jacket): A special purpose device approved for specific activities, such as commercial white water rafting and riding personal watercraft, where other types of life preserver devices would be too constrictive or when more protection is needed.

When choosing a life jacket:

▶ Make sure it is the right type for the right activity.
▶ Make sure it is approved by the U.S. Coast Guard.
▶ Make sure it fits the intended user. Check the stamp on the life jacket for weight limits.
▶ Make sure it is in good condition. Check buckles and straps for proper function. Discard any life jacket with torn fabric or straps that have pulled loose.
▶ Practice putting it on in water and swimming with it. When practicing, have a companion who can help if difficulty is encountered.

Inflatables, such as water wings, swim rings and other flotation devices, are not designed to be used as substitutes for U.S. Coast Guard–approved life jackets or life vests or adult supervision. Swimmers may go beyond their ability and fall off the inflatable, which may lead to a drowning situation. Inflatable materials deteriorate in sun and rough pool surfaces, leading to deflation and leaks.

Safety at Pools and Spas

Home Pools

As more people have above-ground or in-ground pools, more small children have become drowning victims. To prevent drowning, constant supervision and physical barriers are best. In many drownings, the child was left alone for a moment or was thought to be in a safe area.

A fence with a self-latching gate that completely surrounds the pool gives the most security. The gate should have a latch at least 54 inches high to keep a small child from opening it (Fig. 10-4). Often pool fencing uses the home as a part of the barrier, but this does not keep out a child who wanders out through an unlocked door or even crawls out through a pet door. Many states have pool fence laws. Consult local agencies about regulations for home pools.

Pool owners should:

▶ Learn to swim—and be sure everyone in the household knows how to swim.
▶ Never leave a child unattended who may gain access to any water. Even a small amount of water can be dangerous to young children.
▶ Teach children not to go near the water without an adult; the pool area is off limits without adult supervision.
▶ Adult supervision is essential. Adult eyes must be on the child at all times.
▶ Enclose the pool completely with a fence with vertical bars (so that it is not easy to climb) that has a self-closing, self-latching gate. Openings in the fence should be no more than 4 inches wide. The house should not be part of the barrier. If the house is part of the barrier for an existing pool, an additional fence should be installed and the doors and windows leading from the house to the pool should remain locked and be protected with an alarm that produces sounds when the door is unexpectedly opened.
▶ Post the rules for the pool and enforce them without exception. For example, never allow anyone to swim alone, do not allow bottles or glass around the pool, do not allow running or pushing and do not allow diving unless the pool meets the safety standards given in Chapter 6.
▶ Post depth markers and "No Diving" signs, as appropriate. Use a buoyed line to show where the depth changes from shallow to deep. Limit nonswimmer activity to shallow water.
▶ Never leave furniture or toys near the fence that would enable a child to climb over the fence.
▶ Keep toys away from the pool and out of sight when it is not in use. Toys can attract young children into the pool.

▼ FIG. 10-4

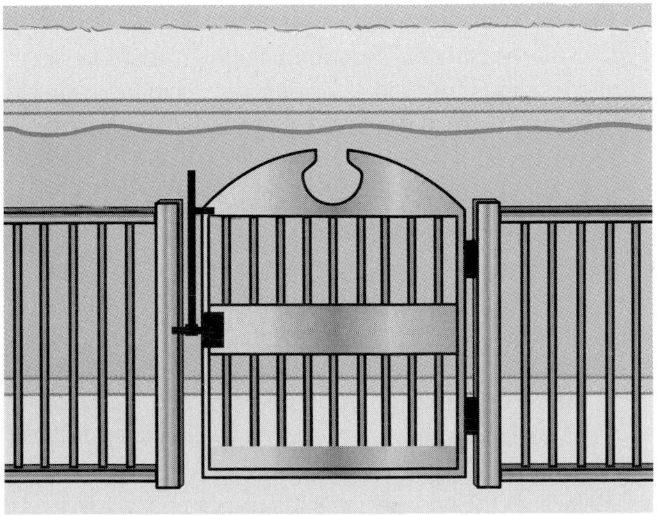

Make a Safety Post

A safety post holds a heaving jug and a reaching pole. It is a useful piece of equipment for a home pool or a private pond that is used for swimming, boating or ice-skating.

Materials Needed

- ❑ Spike post 4″ × 4″, 6 feet long
- ❑ Screw-in hanging hook that is large enough to hang the rope and jug on
- ❑ 1-gallon plastic jug with top
- ❑ 40 to 50 feet of lightweight rope
- ❑ Reaching pole 10 to 12 feet long
- ❑ Two 6-ounce cans, each open-ended
- ❑ Nails for attaching cans to post
- ❑ Safety poster or First Aid Fast booklet (optional)
- ❑ First aid kit
- ❑ Emergency contact information
- ❑ Plastic zipper bag

Procedure

Screw in the hanging hook about 1 foot from the top of the post. Nail the two open-ended cans, one about 1 foot above the other, no lower than 2½ feet from the bottom of the post. Set the post 2 feet in the ground near the water where swimmers, boaters or skaters might get into trouble. Make a heaving jug by putting one-half inch of water or sand in the plastic jug and screwing the top on tightly. (If the jug has a snap-on top, secure it with very strong glue.) Tie the rope to the handle of the jug. Hang the jug and the rope on the hanging screw. Put the reaching pole through the open-ended cans. A safety poster, first aid kit, First Aid Fast booklet and emergency contact information can be put into the plastic zipper bag and attached to the top of the post if desired.

- ▶ Pool covers should always be completely removed prior to pool use and completely secured when in place.
- ▶ Have an emergency action plan to address potential emergencies.
- ▶ Post CPR and first aid instructions.
- ▶ Post the emergency telephone number for the EMS system by the telephone. Keep a telephone near the pool or bring a fully charged cordless or mobile phone poolside. Also post the home's address and the nearest cross streets so that anyone can read them to an emergency dispatcher.
- ▶ Always keep basic lifesaving equipment by the pool and know how to use it. A reaching pole, rope and flotation devices, such as ring buoys, rescue tubes and life jackets, are recommended. A well-stocked first aid kit should also be available. Store the safety gear in a consistent, prominent, easily accessed location. A "safety post" may be used.
- ▶ Learn Red Cross CPR and first aid. Insist that babysitters, grandparents and others who care for the children know these lifesaving skills.
- ▶ If a child is missing, check the pool first. Go to the edge of the pool and scan the entire pool, bottom and surface, as well as the surrounding pool area.
- ▶ Keep the pool water clean and clear. Water should be chemically treated and tested regularly. If it is not possible to clearly see the bottom of the deep end, close the pool. Contact a local pool store or health department for information and instruction.
- ▶ Store pool chemicals—chlorine, soda ash, muriatic acid, test kits—in childproof containers and out of children's reach. Clearly label the chemicals. Follow manufacturer's directions and safety instructions.
- ▶ Consult the National Spa and Pool Institute, state law and local building codes for pool dimension guidelines to help establish rules to ensure safe diving activities. For example:
  - Prohibit all dives into shallow water.
  - Only allow dives from the edge of the pool into deep water.
  - Diving from a diving board should only occur if there is a safe diving envelope (the area of water in front of, below and to the sides of a diving board that is deep enough that a diver will not strike the bottom, regardless of the depth of the water or the design of the pool).
- ▶ Make sure the homeowner's insurance policy covers the pool.

Pool Parties

▶ Make sure that parents or caretakers of all invited guests are aware that the party is a pool party.

▶ If possible, have a lifeguard on duty. Contact the local parks and recreation department or local swimming pools to get names of American Red Cross–trained lifeguards who are willing to guard at private parties. It is the host's responsibility to interview and hire individuals and provide all appropriate rescue equipment.

▶ If not hiring a lifeguard, identify or appoint responsible adults to supervise the pool when it is being used. These individuals must understand and accept responsibility for monitoring the pool and should be trained in CPR, first aid and water safety.

▶ Establish rules for safety, such as:
  • Prohibiting all dives into shallow water
  • Walking—no running on the deck
  • Not permitting glass in the pool area

▶ If the swimming portion of the party goes for more than an hour, set rest breaks. This allows guests the opportunity to rest and warm up and provides a break for the lifeguard or water watcher from watching over the water.

▶ Do not serve alcoholic beverages to guests who are or will be participating in water activities.

▶ Maintain cleanliness of water. Water should be chemically treated and tested regularly.

▶ Check with the homeowner's insurance company to determine the limits of coverage. Additional coverage for the event may be required.

Unsupervised Pools

Unsupervised pools may include hotel, motel, condominium, apartment complex and homeowner's association pools. In addition to the general water safety tips and additional water safety tips, follow these tips when swimming in unsupervised pools:

▶ Read and obey all posted pool rules.

▶ Supervise children at all times. Remember, children are their parents' responsibility (Fig 10-5).

▶ Check for the availability of safety equipment, such as a reaching pole, ring buoy and telephone, and know how to use it.

▶ Make sure rescue equipment is in good condition.

▶ Safety equipment should not be used as pool toys.

Checklist of Questions When Hiring a Lifeguard

Following is a checklist of questions to ask before hiring a lifeguard to guard a private pool. Make sure to go over the list completely and ask for proof of certification prior to the date of hire.

❑ Do you have current American Red Cross Lifeguard Training certification (or equivalent)?

❑ Do you have current CPR certification? If so, through what training agency?

❑ Do you have a current first aid certification? If so, through what training agency?

❑ Do you have a current list of references?

❑ Do you have a current job history list?

❑ What do you charge per hour?

❑ Are there any specific pieces of safety equipment we need to provide for you (rescue tube, ring buoy, reaching pole, backboard with head immobilizer, first aid kit)?

❑ How do you enforce pool rules?

❑ Do you have a list of rules you require while lifeguarding?

❑ Are there any accommodations we need to make for you?

▲ Fig. 10-5

- ▶ Do not rely on inflatables to keep a child safe.
- ▶ Take breaks from water activities. This gives swimmers and those supervising them an opportunity to rest.
- ▶ Make sure the pool is properly marked with depth indicators.
- ▶ Do not swim in a pool that is overly crowded or with swimmers who are not following the rules.
- ▶ Do not bring any glass or breakable objects onto the pool deck.
- ▶ Check the pool area for obvious hazards (slippery decks, debris on the pool bottom, malfunctioning equipment, drop-offs, cracks in the deck).
- ▶ Check to see that fences are in good repair and that gates are self-closing and self-latching. Do not prop gates open or leave furniture near the pool fence that would allow children to easily climb the fence.
- ▶ Check for a well-maintained area.
- ▶ Check the water conditions. The water should be clear and clean without debris. The drain or the bottom of the pool should be visible at the deepest point. If the drain or bottom is not visible, do not enter the water.

Spas and Hot Tubs

Spas and hot tubs in the home or at a facility are often not guarded. According to the National Spa and Pool Institute, the maximum safe water temperature is 104° F (40° C).

Soaking too long at too high a temperature can raise body temperature over safe limits.

- ▶ Spas should be chemically treated and tested regularly. High water temperature can foster bacteria and parasite growth. Check with the health department or a local pool or spa store for information.
- ▶ Time spent in a spa should be limited to 15 minutes or less.
- ▶ Never use a spa or hot tub when drinking alcohol.
- ▶ Do not let children of any age use a spa unsupervised.
- ▶ Do not allow anyone to play near the drain.
- ▶ Children under 5 years of age should not use a spa. Young children are more prone to overheating because their bodies cannot regulate temperature well.
- ▶ Pregnant women or people taking medications or who have a chronic medical condition, such as high or low blood pressure, heart disease, seizures or diabetes, should not use a spa or hot tub without their physician's approval.
- ▶ Know the location of the emergency cut off switch.
- ▶ When not in use, a hot tub should be securely covered to prevent anyone from falling in.
- ▶ After using a spa, always wait at least 5 minutes before swimming. A sudden change in temperature can cause shock.
- ▶ Post the emergency telephone number for the EMS system by the telephone. Keep a cordless or mobile telephone near the spa.

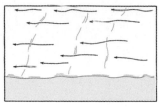

A

Safety in Natural Bodies of Water

Many people enjoy swimming in natural bodies of water, including lakes, rivers and oceans. Although such environments can be safe, they may also pose hazards not found in a pool. The information in this section should help swimmers judge the safety of such areas.

Even when a lifeguard is present, one must be more careful when swimming in open water. In an ocean, river, lake or other open water, swimmers may encounter potentially dangerous conditions that may differ from those they have seen in other waters. Conditions also may change from hour to hour in some waters. Before swimming in a new area, check it out carefully and consider the hazards described in the next sections.

Waves

Any large open-water area may have dangerous waves (Fig. 10-6). The water surface also may change quickly with the weather. A sudden wave may carry or push an inexperienced swimmer into deep water. Any swimmer can be knocked over by a wave breaking close to shore. Children playing at the water's edge can be knocked down and pulled into the water by a sudden, large breaking wave.

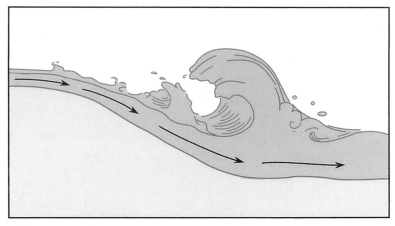

B

▲ FIG. 10-7, *A-B*

Currents

Ocean Currents

Lifeguards at ocean beaches often use flags to alert swimmers to water conditions. Generally, a green flag means the water is safe, a yellow flag means to be cautious when swimming because of currents or other conditions and a red flag means the area is closed because conditions are unsafe. Check the local area for variations. Do not swim at unguarded beaches because of the potential dangers.

If swimming in the ocean, it is important to be aware of the types of currents that present danger. Watch for longshore and rip currents. A longshore current moves parallel to the shore (Fig. 10-7, *A*). Backrush moves down the slope of the beach, straight out and under incoming

waves (Fig. 10-7, *B*). Longshore currents and rip currents can be dangerous if one is not careful. An unexpectedly strong backrush can pull a person's feet out from under them, resulting in a fall. These currents are especially hazardous to small children, who can easily fall into the water. Longshore currents can move a person rapidly away from the original point of entry. If caught in a longshore current, try to swim toward shore while moving along with the current.

Rip currents move straight out to sea beyond the breaking waves. They often occur if a sandbar has formed offshore. A band of water a few feet wide may rush back from the beach through a gap in the sandbar made by breaking waves. A rip current sometimes can be spotted because of the narrow strip of choppy, turbulent water that moves differently from the water on either side of it. A rip current can take persons in over their head or move them a frightening distance from the beach. If caught in a rip current, swim parallel to the shore until free

▶ FIG. 10-6

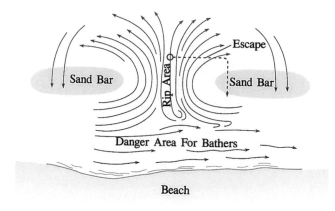

▲ FIG. 10-8

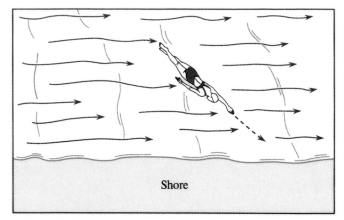

▲ FIG. 10-10

of the current. Once free, turn and swim toward shore (Fig. 10-8).

River Currents

Great care needs to be taken around river currents. River currents are often unpredictable and fast moving. They may change direction abruptly because of bottom changes. The current may not be visible on the water surface even though it may be strong below the surface. A current can slam a swimmer into an unseen object, such as a rock. If being carried by a river current, roll over onto the back and go downstream feetfirst (Fig. 10-9). This can avoid a head-first crash into rocks or other obstacles. When out of the strongest part of the current, swim straight toward shore. Because of the current, the swimmer will actually move downstream at an angle toward the shore (Fig. 10-10).

Hydraulics and Dams

Hydraulics are vertical whirlpools that happen as water flows over an object, such as a low-head dam or waterfall, causing a strong downward force that may trap a swimmer (Fig. 10-11). The reverse flow of the water can trap and hold a person under. The water surface may look calm and fool a swimmer because the hydraulic does not show from the surface. To avoid this hazard, do not swim near areas where the water drops off. It is difficult to escape from a hydraulic. If a swimmer is caught in a hydraulic, instead of fighting it he or she should swim to the bottom and try to get into the downstream current and then reach the surface.

Dams are common on rivers and in large lakes or ponds. When the floodgates open, the water level can rise quickly below the dam, making a wall of water. If the dam is part of a hydroelectric power plant, the current made when the gates are open can pull swimmers and even boaters above the dam into danger. Therefore, always avoid swimming and boating above or below a dam.

▶ FIG. 10-9

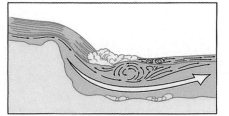

▶ FIG. 10-11

Underwater Obstacles

There may be underwater obstacles like rocks, stumps and remains of old structures in any open water. Even in some ocean waters there may be large unseen obstacles. With wind, currents and heavy rains, some obstacles on the bottom may move or change shape. Swimmers can be seriously injured if they jump, slide or dive into water and hit any object. Always enter open water slowly, carefully and feetfirst.

Aquatic Life

There is aquatic life in natural bodies of water. In a few locations, plants are potentially dangerous. Weeds, grass and kelp often grow thickly in open water and can entangle a swimmer. If swimmers find themselves becoming caught, they should avoid quick movements that may only entangle them more. Try to stay horizontal at the surface and swim slowly and gently out of the plants, preferably along with a current. If swimmers see or feel a patch of plants near the surface, they should avoid the area.

Aquatic animals seldom pose a danger to swimmers. In the ocean, however, one may be stung by a Portuguese man-of-war (Fig. 10-12, *A*), jellyfish (Fig. 10-12, *B*) or other aquatic life with less severe stings. A sting can be very painful and may cause illness or even death if the affected area is large. Swimmers may not see the tentacles of stinging jellyfish below the surface, and they may extend far from what is seen on the surface. Even stepping on a dead jellyfish or Portuguese man-of-war can cause a sting. The stinging cells may be active hours after the creature dies.

A sting can be treated by a simple method. First, rinse the skin with sea water—not fresh water. Do not use ice, and do not rub the skin. Soothe the skin by soaking it in vinegar or isopropyl alcohol. If these are not available, use a baking soda paste. Call for emergency medical help if the victim:

- ▶ Does not know what caused the sting
- ▶ Has ever had an allergic reaction to a sting from marine life or insects
- ▶ Is stung on the face or the neck
- ▶ Develops any problem that seems serious, such as difficulty breathing

In some ocean areas, there are sea urchins with spines that can break off in the foot and cause a painful wound. Another danger comes from coral that sting. Stingrays and other marine animals have stings that may be dangerous. Before going into any ocean, find out what local marine life may be dangerous, how to avoid it and how to care for any injuries. Signs warning of hazardous marine life may be posted at supervised beaches. When entering the ocean, shuffle the feet to avoid stepping on and stirring up marine life that rests on the bottom.

The relative risk of a shark attack is very small, but risks should always be minimized whenever possible in any activity. The chances of having an interaction with a shark can be reduced if one heeds the following advice:

- ▶ Always stay in groups, because sharks are more likely to attack a solitary individual.
- ▶ Do not wander too far from shore—this isolates an individual and additionally places one far away from assistance.

▼ **Fig. 10-12,** *A-B*

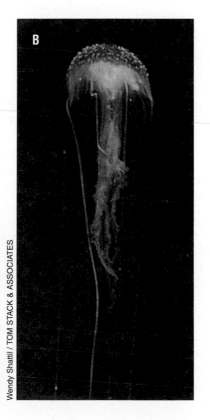

Wendy Shattil / TOM STACK & ASSOCIATES

▶ Avoid being in the water during darkness or twilight hours, when sharks are most active and have a competitive sensory advantage.

▶ Do not enter the water if bleeding from an open wound or if menstruating—a shark's olfactory ability is acute.

▶ Do not wear shiny jewelry, because the reflected light resembles the sheen of fish scales.

▶ Avoid waters with known effluents or sewage and those being used by sport or commercial fisherman, especially if there are signs of bait fish or feeding activity. Diving seabirds are good indicators of such action.

▶ Use extra caution when waters are murky and avoid uneven tanning and brightly colored clothing—sharks see contrast particularly well.

▶ Refrain from excess splashing and do not allow pets in the water because of their erratic movements.

▶ Exercise caution when occupying the area between sandbars or near steep drop-offs—these are favorite hangouts for sharks.

▶ Do not enter the water if sharks are known to be present and evacuate the water if sharks are seen while there.

▶ Do not harass a shark if one is seen.

Snakes or leeches may be encountered in fresh water. Snakes rarely pose a threat. Leave them alone and swim slowly away. Swimmers usually will not see a leech but may come out of the water and find one on their skin. They can be pulled off slowly and are not harmful.

Water Quality

Swimming and other aquatic activities should occur only in areas with good water quality. Many guarded beaches are tested regularly for pollution and disease-causing organisms. In some areas, water quality flags let swimmers know water conditions. For example, blue flags may be used to indicate good swimming conditions and red flags to indicate a potential water quality problem. Whenever possible, swim at beaches that have clean water, are carefully monitored and have strict closure and advisory procedures. Avoid swimming in areas that have been identified as unsafe by state and local health officials. Also, avoid swimming in natural bodies of water for 24 hours after heavy rains. To find out about recreational water quality, contact state and local health departments.

Safety for Special Activities In, On or Around Water

Sailboarding, Kiteboarding and Windsurfing

▶ Always wear a U.S. Coast Guard–approved life jacket.

▶ Wear a wet suit in cold water to prevent hypothermia.

▶ Maintain good physical strength and swimming ability. The Red Cross has swimming courses for people of any age and swimming ability. To enroll in a swim course, contact a local Red Cross chapter.

▶ Take lessons from a qualified instructor.

Snorkeling

When snorkeling, the swimmer uses fins for propulsion, a snorkel for breathing and a mask to observe the underwater world while swimming on the surface. The snorkeler can dive under water by holding the breath and then blowing water out the snorkel, called "clearing the snorkel," upon returning to the surface.

▶ Take lessons from a certified instructor before participating in snorkeling activities.

▶ Check equipment carefully and know how it functions.

▶ Use a U.S. Coast Guard–approved safety vest in open water.

▶ Learn how to clear water from the snorkel.

▶ Learn how to put a mask back on while treading water.

▶ Be careful not to swim or be carried by a current too far from shore or the boat.

▶ Use a diver-down flag to let others know that snorkelers are in the area.

▶ Never snorkel alone.

▶ Always let someone know where a person is snorkeling.

▶ Do not attempt to dive if suffering from sinus infections, a cold or allergies.

▶ Always clear the ears when descending. Pinch and gently blow through the nose.

Clear the ears every several feet upon descent. If there is pain, ascend until pain stops and clear the ears more regularly while descending.

► FIG. 10-13

Brian Parker / TOM STACK & ASSOCIATES

Scuba Diving

Some 3 to 4 million scuba divers enjoy the beauty and excitement of our underwater world (Fig. 10-13). Scuba divers wear a mask and fins and carry a compressed air supply and regulator for breathing under water for extended periods. Scuba divers also use buoyancy control devices, weights, wet suits and a variety of instruments to monitor depth, time and direction under water. Divers enjoy a variety of underwater activities, such as shore diving, boat diving, reef diving, night diving, underwater photography and underwater archeology.

Scuba diving is a very safe sport for the certified diver. Recreational diving has a good safety record because of the comprehensive training required. At least 40 hours of instruction in the pool and the classroom are required before the student starts supervised training in open water. Never scuba dive unless certified or enrolled in a course taught by a certified instructor. Simple actions, such as holding one's breath, can be very dangerous.

A medical examination and a swim test are strongly recommended and often required before learning scuba. Most scuba accidents can be easily avoided. Hazards include running out of air and diving in rough or dangerous waters or in environments for which the diver has not trained. Ice, cave and shipwreck diving are very dangerous for novices. One can easily get lost and then run out of air. Panic on the surface or under water can be disas-

trous for any diver, but poorly trained divers are the most likely to feel panic.

Lung overexpansion, caused by an uncontrolled, rapid ascent to the surface, can result in arterial gas embolism (AGE). Although this is a serious problem, it does not happen to well-trained divers. Decompression sickness, or "the bends," results from diving too deep or for too long. It is seldom fatal. One can easily avoid it by using simple decompression tables and meters. Equipment failures and dangerous marine life attacks, which may scare the non-diver, are very rare. A diver who has a serious problem, such as AGE or the bends, should seek immediate medical attention and the Divers Alert Network should be contacted. Contact information for the Divers Alert Network can be found at the following web site: www.diversalertnetwork.org

Follow these guidelines whenever scuba diving:

► Take lessons from a certified scuba diving instructor at an approved facility before participating.
► Get a medical examination and take a swim test before learning scuba diving.
► Once certified, do not dive in rough or dangerous waters or in environments for which one is not trained. Ice, cave, shipwreck and deep diving require special training. One can easily get lost or trapped and run out of air.
► Use a diver-down flag to let others know that a diver is in the area.
► Never dive alone.
► Always let someone know where a dive is planned. Plan a dive out and dive that plan.
► Get a local diving orientation from a scuba instructor when traveling to new locations.
► Ensure equipment is in good condition and functioning properly before each dive.
► Do not attempt to dive if suffering from sinus infections, a cold or allergies.
► When descending, always clear the ears. Pinch the nose and gently blow through the nose.
► Clear the ears every several feet upon descent. If pain is felt, ascend until pain stops and clear the ears more regularly while descending.
► Always watch the depth, time and amount of air in the tank.

Spencer Swager / TOM STACK & ASSOCIATES

▲ FIG. 10-14

Surfing

Before trying to surf:

▶ Take lessons from a qualified instructor.

▶ Always surf with a buddy and let someone know where you are going and when you expect to return.

▶ Always attach the safety leash to the surfboard and to the ankle.

▶ Wear a wet suit when in cold water.

▶ Learn how to read surf conditions and be sure water and weather conditions are safe.

▶ Because surfing moves one through the water very quickly, watch out for the board and other surfers. A surfer could be injured seriously or knocked unconscious if hit by a board.

Tubing and Rafting

▶ Always wear a U.S. Coast Guard–approved life jacket.

▶ Do not drink alcohol while tubing or rafting.

▶ Do not overload the raft.

▶ Do not go rafting after a heavy rain or if flash flood warnings are posted.

▶ When rafting with a tour company, make sure the guides are qualified. Check with the local chamber of commerce for listings of accredited tour guides and companies (Fig. 10-14).

▶ Develop a float plan.

Personal Watercraft

▶ Riders should wear helmets and U.S. Coast Guard–approved life jackets.

▶ Know the local laws and regulations. Some states have special laws governing the use of personal watercraft—such as jet skis—that address operations, registration and licensing requirements, education, environmental restrictions, required safety equipment and minimum ages.

▶ Operate a personal watercraft with courtesy and common sense. Pay attention to surroundings and follow the traffic pattern of the waterway. Obey no-wake and speed zones.

▶ Use extreme caution around swimmers and surfers. Run the personal watercraft at a slow speed until the craft is away from shore, swimming areas and docks. Avoid passing close to other boats and jumping wakes. This behavior is dangerous and often illegal.

▶ Ride with a buddy. Personal watercraft should always travel in groups of two or three. You never know when an emergency might occur.

▶ Always attach the ignition cutoff cord to oneself and the personal watercraft during operation.

▶ Alcohol and personal watercraft do not mix. Alcohol impairs your judgment, balance and coordination. For the same reasons it is dangerous to operate an automobile, people should not operate a boat or personal watercraft while drinking alcohol.

▶ Do not ride in a personal watercraft being operated by someone who has been drinking.

▶ Develop a float plan. Anytime people go out on the water, they should give a responsible person details about where they will be and how long they will be gone. This is important because if one is delayed because of an emergency, becomes lost or encounters other problems, help needs to be able to reach the group.

Fishing and Hunting

In most fishing- and hunting-related drownings, the victim never intended to get in the water. When fishing or hunting near water or from a boat:

▶ Always wear a U.S. Coast Guard–approved life jacket.

▶ Dress properly for the weather and have some type of reaching device nearby.

▶ Watch footing when walking next to water.

▶ Guard against losing balance when in a boat by keeping a wide base of support and low center of gravity and using hands to balance.

▶ Do not drink alcohol. Alcohol is a cause of many hunting and fishing mishaps.

Safety for Group Aquatic Activities

Summer Camps

Water activities are a major attraction of many summer camps. Before enrolling a child, check to see that the camp has the necessary state permits. State regulations often address aquatic safety. Because codes vary from state to state, it is also appropriate to determine if the camp follows the aquatic safety standards of a national organization, such as the American Camping Association, the Boy Scouts of America or the YMCA of the USA. Also, check to see if the standards are being followed. Observe the condition of the pool, waterfront or any other aquatic feature and find out how it is being supervised. All activities, such as swimming, canoeing, water skiing and scuba diving, should be supervised and taught only by qualified staff.

The aquatic activity areas should be well designed and maintained, free of obvious hazards, and closely supervised by adequate numbers of alert, trained staff. All equipment should be in good condition. The camp should have a system that ensures that supervisors can quickly account for all swimmers at all times. Such systems include roll calls, buddy checks and buddy tags (Fig. 10-15). All campers should be classified by swimming ability and provided instructional and recreational activities consistent with their abilities. For example, nonswimmers should not be permitted in deep water other than during special instructional situations. A system should be in place so that the staff can easily identify a camper's swimming ability. Such systems include color-coded tags or swim caps. Everyone, campers and staff, should wear U.S. Coast Guard–approved life jackets during all boating activities. The camp should request information on any temporary or chronic medical conditions that require special precautions in or on the water.

Group Trips

Before taking a group to a water recreational facility, plan in advance. Most facilities appreciate knowing when a group will be coming, the names of contact persons and the general age range and size of the group. The facility manager can ensure adequate supervision and can help make the visit safer and more enjoyable if there is advance notification.

▼ FIG. 10-15

Before the trip, talk to the group about what behavior is or is not allowed at the facility. If one is not sure of the swimming abilities of some in the group, pretest their skills to be sure they use only the appropriate parts of the facility. If possible, visit the site in advance and look for ways to help the group prepare for the outing. Review the rules and regulations and study a diagram of the facility. Do not take a group, especially children, to open water unless certain there is enough supervision.

Safety Around Cold Water and Ice

Exposure to Cold Water

Falling off a pier, breaking through ice on a lake, being thrown into the water as a boat swerves—these accidents can suddenly put a person in cold water. Exposure to cold water leads to the danger of immersion hypothermia (Fig. 10-16). Hypothermia is a life-threatening condition in which the body cannot maintain normal body temperature and the body cools. Hypothermia occurs when cold or cool temperatures cause the body to lose heat faster than it can produce it.

Here is what happens when a person falls into cold water:

- The temperature of the skin and of the blood in the arms and legs drops quickly.
- At first the victim may have trouble breathing and then may slowly become unable to use the arms and legs.

▼ Fig. 10-16

- The temperature of the heart, brain and other vital organs gradually drops.
- Shivering begins.
- The victim may become unable to think clearly.
- The victim may become unconscious. If the temperature drops more, death from heart failure is possible, but drowning may occur first.

Care for a victim of a cold-related emergency, such as hypothermia, is described on page 255.

Preventing Hypothermia

Protect against hypothermia in the following ways:

- When near cold water—playing, working, hunting, fishing—remember that cold water is dangerous even if one does not intend to go in.
- Join in water activities only when and where it is possible to get help quickly in an emergency.
- Always wear a U.S. Coast Guard–approved life jacket while boating in cold water. Have life jackets at hand whenever near cold water; wearing it is best.
- If one will be in cooler weather, wear rain gear, a warm hat and layers of clothes or insulated clothes. Avoid cotton and wear fabrics containing wool or synthetic blends instead.
- Wear a wet suit for skin diving, surfing and kayaking.
- Carry matches in a waterproof container. It may be necessary to build a fire to warm up after a fall into cold water.
- Do not drink alcohol for the sensation of warmth. Alcohol actually increases loss of body heat.

Benefits of Winter Clothes

People who fall into the water wearing winter clothes, especially heavy boots or waders, usually panic because they think they will sink immediately. But winter clothes can actually help you float. Heavy clothes also help delay hypothermia. Tight-fitting foam vests and flotation jackets with foam insulation can double the survival time.

If a person falls into the water wearing a snowmobile suit or other heavy winter clothes, air will be trapped in the clothes and will help the person float.

- Simply lie back.
- Spread the arms and legs.

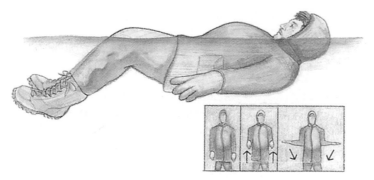

► FIG. 10-17

► Perform a "winging" motion with the arms to move toward safety (Fig. 10-17).

Hip boots, waders and rubber boots often trap air when someone falls into water. Relax, bend the knees and let the trapped air in the boots bring one to the surface quickly.

While on the back, one can float in a tuck position.

► Bring the knees up to the chest.
► Let the hips drop.
► Keep the head up and back.
► Paddle backward with the hands to safety.

One can also float on the front:

► Keep the head raised.
► Bend the knees.
► Paddle forward with the arms in the water (Fig. 10-18).

▲ FIG. 10-18

Ice Safety

Outdoor ice sports and activities can be safe and enjoyable (Fig. 10-19), but first learn about ice and what precautions to take to protect oneself.

Ice over open water may be unsafe if any of the following are present:

► Springs or fast-moving water
► Wind and wave action
► Waterfowl and schooling fish
► Decomposing material in the water
► Water bubblers (devices designed to keep the water near boat docks from freezing thick)
► Discharge from an industrial site or power production facility
► Objects protruding through the ice, such as tree stumps

Preventing Ice Accidents

Follow these guidelines to avoid accidents when on or near ice:

► Check the ice thickness before going out. To be safe, ice should be solid and at least 4 inches thick. Remember, the ice may not be the same thickness over the entire area of a lake or pond.
► Solid, 4-inch-thick ice is generally safe to walk on but not thick enough to drive a vehicle on.

► To be safe, the ice should be thicker as more people are on it.
► Ice on smaller, shallower and slower-moving bodies of water is usually more solid. Use these for ice activities.
► Look for objects sticking up through the ice and mark them as hazards.
► Do not go out on ice that has recently frozen, thawed and then frozen again. This happens in the spring and early winter as temperatures change often. Wait until the outside temperature has been below freezing long enough that at least 4 inches of solid ice forms over the entire area.
► Always stay with at least one other person. (Remember, more people require thicker ice for safety.)

Earth Scenes / Michael Gadomski

▲ FIG. 10-19

▶ Someone should be told where the group will be and when they intend to return.

▶ Wear warm clothes. Wool is good for holding warm air next to the body and for insulation, even when wet.

▶ Have something at hand to throw or extend to a person who needs help—a life jacket, a rope with a weighted end, a long tree branch, a wooden pole or a plastic jug with a line attached.

▶ Carry matches in a waterproof container. It may be necessary to build a fire to warm up after a fall into cold water.

Emergency Action Steps

In the excitement of an emergency, one may be frightened or confused about what to do. Stay calm—one can help. An emergency scene might look complicated at first, but the three emergency action steps will help organize one's response to the situation.

1. **Check**   Check the scene and the victim.
   - Check the scene for unsafe conditions that would prevent one from helping.
   - Check the victim for consciousness, breathing and signs of circulation.
2. **Call**   Call 9-1-1 or the local emergency number.
3. **Care**   Care for the victim.
   - Care for the conditions found (first aid, rescue breathing, CPR).
   - Make the victim comfortable until emercency medical services (EMS) personnel arrive.

Emergency Action Plan

Emergency action plans are detailed plans for how everyone should act in an emergency. It is best to swim in a supervised area where emergency action plans are established. If there is an emergency, follow the lifeguard's instructions. A plan should be established if there is body of water around or near the home, such as a pool, pond or canal. To create a plan:

▶ Identify types of emergencies that could occur, such as someone falling into the water.

▶ Identify rescue equipment available, such as a telephone near the body of water, ring buoy with a line attached and reaching pole.

▶ Create an emergency contact list that includes telephone numbers of emergency medical services and names of the nearest cross streets to the home.

The basic elements of an emergency action plan include:

▶ An emergency signal. Blow a whistle or horn or wave a flag to alert swimmers that they should leave the water immediately. At a home pool or pond, the signal will tell other family members and neighbors that there is an emergency and help is needed quickly.

▶ Safety equipment. For the home pool or pond, safety equipment includes a telephone and rescue equipment near the water. Make a safety post for emergency equipment and set it close to the water. The safety post should have a heaving jug or other device, such as a reaching pole, along with a well-stocked first aid kit.

▶ Emergency procedures. Develop and post procedures for what to do in a water emergency. Emergency procedures must be carefully planned and should outline:
   - Steps a responder should take to remove the victim from danger, without putting the responder in danger.
   - Who, how and where the call to 9-1-1 or the local emergency number is made. Take into account how a mobile phone can access emergency numbers.
   - How EMS personnel is directed to the specific scene of the emergency. For example, someone should be appointed to meet EMS personnel at the street.
   - Who should be contacted, such as the victim's physician and immediate family members.

At home pools or ponds, family and friends should be taught the emergency procedures. Neighbors should also know those procedures to provide assistance, if necessary.

Aquatic Emergencies

There may be a time when someone is in trouble in the water. There are some basic skills one can learn to help oneself if there is trouble in the water. There are other basic skills that one can use to aid a person in the water. Always remember to stay safe when helping others. If there is any chance that one cannot easily assist the per-

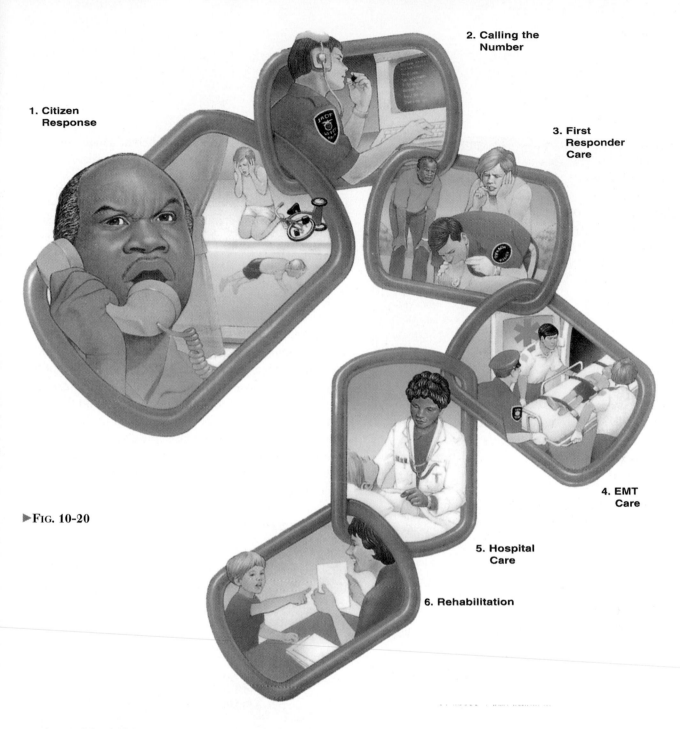

1. Citizen Response

2. Calling the Number

3. First Responder Care

4. EMT Care

5. Hospital Care

6. Rehabilitation

▶FIG. 10-20

son in trouble, call for advanced medical help before trying to help. Red Cross courses in swimming, water safety, lifeguard training, first aid and CPR help people be prepared to handle aquatic and other emergencies.

The Emergency Medical Services System

The EMS system is a network of professionals linked together to give the best care for victims in all emergencies, both in and out of the water. The system begins when someone sees an emergency occurring and takes action. When someone calls 9-1-1 or the local emergency number, the EMS dispatcher takes the information and summons trained professionals to the scene. These may include police or fire personnel, special rescue squads and an ambulance with emergency medical technicians (EMTs) (Fig. 10-20).

These professionals will take over the care of the victim, including transporting the victim to a hospital or other facility for the best medical care. One's role in this system is to recognize the emergency, decide to act, call EMS for help and provide assistance consistent with one's knowledge until EMS arrives.

Recognizing an Emergency

An emergency can happen to anyone in or around the water, regardless of how good a swimmer the person is or what he or she is doing at the time. A strong swimmer can get into trouble in the water because of sudden illness or injury. A nonswimmer playing in shallow water can be knocked down by a wave or pulled into deeper water by a rip current. The key to recognizing an emergency is staying alert and knowing the signals that indicate an emergency is happening.

Use all the senses when observing others in and around the water. A swimmer may be acting oddly or a scream or sudden splash may be heard. One may smell an unusual odor, such as a strong chlorine odor, that could indicate a problem. Watch for anything that seems unusual.

Being able to recognize a person who is having trouble in the water may help save that person's life. Most drowning people cannot or do not call for help. They spend their energy just trying to keep their heads above water to get a breath. They might slip under water quickly and never resurface. There are two categories of water emergency situations: a swimmer in distress and a drowning person.

Each kind of emergency poses a different danger and can be recognized by different behaviors.

A swimmer in distress may be too tired to get to shore or to the side of the pool but is able to stay afloat and breathe and may be calling for help. The person may be floating, treading water or clinging to a line for support. Someone who is trying to swim but making little or no forward progress may be in distress (Fig. 10-21). If not helped, a person in distress may lose the ability to float and become a drowning victim.

An active drowning victim is vertical in the water but unable to move forward or tread water. His or her arms are at the side pressing down in an instinctive attempt to keep the head above the water to breathe (Fig. 10-22). All energy is going into the struggle to breathe, and the person cannot call for help. A passive drowning victim is not moving and will be floating face down on the bottom or near the surface of the water (Fig. 10-23). Table 10-1 compares the behaviors of distressed swimmers and drowning victims to those of swimmers.

Deciding to Act

Once a person recognizes that there is an emergency, he or she needs to decide to act—and how to act. This is not always as simple as it sounds. Often people are slow to act in an emergency because they are not sure exactly

▲ FIG. 10-23

what to do or they think someone else will do whatever is needed. What if no one else is present or no one is taking action? If a person decides to act, he or she may save someone's life.

Once one has decided to act, proceed safely. Make sure the scene is safe—do not go rushing into a dangerous sit-uation where the responder too may become a victim. If the victim is in the water, decide first whether he or she needs help getting out and then act based on one's train-ing. If the victim is out of the water, quickly try to deter-mine what help the victim needs and check for any dan-gers to oneself or others helping. Look for any other victims. Look for bystanders who can help give first aid or call for help.

Calling for Help

If the victim is in the water, the first goal is for the rescuer to stay safe. Rushing into the water to help a victim may lead to the rescuer becoming a victim too. Once one's safety is ensured, the goal is to help get the victim out of the water. If the victim is unconscious, send someone else to call EMS personnel while starting the rescue. If the vic-tim is conscious, first act to get the victim out of the water and then determine whether EMS is needed.

If the victim is not in the water, as soon as it is deter-mined that there is an emergency, call EMS immediately. If in doubt about whether the victim needs professional help, do not hesitate—call EMS personnel. The following conditions and situations are serious and require one to call EMS:

TABLE 10-1 Behaviors of Distressed Swimmers and Drowning Victims Compared with Swimmers

BEHAVIORS	SWIMMER	DISTRESSED SWIMMER	ACTIVE DROWNING VICTIM	PASSIVE DROWNING VICTIM
Breathing	Rhythmic breathing	Can continue breathing and may call for help	Struggles to breathe; can-not call out for help	Not breathing
Arm and Leg Action	Relatively coordinated	Floating, sculling or treading water; may wave for help	Arms to sides alternately moving up and pressing down; no supporting kick	None
Body Position	Horizontal	Horizontal or diagonal, depending on means of support	Vertical	Horizontal or vertical; face down, face up or submerged
Locomotion	Recognizable	Little or no forward progress; less and less able to support self	None; has only 20–60 sec-onds before submerging	None

- Any drowning or near-drowning situation
- Injury to the head, neck or back
- Difficulty breathing
- Persistent chest or abdominal pain or pressure
- No pulse
- Unconsciousness
- Severe bleeding, vomiting or passing blood
- Seizure, severe headache or slurred speech
- Poisoning
- Possible broken bones
- Multiple injuries

Make the call to EMS personnel, or ask someone else at the scene to call (Fig. 10-24). If possible, send two people to make the call. Tell the callers to report back what the dispatcher said.

Be sure the callers stay on the phone after giving all the information to the dispatcher, in case there are any questions. Make sure that the dispatcher has all the correct information to get the right type of help to the scene quickly. Be prepared to tell the dispatcher the following:

- The location of the emergency (exact address, city or town, nearby intersections or landmarks, name of the facility)
- The telephone number of the telephone being used
- The caller's name

▼ Fig. 10-24

- What happened
- The number of victims
- The help being given so far

Remember, do not hang up first, because the dispatcher may need more information.

If a person is in a situation where he or she is the only person other than the victim, the person should Call First, that is, call 9-1-1 or the local emergency number—before providing care for:

- An unconscious adult or child 8 years old or older
- An unconscious infant or child known to be at high risk for heart problems

Call First situations are likely to be cardiac emergencies, such as sudden cardiac arrest, where time is critical.

Call Fast, that is, provide 1 minute of care, then call 9-1-1 or the local emergency number, for:

- An unconscious victim less than 8 years old
- Any victim of submersion or near drowning
- Any victim of cardiac arrest associated with trauma
- Any victim of drug overdose

Call Fast situations are likely to be related to breathing emergencies, rather than sudden cardiac arrest. In these situations, provide support for airway, breathing and circulation through rescue breaths and chest compressions, as appropriate.

Self-Rescue

Muscle Cramps

Muscle cramps can occur when muscles become tired or cold from swimming or other activity. A cramp is an involuntary muscle contraction, usually in the arm, foot or calf. If one gets a muscle cramp in shallow water:

- Try to relax the muscle by stopping the activity or changing the swimming stroke.
- Change the position of the limb to stretch the cramped muscle and massage the area to help relieve the cramp.

For a muscle cramp in deep water:

- Take a deep breath, roll forward face down and float.
- Extend the leg and flex the ankle or toes.
- Massage the cramp (Fig. 10-25).

▲ Fig. 10-25

Abdominal cramps, although rare, can happen if a person is tired and cold. If one has an abdominal cramp, try to relax and maintain the position in the water until the cramp passes.

Exhaustion

Exhaustion simply means that a person no longer has the energy to keep swimming or floating. Exhaustion can occur:

▶ In reaction to cold water
▶ After lying in the sun too long
▶ From swimming when very tired
▶ From swimming too long and too hard
▶ From being dehydrated
▶ From any combination of these factors

Fatigue early in the swimming season can be a serious problem. Exhaustion is more likely for swimmers who swim too much before they are really in shape. Exhaustion is also more likely to overtake those who do not know the restful swimming strokes discussed in Chapter

9. Compared with a poorly executed front crawl, the elementary backstroke takes very little energy.

Prevent exhaustion by resting often while swimming or doing other water activities. Especially look out for younger inexperienced swimmers, who may become exhausted before they realize they are in danger.

Hyperventilation

Hyperventilation is a dangerous technique some swimmers use to try to stay under water longer. By taking a series of deep breaths and forcefully exhaling, the carbon dioxide in the blood is reduced. This delays the time when the carbon dioxide level triggers the demand for the body to take a breath. The practice is risky because the level of carbon dioxide in the blood is what signals the body to take each breath. If a person hyperventilates and then swims under water, he or she could pass out before the brain signals it is time to breathe. By the time someone notices the swimmer has been under too long, it could be too late. If people enjoy underwater swimming, they should work on their skills with a certified Red Cross instructor. Do not hyperventilate!

Submerged Vehicle

In most cases when vehicles plunge into the water, the occupants try frantically to open the doors but cannot because of the external water pressure. They begin to panic and are unable to help themselves.

People can help themselves in this kind of emergency if they remain calm and remember the following guidelines:

▶ Wearing a vehicle safety belt will reduce the chances of injury when the vehicle hits the water.
▶ Tests indicate that even a heavy vehicle will float for up to 45 seconds after it enters the water. During this time, release the safety belt, try to open the nearest window and exit immediately through that window.
▶ If the vehicle begins to sink, move to the higher end to breathe the trapped air. Do not try to open the door to exit.
▶ Use one of three routes to escape:
  ● Open a window.
  ● Open an undamaged door when the water pressure is equal inside and out (when the vehicle is nearly full of water).

- Break or push out a window when the water pressure is equal inside and out (when the vehicle is nearly full of water).

If someone witnesses a vehicle plunging into the water, he or she should get immediate assistance. Activate the EMS system by calling 9-1-1 or the local emergency number.

Falling into Water

Water emergencies often happen to people who did not intend to go into the water in the first place. In most cases, people who fall in end up in the water fully clothed. There are some advantages to keeping clothes on in this case. Many types of clothing will actually aid floating and provide protection against cold

water. If shoes are light enough to allow swimming comfortably, leave them on. If they are too heavy, assume a jellyfish float position and remove them.

Survival Floating in Warm Water

Survival floating involves floating face down in warm water. Use this method if it is not possible to reach safety and it is necessary to wait for help or to rest while making the way to safety.

To survival float:

1. Hold one's breath and put the face in the water. Allow the arms and legs to hang freely. Rest in this position for a few seconds (Fig. 10-26, *A*).
2. To take a breath, slowly lift the arms to about shoulder height and move the arms forward. Separate the legs, moving one leg forward and one leg back.
3. Gently press down with the arms and at the same time bring the legs together. This movement lifts the mouth above the water, allowing one to take another breath (Fig. 10-26, *B*).
4. Return to the resting position. Repeat these movements to take the next breath.

Survival Swimming in Warm Water

Survival swimming should be used together with the survival float in a warm water emergency only. It allows one, regardless of buoyancy, to cover a considerable distance with a minimal use of energy. Remember that swimming long distances to

▼ Fig. 10-26, *A-B*

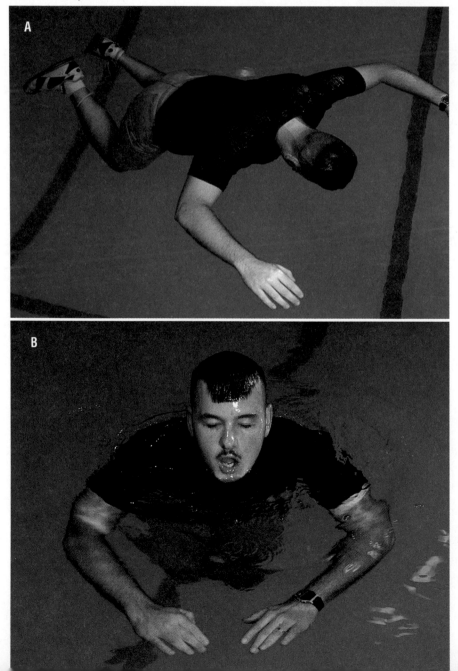

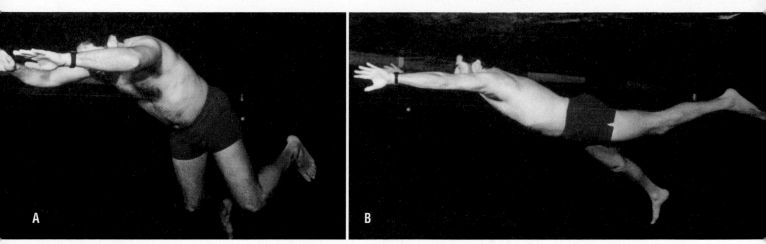

A

B

▲ FIG. 10-27, *A-B*

safety should be used as a last resort.

1. After taking a breath (Fig. 10-27, *A*), bend forward at the waist, bring the hands up alongside the head, separate the legs in the stride position, extend the arms forward and then bring the legs together again, propelling diagonally toward the surface (Fig. 10-27, *B*).
2. Sweep the arms out and back to the thighs and glide easily near and almost parallel to the surface.
3. When a breath is needed, bend the legs and draw them toward the torso and bring the hands up again alongside the head. One who does not float well may need to pull harder with the arms and then quickly assume the body position just described to prevent the body from sinking.
4. Extend the arms forward and separate the legs in the stride position once again. Tilt the head back and prepare to breathe out, as in survival floating.
5. Repeat the full cycle.

A person who is not very buoyant must do these movements slightly faster to prevent sinking before the breath.

Using a Shirt or Jacket for Flotation

With air trapped in the shoulders of a shirt or jacket, one may be able to swim toward safety. If it is necessary to use one hand to hold the shirt or jacket closed, stroke with the other.

There are two ways to use a shirt or jacket for flotation:

1. Tuck the shirt in or tie the shirt-tail ends together around the waist. Fasten the top button of the shirt up to the neck. Take a deep breath, bend the head forward, pull the shirt up to the face and blow into the shirt between the second or third button (Fig. 10-28). The front of the

◄ FIG. 10-28

A

B

◀ Fig. 10-29, *A-B*

Falling into Cold Water with a Life Jacket

Even if the air is warm and one is a good swimmer, wear a life jacket when near cold water. In cold water, one must decide whether to try to reach safety or float and wait for help. Remember that people cannot swim as far in cold water as in warm water. Use only strokes with underwater arm recovery. If it is possible to get to safety with a few strokes, do so. If not, float quietly and wait for rescue.

If one falls into cold water wearing a life jacket:

► Keep the face and head above the surface. If in a boating accident, try to climb up onto the capsized boat to get more of the body out of the water.
► Keep all clothes on, especially a hat. Even wet clothes help retain body heat.
► Swim to safety if a current is carrying one toward some danger. Unless it is necessary to swim away immediately, float on the back and go downstream feetfirst until breathing is slowed. Breathe normally for a few seconds before starting to swim to shore.
► If not in immediate danger but far from shore, stay still and let the life jacket provide support until help arrives. To stay warmer, assume the heat escape lessening posture as described in the next section.

Treading water chills the body faster than staying still with a life jacket on in the water. In cold water, tread water only if one cannot stay afloat any other way.

Heat Escape Lessening Posture

The heat escape lessening posture (HELP) can increase the chances of survival by reducing the amount of body surface area that is directly exposed to cold water. In this position, the chest and knees are in contact with each other rather than being in contact with cold water.

► Draw the knees up to the chest.
► Keep the face forward and out of the water.
► Hold the upper arms at the sides and fold the lower arms against or across the chest (Fig. 10-30).

Do not use the HELP in swift river currents or whitewater.

Huddle

The huddle position is much like the HELP. Body surface area is in contact with other bodies rather than with cold water. This position is for two or more persons.

shirt must be under water. The air will rise and form a bubble in the shoulders of the shirt, which will help one float.
2. Inflate the shirt or jacket by splashing air into it (Fig. 10-29, *A*). Float on the back and hold the front of the shirttail or jacket with one hand, keeping it just under the surface of the water. Strike the water with the free hand palm down from above the surface of the water to a point below the shirttail or jacket. The air, carried down from the surface, will bubble into the shirt or jacket, allowing it to inflate (Fig 10-29, *B*).

▲ FIG. 10-30

- ► With two people, put the arms around each other so that the chests are together.
- ► With three or more people, put the arms over each other's shoulders so that the sides of the chests are together.
- ► Sandwich a child or elderly person between adults (Fig. 10-31).

Falling into Cold Water Without a Life Jacket

- ► Look around for a log or anything floating for support. If near a capsized boat, climb or hold onto it.
- ► Move as much of the body as possible out of the water. Keep the face and head above the water. Turn back to waves to help keep water out of the face.
- ► Keep all clothes on, especially a hat. Try to inflate clothing with air for flotation.
- ► Do not splash around trying to warm up. The heat this movement creates will not last. Splashing increases blood circulation in the arms and legs and will drain energy.
- ► Swim only if one is close enough to reach shore safely. How far one can swim depends on one's swimming skill, the amount of insulation one is wearing and water conditions. Remember, one cannot swim as far in cold water as in warm water. Be careful not to underestimate the distance to shore. In emergencies it is hard to judge distance. When the water is 50° F (10° C) or colder, even a good swimmer may have difficulty reaching shore.

Once Ashore

Hypothermia is still a risk even after reaching safety. Care for a victim of hypothermia is described on page 255.

Falling Through the Ice

When falling through the ice:

- ► Resist the urge to try to climb out onto the ice. It is likely to be weak in the area where the fall took place.
- ► Quickly get into a floating position on the stomach. Bend the knees to help trap air in pant legs and boots.
- ► Reach forward onto the broken ice, but do not push down on it. Use a breaststroke or other kick to push farther onto the ice.
- ► Do not stand up once on the ice. Crawl or roll away from the break area, with arms and legs spread out as far as possible.
- ► Have someone throw or extend something if needed. Remember not to stand on the ice.

▲ FIG. 10-31

Once safely off the ice, follow the guidelines for caring for hypothermia, described on page 255.

Helping Others

Out-of-Water Assists

Help a person in trouble in the water by using reaching and throwing assists. Out-of-water assists are safer for the rescuer. Wherever possible, start the rescue by talking to the victim. Let him or her know help is coming. If it is too noisy or if the victim is too far away to hear, use gestures. Tell the victim what he or she can do to help with the rescue, such as grasping a line, rescue buoy or any other floating device. Ask the victim to move toward safety by kicking or stroking. Some people have reached safety by themselves with the calm and encouraging assistance of someone calling to them.

Reaching Assists

If the victim is close enough, use a reaching assist to help him or her out of the water. If available, use any object that will extend the reach, such as a pole (Fig. 10-32), an oar or paddle, a tree branch, a shirt, a belt or a towel. Community pools and recreational areas, as well as hotel and motel pools, often have reaching equipment beside the water, such as a shepherd's crook (an aluminum or fiberglass pole with a large hook on one end). If using a

rigid object, such as a pole or oar, sweep it toward the victim from the side until it makes contact with an arm or hand. If using a shirt or towel, lie down and flip it into the victim's hands.

If there is equipment available:

1. Brace oneself on a pool deck, pier surface or shoreline.
2. Extend the object to the victim.
3. When the victim grasps the object, slowly and carefully pull him or her to safety. Keep the body low and lean back to avoid being pulled into the water.

If there is no equipment available to perform a reaching assist, the responder should:

1. Brace oneself on the pool deck or pier surface.
2. Reach with an arm and grasp the victim.
3. Pull the victim to safety.

If already in the water:

1. Hold onto a pool ladder, overflow trough (gutter), piling or another secure object with one hand.
2. Extend a free hand or one leg to the victim. Do not let go of the secure object or swim out into the water (Fig. 10-33).
3. Pull the victim to safety.

▼ Fig. 10-32

▼ Fig. 10-33

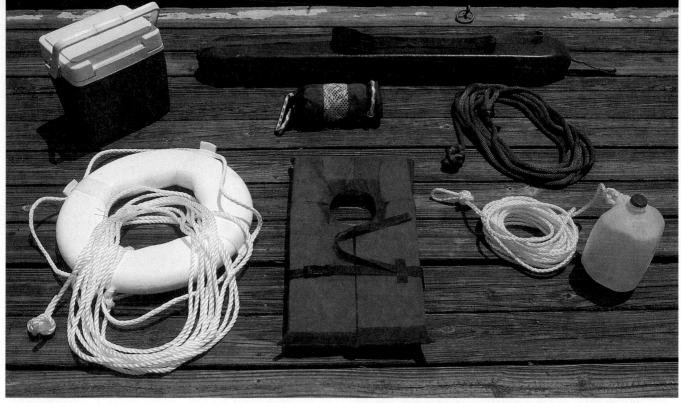

▲ Fig. 10-34

Throwing Assists

Rescue a conscious victim out of reach using a throwing assist. Use anything that will provide the victim support. A floating object with a line attached is best. The victim can grasp the object and then be pulled to safety. However, lines and floats can also be used alone. Suitable throwing objects include a heaving line, ring buoy, throw bag, rescue tube or homemade device (Fig. 10-34). Use any floating object at hand, such as a picnic jug or innertube. A throwing object with a coiled line should be kept in a prominent location that is accessible to the water so that anyone can quickly grasp it to throw to someone in trouble.

A heaving line should float. It should be white, yellow or some other highly visible color. Tying a buoyant, weighted object on the end will make throwing easier and more accurate. Hang about half of the coiled line on the open palm of the nonthrowing hand, and throw the other half underhand to the victim.

A ring buoy is made of buoyant material and weighs about 2 pounds. It should have a towline or lightweight line with something at the end to keep the line from slipping out from under the foot as it is thrown. Hold the underside of the ring with the fingers, and throw it underhand.

The throw bag is a small, useful device. It is a nylon bag containing 50 to 75 feet of coiled floating line. A foam

disk in the bag gives it shape and keeps it from sinking. Throw bags are often used in canoes and other boats. Throw the throw bag with an underhand swing.

The rescue tube is a vinyl, foam-filled floating support about 45 to 54 inches long. It is the most effective equipment in lifeguarding. It is popular because it is easy to use and can support three to five people, depending on its size. Attached to the rescue tube is a tow line and shoulder strap with a total length of 6 to 12 feet.

A homemade heaving jug can be thrown to a victim. Put a half-inch of water or sand in a gallon plastic container, seal it and attach 50 to 75 feet of floating line to the handle. Throw it by holding the handle and using a swinging motion. The weight of the water in the jug helps direct the throw.

To perform a throwing assist, follow these guidelines:

▶ Get into a stride position: The leg opposite the throwing arm is forward. This helps maintain balance during the throw.
▶ Step on the end of the line with the forward foot. Avoid stepping on the coiled line with the other foot (Fig 10-35, *A*).
▶ Shout to get the victim's attention. Make eye contact and say that the object is going to be thrown now. Tell the victim to grab it.

A

B

C

▶ Bend the knees and throw the object to the victim. Try to throw the object upwind or up current, just over the victim's head, so the line drops within reach (Fig 10-35, *B*).

▶ When the victim has grasped the object or the line, slowly pull him or her to safety. Keep weight low and back. Lean away from the water while bringing the victim to safety (Fig 10-35, *C*).

▶ If the object does not reach the victim, quickly pull the line back in and throw it again. Try to keep the line from tangling, but do not waste time trying to coil it. If the object is a throw bag, partially fill the bag with some water and throw it again.

If the throwing assist does not work and the water is shallow enough for wading, try a wading assist with equipment.

Helping Someone Who Has Fallen Through Ice

If a person falls through ice, never go out onto the ice to attempt a rescue. This is a very dangerous situation, and the responder is likely to become a victim. Instead, follow these guidelines:

1. Send someone to call EMS immediately. Trained rescuers may be needed to get the person out of the ice, and even if one succeeds in rescuing the person, he or she will probably need medical care.
2. From a secure place on land, try a reaching or throwing assist. Use anything at hand that the person can grasp for support, such as a tree branch, pole, life jacket, weighted rope and so on (Fig. 10-36). Act quickly because within 1 minute, the victim's hands may be too numb to grasp the object.
3. If it is possible to do it safely, pull the victim to shore. If it is not, talk to the victim and make sure he or she is secure as possible with the object until help arrives.

In-Water Assists

Wading Assist with Equipment

If the water is shallow enough that one can stand with the chest out of the water, wade into the water to assist the person using a rescue tube, ring buoy, kickboard or a life jacket. A tree branch, pole, air mattress or paddle can

► FIG. 10-36

also be used (Fig. 10-37, *A* and *B*). If a current or soft bottom makes wading dangerous, do not enter the water. If possible, wear a life jacket when attempting a wading assist with equipment.

1. Take a buoyant object to extend out to the victim.
2. Wade into the water and extend the object to the victim.
3. When the victim grasps the object, tell him or her to hold onto the object tightly for support and pull him or her to safety. Keep the object between the responder and the victim to help prevent the victim from grasping the responder.

A victim who has been lying motionless and face down in the water for several seconds is probably unconscious.

1. If the water is not over one's chest, wade into the water care-fully with some kind of flotation equipment and turn the person face up.
2. Bring him or her to the side of the pool or to the shoreline.
3. Remove the victim from the water.

Submerged Victim

If a victim is discovered on or near the bottom of the pool in deep water, call for trained help immediately. If in shallow water less than chest deep and a head, neck or back injury is not suspected:

1. Reach down and grasp the victim.
2. Pull the victim to the surface.
3. Turn the victim face up and bring him or her to safety.
4. Remove the victim from the water.
5. Provide emergency care.

Helping Victims from the Water

Walking Assist

If the victim is in shallow water where he or she can stand, he or she may be able to walk with some support. Use the walking assist.

1. Place one of the victim's arms around the neck and across the shoulder of the responder.
2. Grasp the wrist of the arm that is across the responder's shoulder, and wrap the free arm around the victim's back or waist.
3. Maintain a firm grasp, and help the victim walk out of the water (Fig. 10-38).

▼ FIG. 10-37, *A-B*

▲ Fig. 10-38

▲ Fig. 10-40

Beach Drag

One may use the beach drag with a victim in shallow water on a sloping shore or beach. This method works well with a heavy or unconscious victim.

1. Stand behind the victim, and grasp him or her under the armpits, supporting the victim's head, when possible, with the forearms.
2. While walking backward slowly, drag the victim toward the shore (Fig. 10-39).
3. Remove the victim completely from the water or at least to a point where the head and shoulders are out of the water.

One may use a two-person drag if another person is present to help (Fig. 10-40).

▼ Fig. 10-39

Two-Person Lift

Do not use the two-person lift or the two-person removal from water using a backboard if it is suspected the victim has a head, neck or back injury.

To perform a two-person lift:

1. Place the victim's hands, one on top of the other, on the deck or overflow trough (gutter).
2. Take the victim's hands and pull the victim up slightly to keep the head above the water. Be sure the victim's head is supported so that it does not fall forward and strike the deck (Fig. 10-41, *A*). Note: If in the water, climb out to help the second person.
3. Each person grasps one of the victim's wrists and upper arms (Fig. 10-41, *B*). Lift together until the victim's hips or thighs are at deck level.
4. Step backward and lower the victim to the deck. Be sure to protect the victim's head from striking the deck (Fig. 10-41, *C*).
5. If necessary, pull the victim's legs out of the water, taking care not to twist the victim's back. Roll the victim onto his or her back. Support the victim's head, and take care not to twist the victim's body as it is rolled.

Two-Person Removal from Water Using a Backboard

If a backboard is available, perform the two-person removal from water using a backboard:

1. One responder grabs the victim's opposite wrists and pulls the victim up slightly to keep the head above

▲ FIG. 10-41, *A-C*

the water and away from the pool edge (Fig 10-42, *A*). Support the victim's head so that it does not fall forward.

2. A second responder gets a backboard and removes the head immobilizer and the straps, if possible.
3. The first responder guides the backboard, foot-end first, straight down into the water next to the victim.
4. The second responder then turns the victim onto the backboard (Fig 10-42, *B*). Each responder then quickly grasps one of the victim's wrists and one of the handholds of the backboard.
5. When the first responder gives the signal, both responders pull the backboard and victim onto the deck, resting the underside of the board against the edge of the pool. (Remember to lift with the legs and not the back.) Step backward and then lower the backboard onto the deck (Fig 10-42, *C*).

Injuries to the Head, Neck or Back

Head-first entries into shallow water and other unsafe activities can cause injuries to the head, neck or back. Usually a head, neck or back injury is caused by hitting the bottom or an object in the water. The major concern is to keep the victim's face out of the water to let him or her breathe and to prevent the victim's head and back from moving further. Movement can cause more injury and increase the risk of the victim being paralyzed. A goal is to keep the spine from moving until help arrives. To do this, it helps to understand the spine and know how to recognize a possible head, neck or back injury.

The spine is a strong, flexible column of bones called vertebrae. It supports the head and trunk and protects the spinal cord. The spinal cord is a bundle of nerves that run through the vertebrae and go out to all parts of the body (Fig. 10-43). Any injury to the spine can dam-

▼ FIG. 10-42, *A-C*

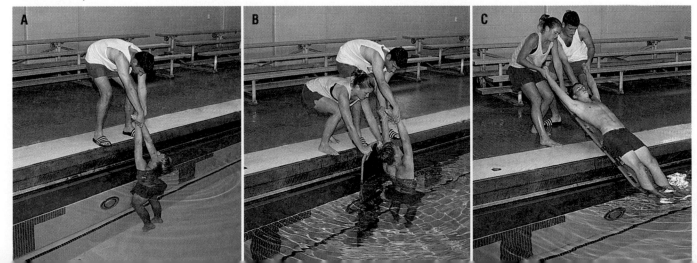

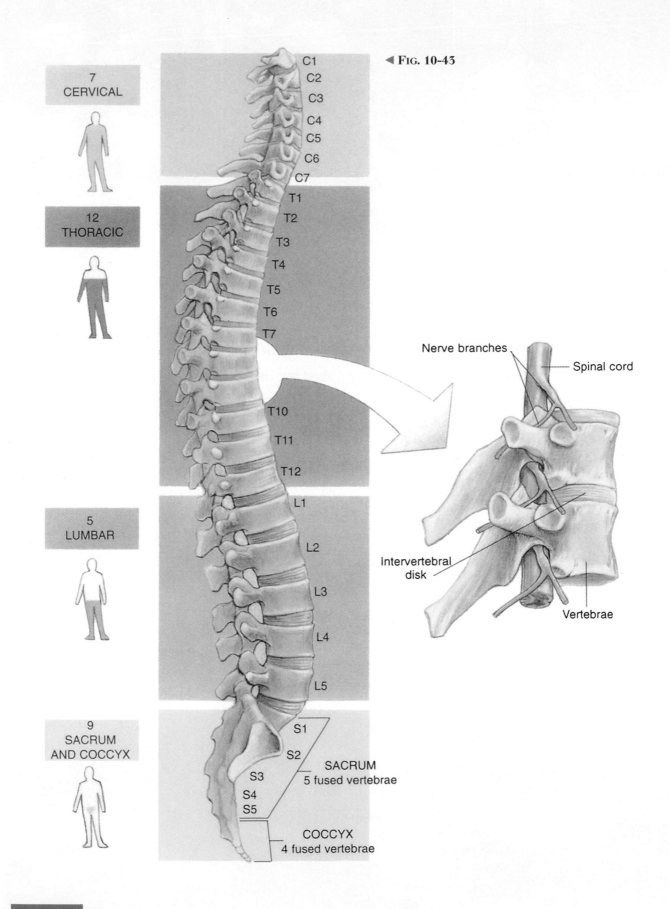

7
CERVICAL

12
THORACIC

5
LUMBAR

9
SACRUM
AND COCCYX

C1
C2
C3
C4
C5
C6
C7

T1
T2
T3
T4
T5
T6
T7

T10
T11
T12

L1
L2
L3
L4
L5

S1
S2
S3
S4
S5

SACRUM
5 fused vertebrae

COCCYX
4 fused vertebrae

Nerve branches

Spinal cord

Intervertebral
disk

Vertebrae

age these nerves and cause paralysis or death. An injury can happen anywhere along the back or neck up to the head, but neck injuries most commonly result from head-first entries into the water.

If one is unsure whether a victim has a head, neck or back injury, think about what the victim was doing and what happened to cause the injury. The following are situations in which head, neck or back injury is possible:

▶ Any head-first entry into shallow water
▶ Any fall onto land from a height greater than the victim's height
▶ Any injury involving a diving board or water slide
▶ Entering water from a height, such as a bank or cliff

Signals of a possible head, neck or back injury include:

▶ Head, neck or back pain
▶ Loss of balance
▶ Difficulty breathing
▶ Loss of movement in the arms and legs or below the injury site
▶ Tingling or loss of sensation in the arms, legs, hands or feet
▶ Bumps, bruises or depressions on the head, neck or back
▶ Altered consciousness or seizures
▶ Fluid or blood in the ears

If a head, neck or back injury is suspected, give care assuming there is an injury. If the victim is in the water, the goal is to prevent any further movement of the head or neck and to move the victim to safety. Always check first whether a lifeguard or other trained professional is present before touching or moving a victim who may have a head, neck or back injury. This section describes what one can do alone or with the assistance of bystanders to care for a victim of a head, neck or back injury.

General Guidelines for Care

A victim's head, neck or back can be stabilized in several ways while the victim is still in the water. These methods are described in the next sections. Follow these general guidelines for a victim with suspected head, neck or back injury in shallow water:

▶ Be sure someone has called 9-1-1 or the local emergency number. If other people are available, ask someone else in the group or a bystander to help.
▶ Minimize movement of the victim's head, neck and back. First, try to keep the victim's head in line with the body. This technique is called in-line stabilization. Do this without pulling on the head. Three methods described in the next section can be used.
▶ Position the victim face up at the surface of the water. This may require one to bring a submerged victim to the surface and to a face-up position. Keep the victim's face out of the water to let the victim breathe.
▶ Check for consciousness and breathing once the victim's head, neck and back are stabilized. A victim who can talk or is gasping for air is conscious and breathing.
▶ Support the victim with his or her head, neck and back immobilized until help arrives.

Specific Immobilization Techniques

The following sections describe three methods for stabilizing the victim's head, neck and back in the water. These methods will enable one to provide care for the victim whether he or she is face up or face down.

Hip and Shoulder Support

This method helps limit movement to the head, neck and back. Use it for a victim who is face up. Support the victim at the hips and shoulders to keep the face out of the water.

1. Approach the victim from the side, and lower oneself to chest depth.
2. Slide one arm under the victim's shoulders and the other under the hip bones. Support the victim's body horizontally, keeping the face clear of the water (Fig. 10-44, *A* and *B*).
3. Do not lift the victim, but support him or her in the water until help arrives.

Head Splint

This method provides better stabilization than the hip and shoulder support. Use it for a victim who is face down at or near the surface in the water. This victim must be turned face up to breathe.

1. Approach the victim from the side.

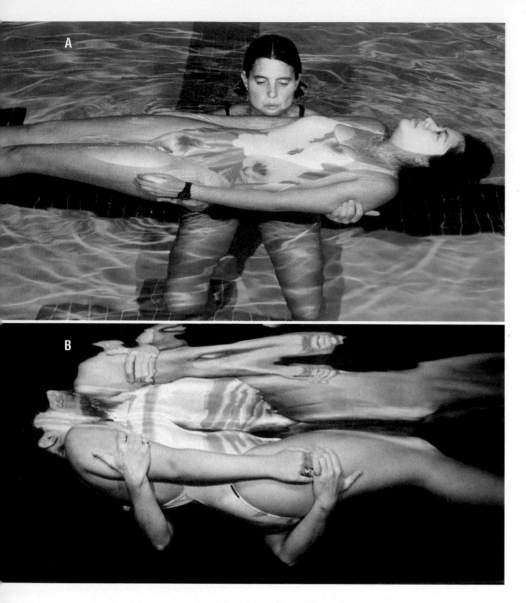

6. Position the victim's head in the crook of one's arm with the head in line with the body (Fig. 10-45, *C*).
7. Maintain this position in the water until help arrives.

Head and Chin Support

The head and chin support is used for face-down or face-up victims, at or near the surface, in shallow water at least 3 feet deep or in deep water. To perform the head and chin support for a victim in shallow water at or near the surface:

1. Approach the victim from the side.
2. With one's body at about shoulder depth in the water, place one forearm along the length of the victim's breastbone and the other forearm along the victim's spine.
3. Use one's hands to gently hold the victim's head and neck in line with the body. Place one hand on the victim's lower jaw and the other hand on the back of the lower head (Fig. 10-46, *A* and *B*). Be careful not to touch the back of the neck.
4. Squeeze the forearms together, clamping the victim's chest and back. Continue to support the victim's head and neck.
   ▶ If the victim is face down, turn him or her face up. Using the head and chin support to stabilize the spine, slowly move the victim forward to help lift the victim's legs. Turn the victim toward the responder as he or she submerges (Fig. 10-46, *C*).

2. Gently move the victim's arm up alongside the head. Do this by grasping the victim's arms midway between the shoulder and elbow. Grasp the victim's right arm with one's right hand. Grasp the victim's left arm with one's left hand.
3. Squeeze the victim's arms against his or her head. This helps keep the head in line with the body (Fig. 10-45, *A*).

4. With one's body at about shoulder depth in the water, glide the victim slowly forward.
5. Continue moving slowly, and rotate the victim until he or she is face up. This is done by pushing the victim's arm that is closest to the responder under water, while pulling the victim's other arm across the surface (Fig. 10-45, *B*).

▲ Fig. 10-45, *A-C*

► Roll under the victim while turning the victim over (Fig. 10-46, *D*). Avoid twisting the victim's body. The victim is face up when the responder surfaces on the other side (Fig. 10-46, *E*).

5. Hold the victim face up in the water until help arrives.

► Fig. 10-46, *A-E*

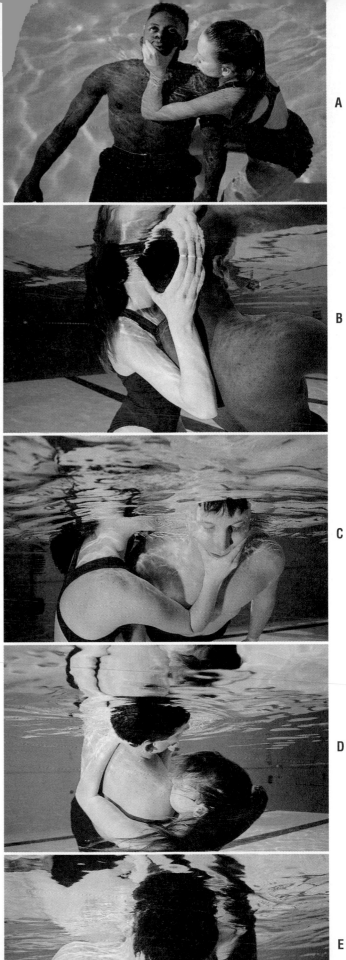

Using the Backboard

At least two trained people are needed to immobilize a victim on a backboard, but additional people should also help if available. Backboarding is a skill that should be practiced regularly. After stabilizing the victim's head and neck with either the head splint or the head and chin support, immobilize the victim on a backboard. Follow these steps to immobilize a victim in shallow water:

1. The FIRST responder brings the victim to the side of the pool using the head and chin support or head splint. The SECOND responder enters the water, submerges the backboard and positions it under the victim so that it extends slightly beyond the victim's head (Fig. 10-47, *A* and *B*).
2. While the SECOND responder raises the backboard into place, the FIRST responder carefully removes his or her arm from beneath the victim.

▶ If the head splint technique is used:
  • The FIRST responder moves the arm that is under the victim toward the top of the victim's head and continues to apply pressure on both arms, while the SECOND responder uses the head and chin support to stabilize the victim (one hand and arm on the chin and chest, the other hand and arm under the backboard) (Fig. 10-48, *A*).
  • Once the backboard is in place, the FIRST responder lowers the victim's arms, moves to the victim's head, submerges to shoulder depth, and supports the backboard against his or her chest and shoulders while squeezing the sides of the backboard with his or her forearms. The FIRST responder then stabilizes the victim's head by placing his or her hands along each side of the victim's head (Fig. 10-48, *B*).

▼ Fig. 10-47, *A-B*

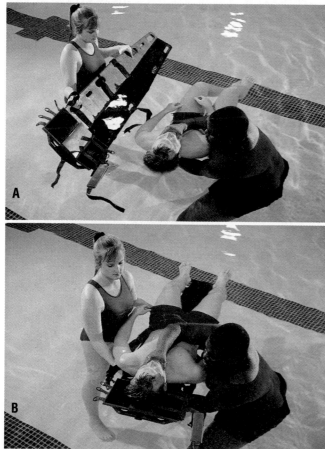

▼ Fig. 10-48, *A-B*

▲ FIG. 10-49, *A-B*

3. The responder who is not positioned at the victim's head secures the victim on the backboard. The responder places straps at least across the victim's chest, hips and thighs. Secure the straps in the following order:
   a. Strap across the chest and under the victim's armpits. This helps prevent the victim from sliding on the backboard during the removal (Fig 10-50, *A*).
   b. Strap across the hips with the victim's arms and hands secured (Fig 10-50, *B*).
   c. Strap across the thighs (Fig. 10-50, *C*).
   d. Recheck straps to be sure that they are secure.
4. After all the straps have been checked and properly secured, the responder immobilizes the victim's head to the board, using a head immobilizer and a strap across the victim's forehead.

▼ FIG. 10-50, *A-C*

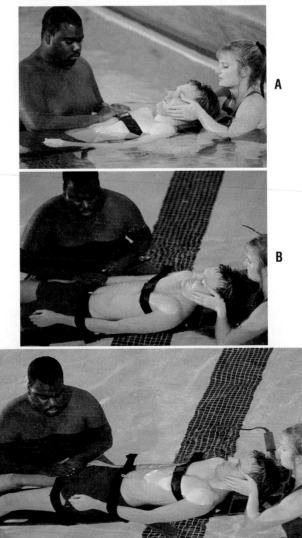

▶ If the head and chin support technique is used:
   • The FIRST responder keeps the hand on the chin and arm on the chest and places the other hand and arm under the backboard (Fig. 10-49, *A*).
   • Once the backboard is in place, the SECOND responder moves to the victim's head, submerges to shoulder depth, supports the backboard against his or her chest and shoulders and squeezes the sides of the backboard with his or her forearms. The SECOND responder then stabilizes the victim's head by placing his or her hands along each side of the victim's head (Fig. 10-49, *B*).

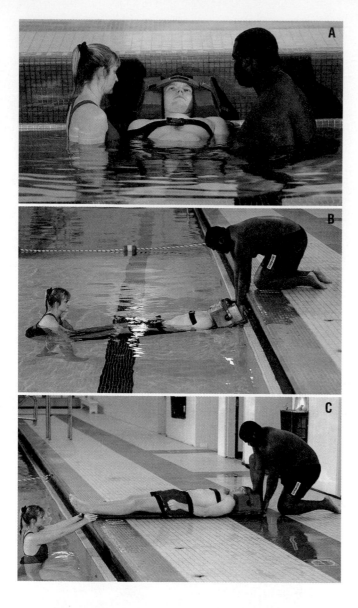

pushes on the backboard. Use proper lifting techniques to prevent injury:

- ▶ Keep your back straight.
- ▶ Bend at the knees.
- ▶ Move in a controlled way without jerking or tugging.

5. Together both responders slide the backboard up over the edge of the deck out of and away from the water (Fig. 10-51, *C*).

Anyone else helping stays in the water at the side of the backboard and helps guide the backboard and victim onto the deck.

Basic First Aid

In addition to rescuing a victim from the water, one should also be prepared for other kinds of emergencies in, on and around the water that may require first aid (Fig. 10-52). People may need first aid because of injuries or sudden illness. One needs to act quickly to save the victim's life or prevent further problems or disability.

Before giving first aid, the responder needs the victim's consent if the victim is conscious. When the victim is first reached, the responder should advise the victim of his or her level of training and what actions are intended. Ask the victim if that is okay. Consent can be assumed with unattended children or an adult who is unconscious or unable to respond, and first aid can be given.

Removal from the Water

Once the victim is secured on the backboard, remove him or her from the water:

1. Position the backboard with the head end by the side of the pool and the foot end straight out into the pool.
2. With one responder at each side, lift the head of the backboard slightly and place it on the edge of the gutter, if possible (Fig. 10-51, *A*).
3. One responder gets out of the pool and grasps the head end of the backboard. The other responder helps lift the head end of the board onto the deck and then moves to the foot end of the backboard (Fig 10-51, *B*).
4. As the responder on deck stands and steps backward pulling the backboard, the responder at the foot end

▼ Fig. 10-52

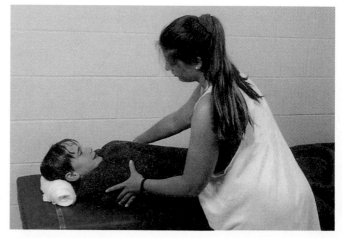

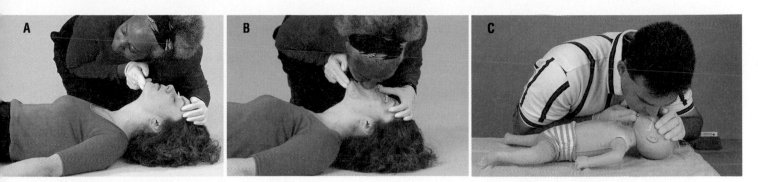

▲ Fɪɢ. 10-53, *A-C*

In any emergency situation, remember to call 9-1-1 or the local emergency number as soon as it is known that there is an emergency, or ask someone else to call. Remember also to make sure the scene is safe before going to the victim—do not risk personal safety or that of others at the scene. Once it is decided that it is safe to go to the victim, the goal then is to provide first aid for the short time until help arrives.

This section only covers first aid for a few types of injuries and illnesses that may occur in the aquatic environment. These are:

▶ Absence of breathing
▶ Choking
▶ Heat emergencies

Contact a local Red Cross chapter to enroll in a first aid and CPR course.

Rescue Breathing

Rescue breathing is a way to help a nonbreathing victim get air. Air is breathed into the victim to supply the oxygen needed to survive. Rescue breathing is given to a victim who is not breathing but whose heart is still beating.

Rescue breathing for a victim in the water is extremely difficult. When responding to a victim who is not breathing, get the victim out of the water as quickly as possible and have someone call EMS.

Once the victim is out of the water:

▶ CHECK the scene and victim.
▶ Send someone to CALL 9-1-1 or the local emergency number.
▶ To find out whether the victim is breathing, position the victim on his or her back on a flat surface. Tilt the head back and lift the chin to open the airway (Fig 10-53, *A*).

▶ Look, listen and feel for breathing for about 5 seconds.

If the victim is breathing but remains unconscious:

▶ Place the victim on the side in case he or she vomits, and monitor breathing and signs of circulation.

If the victim is NOT breathing:

▶ Pinch the victim's nose shut, the responder opens his or her mouth wide and makes a tight seal around the victim's mouth. (For an infant, both the mouth and nose are covered with the responder's mouth.)
▶ Give two slow breaths, until the chest clearly rises.
▶ Check for movement (coughing or response to breaths) for about 10 seconds.

If the breaths do not go in:

▶ Reposition the head and reattempt breaths.

When the breaths go in:

▶ Check for signs of movement (coughing or response to breaths) for about 10 seconds.

If victim is NOT breathing but shows some movement (coughing or response to breaths):

▶ Perform rescue breathing.
  • **Adult:** Give one slow rescue breath about every 5 seconds (Fig 10-53, *B*).
  • **Child or infant:** Give one slow rescue breath about every 3 seconds (Fig 10-53, *C*).
▶ Recheck for breathing and movement about every minute.

Choking

Emergencies in, on and around water can result in a victim's airway being blocked. This can happen when someone is chewing gum while swimming, goes into the water with food in the mouth or becomes a drowning victim.

▲ FIG. 10-54

When a victim's airway is blocked, the goal is to open the airway as quickly as possible (Fig. 10-54).

▶ Check the scene and the victim.
▶ Send someone to call 9-1-1 or the local emergency number and get consent before providing care.
▶ Place the thumb side of the fist against the middle of the abdomen just above the navel. Grasp the fist with the other hand.
▶ Give a quick, upward thrust.
▶ Repeat until the object is coughed up and the victim breathes on his or her own or the victim becomes unconscious.

Heat-Related Emergencies

It is best to try to prevent heat emergencies from occurring in the first place. One should know how to care for someone with heat cramps, heat exhaustion or heat stroke.

Heat cramps are painful muscle spasms, usually occurring in the arms and legs. To care for heat cramps:

▶ Have the victim rest in a cool place.
▶ Give cool water to drink.
▶ Lightly stretch and gently massage the muscle.
▶ Do not give a salt tablet.
▶ Watch for signals of heat illness.

Heat exhaustion can be caused by strenuous work or exercise in the heat that results in fluid losses due to heavy sweating. A victim may be experiencing heat exhaustion if the skin is cool, moist, pale or flushed and he or she has a headache or feels nauseated, faint, dizzy or exhausted. To care for heat exhaustion:

▶ Move the victim to a cool place.
▶ Loosen tight or remove perspiration-soaked clothing.
▶ Apply cool, wet cloths to the skin or mist with cool water and fan the victim.
▶ If the victim is conscious (Fig. 10-55), give cool water to drink.

If the victim's condition does not improve or if the victim vomits, refuses water or becomes less alert or unconscious, call for medical help immediately. These may signal that the victim is developing heat stroke.

Heat stroke is a life-threatening condition and usually occurs when people ignore the signals of heat exhaustion and stay in the heat. Heat stroke occurs when a victim's temperature control system, which produces sweating to cool the body, stops working. The body temperature can rise so high that brain dam-

age and death may result if the body is not cooled quickly. Sweating stops, and the victim has hot, red, dry skin. The victim may vomit and may lose consciousness. Call EMS personnel immediately, place the victim on his or her side and administer the following first aid:

▶ Move the victim to a cool place.
▶ Cool the victim. Apply cool, wet cloths, such as towels or sheets, to the victim's body if this has not already been done. If ice packs or cold packs are available, put them on the victim's wrists, ankles, groin, neck and armpits.
▶ If the victim becomes unconscious, give rescue breathing or CPR if needed.

Cold-Related Emergencies

Exposure to cold water leads to the danger of immersion hypothermia, which is a life-threatening condition. Hypothermia develops when the body can no longer generate suffi-

▼ FIG. 10-55

cient heat to maintain normal body temperature. The air temperature does not have to be below freezing for people to develop hypothermia. Anyone remaining in cold water or wet clothing for a prolonged time may also easily develop hypothermia. It is a medical emergency that requires prompt care.

To care for hypothermia:

► Remove the victim from the cold water.
► Check and care for any life-threatening conditions. Give rescue breathing or CPR, if needed.
► Call EMS personnel immediately.
► Remove any wet clothing and dry the victim.
► Warm the victim slowly by wrapping in blankets or by putting dry clothing on the victim.

Hot water bottles and chemical hot packs may be used when first wrapped in a towel or blanket before applying. Do not warm the victim too quickly, such as immersing the victim in warm water. Rapid warming can cause dangerous heart rhythms.

Frostbite is another type of cold-related emergency that occurs in body parts exposed to the cold.

Frostbite is the freezing of body tissues. It usually occurs in exposed areas of the body, depending on the temperature, length of exposure and the wind. Signals of frostbite include:

► Lack of feeling in the affected area
► Skin that appears waxy
► Skin that is cold to the touch
► Skin that is discolored (flushed, white, gray, yellow or blue)

To care for frostbite:

► Call for medical help immediately.
► Attempt to remove jewelry or restrictive clothing.
► Handle the affected area gently; never rub the affected area. Rubbing causes further damage.
► If there is no chance that the frostbitten part will refreeze, you may begin rewarming the affected area gently by soaking the affected part in water (100° F to 105° F) until it appears red and feels warm.
► Loosely bandage area with a dry, sterile dressing.
► If fingers or toes are frostbitten, place dry, sterile gauze between them to keep them separated.
► Avoid breaking any blisters.

Swimming and water activities can be challenging, fun, and relaxing, but any activity in, on or around the water can be dangerous. For all water activities, always learn and follow the appropriate safety rules. Water is safe only when one respects its power, regardless of one's abilities and the setting. Whether planning a dip in a backyard swimming pool, an excursion to the beach or a tube trip down a nearby river, one should learn, know and practice proper rescue techniques and procedures. People can learn additional first aid and safety techniques in courses offered by a local Red Cross chapter.

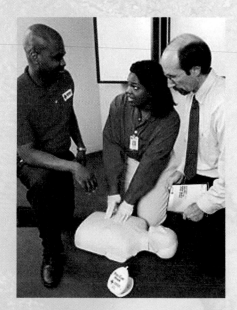

Appendix A
Instructions for Emergency Telephone Calls

Directions: Complete this form and post a copy near each telephone.

Emergency Telephone Numbers

Emergency Medical Services (EMS) _____

Fire _____

Police _____

Poison Control Center _____

Doctor _____

Information for Emergency Call

(Be prepared to give this information to the EMS dispatcher.)

1. Location

   Street address _____

   City or town _____

   Directions (cross streets, roads, landmarks, etc.)

   _____

   _____

2. Telephone number from which the call is being made

   _____

3. Caller's name

4. What happened?

5. How many people injured?

6. Condition of victim(s)

7. Help (first aid) being given

NOTE: Do not hang up first. Let the EMS dispatcher hang up first.

Additional Information

Family members' names	Medical conditions	Allergies

Appendix B
Equipment

Swimming and aquatic exercise require very little special equipment. Other than a pool, all that is really needed is a swim suit. As with many sports, however, high-tech equipment is being developed for swimming and aquatic exercise. A "swimman" can be purchased to listen to favorite music or a stopwatch to help count laps or to give an instant split recall. One is only limited by one's pocketbook. The more traditional equipment, such as hand paddles, fins, and kickboards, can be found at almost any pool. These and other devices can help one learn skills faster, improve one's technique, and provide some basic equipment. If not, one can always bring one's own. Much of the equipment discussed can be purchased at any well-equipped sporting goods store.

Swimsuit and Cap

Most fitness swimmers prefer Lycra swim suits because they dry quickly between workouts. Females usually prefer one-piece suits, although two-piece suits may be worn. Males usually choose brief-style trunks, which produce less drag than boxer-style trunks. Swim suits should be rinsed with fresh water.

Caps are worn to reduce drag. Caps also keep hair out of the eyes while swimming (Fig. B-1).

▲ Fig. B-1

Goggles

Goggles increase underwater visibility and protect the eyes from swimming pool chemicals. Goggles are made in a variety of sizes, shapes, and colors. Most have an adjustable nose piece and head strap. Goggles should fit comfortably in or over the eye socket (Fig. B-2).

▲ Fig. B-2

Check the fit by pressing the eyepieces to see if they develop suction around the eye. Then adjust the strap or nose piece to keep the goggles in place. The pressure of the water should help keep the goggles in place without an excessively tight strap. When swimming outdoors, one may choose to use goggles with colored lenses to reduce glare.

Kickboard

The kickboard is one of the most commonly used pieces of equipment in swimming. This simple device supports the upper body and allows for easy breathing when practicing kicks. This way, one can learn a new kick or practice a familiar one. The kickboard also provides some resistance, so it can be used to increase the workload during either the aerobic segment of a workout or during the strengthening and toning portion.

A kickboard can also be used for support during stroke drills. This allows for isolation of one arm at a time. Rotate the board so that one faces the long edge, providing a greater base of support for balance when using it to learn new strokes.

Pull Buoy and Leg Float

A pull buoy is usually made up of two cylinders of Styrofoam joined together with a nylon cord or strap. Held between the thighs or lower legs to prevent kicking, a pull buoy provides buoyancy for the legs so that the arms can be isolated. With this support, one can learn new strokes, improve arm action, and build upper-body strength. A pull buoy can be used with or without paddles.

Leg floats are made of foam in the shape of a figure eight. The narrow middle section is squeezed between the thighs or the lower legs. It is used just like a pull buoy.

Hand Paddles, Webbed Gloves, and Resistance Cuffs

Hand paddles are devices worn on the hands (and sometimes on the arms) during portions of a fitness or training workout. Paddles help strengthen the shoulders, chest and arms by increasing form drag. They come in a variety of shapes and sizes. Choose paddles that extend up to an inch around the hand in a shape that feels comfortable while swimming.

Hand paddles can also improve one's awareness of the hand moving through the water. If they twist or pull away from the palm, something is probably being done wrong, such as dropping the elbow or twisting the hand. One can use hand paddles alone or combine them with a pull buoy or other devices to concentrate on the arm stroke. They should be used sparingly, because the increased resistance can produce strain on the shoulder muscles. Stop using them if shoulder pain develops.

Hand paddles can also be used during aquatic exercise workouts. Paddles are used to improve upper body muscle tone and to build endurance.

Webbed gloves also rely on increased form drag to help make upper-body strength training more efficient. These may be used during the aerobic portion or the strengthening and toning segments of a workout.

Resistance cuffs are worn during aquatic exercise to increase the cardiovascular workout in deep or shallow water. They may be made of soft, durable foam and are worn around the wrists.

Weights and Weight Belts

Wrist and ankle weights can also be used to increase the intensity of the aerobic or muscular development segment of a workout. However, because they increase the impact of the body on the bottom of the pool, there is greater risk for injury using weights than there is when using equipment designed to increase the water's resistance only.

Individual dumbbells, one for each hand, are used for upper body and abdominal strengthening. They come in different sizes and shapes for more or less resistance. Some are inflatable, so they can be filled with water to adjust the weight.

Weight belts are used to help those who are very buoyant maintain a balanced position in chest-deep water when they are doing aquatic exercise.

Fins

Fins are useful for both the beginner and the accomplished swimmer. They provide increased propulsion while improving strength in the leg muscles and promoting greater ankle flexibility. The less skilled swimmer builds confidence, moves through the water faster and increases awareness of body position in the water. Swimmers of all skill levels might find fins very helpful in training and in the learning of new skills. They can be used while swimming or with a kickboard to emphasize leg work.

Fins come in a variety of styles. Flexible blades are easier to use than the stiffer ones. Be sure to choose fins that are comfortable and will not rub against the ankle or heel. If fins are too small, they could cause cramps in the foot. If they are too large, they could cause blisters, although wearing socks or the aqua shoes mentioned later should help prevent this. It is a good idea to try fins out before purchasing them.

Barbells and Swim Bars

Barbells take advantage of the laws of buoyancy to increase the water's resistance and therefore increase upper-body strength and endurance. Instead of weights, Styrofoam or plastic is attached to both ends of the bar to inhibit movement through the water. They may be used during strengthening and toning exercises performed in the water.

A swim bar is a longer version of a barbell but is held with both hands and primarily helps maintain balance during water walking or jogging (Fig. B-3). It can also be used instead of holding onto the wall when working on the abdomen and lower body or like a kickboard for support when practicing kicks.

▲ FIG. B-3

Swim Belts and Vests

A swim belt is worn around the waist to keep a person stable and afloat while walking or jogging in the water without touching the pool bottom (Fig. B-4). A life jacket serves the same purpose. However, nonswimmers should not rely on these devices for support in deep water.

▲ FIG. B-4

A swim vest is worn during an aquatic exercise workout in cooler water. Swim vests are sleeveless to allow for full range of motion while exercising.

Steps or Bench

Taking advantage of the pool stairs or a weighted bench, one steps up and down rhythmically for an intense yet low-impact aerobic workout that focuses on the lower body. One must work against the resistance of the water on the step up, as well as the step down. One can improve the muscular strength of the upper body at the same time by using wrist or ankle weights or any of the buoyant hand, arm or ankle equipment mentioned previously.

Drag Devices

Drag boards or "pull boards" force one to work harder against the added resistance they provide. A drag board looks like a kickboard, except that it has two holes for the feet so the board is around the ankles. As one swims, the drag board becomes vertical, increasing drag. The drag board may be used in conjunction with the pull buoy.

The drag suit has large outer pockets that fill with water as one swims, which increases drag. The drag suit should allow for normal body position in the water, and one should be able to swim any stroke.

A training tube is placed around the ankles in a figure eight. It can help one work on arm strokes, and the inflation can be changed to vary the buoyancy and drag. The training tube may also be used as a substitute for a kickboard.

The stretching tether, usually constructed of surgical tubing, is a device for providing resistance other than drag. One end of the tether is secured to the swimmer's waist with a belt, while the other end is looped around a starting block. The swimmer first swims a lap against the resistance of the elasticized tether. The greater the distance attempted, the harder it becomes to get anywhere. Then, during the second lap, the swimmer springs faster than is normally possible because he or she is aided by the pull of the tether.

Dry Land Resistance Equipment for Swimmers

Any resistance equipment used to increase muscular strength should concentrate on exercises that help improve swimming speed and endurance. When using dry-land equipment, keep in mind the principle of specificity of training discussed in Chapter 9.

During dry-land training, one works with the device against gravity, gradually increasing the resistance—that is, the weight—and the number of times one moves the added weight to build muscle strength and endurance. More traditional dry-land resistance devices (stationary weight machines such as Nautilus and Universal) (Fig. B-5); free weights, such as barbells and dumbbells; and stretch cords (Fig. B-6) or pulleys may be used if the routines involve the muscles used in swimming and if the movements are as similar to those of swimming as possible.

The mini-gym and isokinetic swim bench (Fig. B-7) were designed specifically with swimmers in mind, and they permit swimmers to duplicate a full range of swimming motions. What is also unique about these devices is that they are isokinetic. This means that the resistance auto-

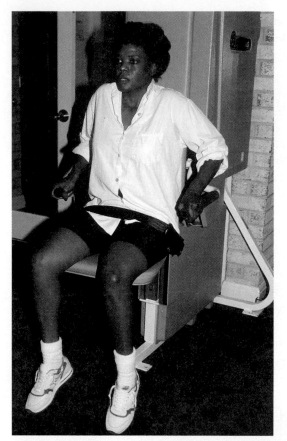

▲ Fig. B-5

▲ Fig. B-6

matically adjusts to the force applied by the muscles, so that as muscles tire and effort weakens, the resistance also decreases, lessening the chance of injury. The swim bench has the added feature of measuring the force of the pull during simulated swimming movements.

▲ FIG. B-8

Pace clocks are either digital or have sweep hands. Many pools have a pace clock at one or both ends of the pool. If a pace clock is not available, a water resistance watch works almost as well.

▲ FIG. B-7

Pace Clock

One of the most useful pieces of equipment for the fitness swimmer is the pace clock. A pace clock is simply a large stopwatch used on the pool deck to assist in timing predetermined distance, interval sets, or even an entire workout (Fig. B-8). In addition, the pace clock makes it easy to do quick pulse checks throughout a workout.

Aqua Shoes

Aqua shoes are flexible shoes constructed with nylon uppers and rubber or neoprene nonslip soles. They help prevent injury in people who lack sensation in the lower extremities. They may be worn in the water, and if they have some arch support they are excellent for aquatic exercise, especially if the bottom of the pool has a rough surface.

Glossary

Above-ground pool: A portable pool of limited depth that sits on the ground.

Active drowning victim: A person exhibiting universal behavior that includes struggling at the surface for 20 to 60 seconds before submerging.

Adipose tissue: Body tissue that stores fat.

Aerobic exercise: Sustained, rhythmic, physical exercise that requires additional effort by the heart and lungs to meet the increased demand by the skeletal muscles for oxygen.

Anaerobic exercise: Exercise at an intensity such that oxygen demand by skeletal muscles is not consistently met. Anaerobic exercise involves high-intensity events that last 1 minute or less.

Approach: The walk toward the end of a diving board before the hurdle.

Aquatic exercise: Fitness activities conducted in water; generally performed in a vertical position with the face out of the water.

Back glide: Coasting through the water in a horizontal, face-up position after pushing off from a solid surface.

Backwash: Seaward flow of water returning down slope after being cast on the beach by a wave.

Basal metabolic rate: The amount of calories the body burns at rest.

Bobbing: The skill of repeatedly submerging and pushing off from the bottom to return to the surface.

Body alignment: The position of the body in preparation for an entry.

Body roll: A rotating movement of the body around the long axis.

Breakpoint: The area of the pool where the depth changes from shallow to deep.

Buoyancy: The upward force a fluid exerts on bodies floating on or submerged in it.

Cardiovascular endurance: The ability of the heart, lungs and circulatory system to sustain vigorous activity.

Cardiovascular system: The heart and blood vessels, which bring oxygen and nutrients to the body through the circulation of blood.

Catch: The stage in an arm stroke when the swimmer first engages the water in a way to start moving; the start of the power phase.

Center of buoyancy: The point around which the buoyant properties of all segments of a body balanced.

Center of mass: The point around which the weight of all segments of the body balanced.

Disability: A limitation resulting from an impairment.

Displacement: The volume of fluid displaced by a floating or immersed body.

Diving board: A diving apparatus that consists of a flexible board secured at one end and a fulcrum below the board. Also called a springboard.

Diving platform: An elevated platform stationary structure for diving.

Diving tower: An elevated structure used for diving that includes diving platforms at several heights. Towers used for competitive diving often have platforms that are 1 meter, 3 meters, 5 meters, $7^1/_2$ meters and 10 meters high.

Down syndrome: A genetic condition that usually causes delays in physical and intellectual development.

Drag: The resistance of water on a body moving through it.

Drowning: Death by suffocation in water.

Duration: The amount of time spent during each exercise session.

Emergency medical services (EMS) personnel: Trained and equipped community-based personnel dispatched through a local emergency number to provide emergency care for ill or injured people.

Emergency medical services (EMS) system: A network of community resources and medical personnel that provides emergency care to victims of injury or sudden illness.

Entry: The part of a dive in which the body passes through the surface of the water.

Equilibrium: A state of balance between opposing forces.

Feet-first scull: A sculling technique for moving the body feetfirst through the water in a horizontal, face-up position using only back and forth movements of the arms and hands.

Feet-first surface dive: A technique for descending under water from the surface with the feet leading.

Figures: In synchronized swimming, movements in the water composed of basic positions and transitions from one position to another.

Finning: A technique for moving through the water on the back using a pushing motion with the arms under water.

Fitness swimming: A swimming program in which the workouts have a specified level of intensity and are sustained for a set duration.

Flat scull: A sculling technique using only back and forth movements of the arms and hands to stay floating in a horizontal, face-up position on the surface of the water.

Flexibility: The range of motion in a joint or group of joints.

Flight: The movement of the body through the air during a dive.

Flip turn: A fast and efficient turn done in a tuck position; used in lap swimming and in the freestyle and backstroke events in competition.

Force of gravity: The pull of the earth on a body.

Form drag: The resistance force caused by an object's shape and profile as it moves through a fluid.

Freestyle: A competitive event that allows any stroke, although the front crawl is generally used.

Freestyle relay: A common competitive event in which each member of a four-member team swims any stroke one quarter of the total distance.

Frequency: The number of occurrences of exercise sessions.

Frictional drag: The resistance force caused by an object's surface texture as it moves through a fluid.

Fulcrum: A pivot point near the center of a diving board that lets the board bend and spring.

Glide: The stage of a stroke after the power phase when the body keeps moving without additional swimmer effort.

Grab start: A competitive start in which the hands grasp the front of the starting blocks for a fast takeoff.

Head-first scull: A sculling technique for moving the body headfirst in a horizontal, face-up position on the surface of the water using only back and forth movements of the arms and hands.

Hearing impairment: Partial or total loss of hearing.

Heat: A race in which times are compared with those from other races to determine overall ranking. A heat is used when there are more entrants in a swimming event than there are lanes in the pool.

Heat cramps: Painful muscle spasms, usually in an arm or leg.

Heat exhaustion: A form of shock, often resulting from strenuous work or exercise in a hot environment.

Heat stroke: A life-threatening condition that develops when the body's cooling mechanisms are overwhelmed and body systems begin to fail.

Hopper-bottom pool: A pool with a bottom that angles sharply up on all four sides from the deepest point. Many fulcrums are adjustable to alter the amount of spring.

Hurdle: The jump to the end of a diving board after the approach.

Hurdle leg: The leg lifted in the hurdle.

Hydraulic: Whirlpools created as water flows over a ledge, such as a low-head dam or waterfall; an unwary swimmer may be trapped in the circulation.

Hydrodynamics: The science that studies the motion of liquids and forces on solid bodies in liquids.

Hyperventilation: A potentially dangerous technique some swimmers use to stay under water longer by taking several deep breaths followed by forceful exhalations, then inhaling deeply before swimming under water.

Hypothermia: A life-threatening condition in which the body is unable to maintain warmth and the entire body cools.

Impairment: Any loss or abnormality of psychological, physiological or anatomical structure or function.

Individual medley: An event in which the competitor swims each quarter of the total distance using a different competitive stroke in a prescribed order (butterfly, backstroke, breaststroke, freestyle).

In-line stabilization: A technique used to minimize movement of a victim's head and neck while providing care.

Intensity: How hard one works out when exercising.

Jumpboard: A recreational mechanism with a spring beneath the board that is activated by jumping on the board.

Kinesthetic awareness: The conscious sense of where the body or its parts are positioned or how they are moving at any given moment.

Laminar flow: The principle by which the molecules of a fluid that is moving around an object speed up or slow down to stay parallel to each other.

Law of acceleration: The principle by which the change in speed of a body depends on how much force is applied to it and the direction of that force.

Law of action and reaction: The principle that for every action there is an equal and opposite reaction.

Law of inertia: The principle that a force must be applied to change the motion of a body.

Law of levers: The principle that movement of levers is related to the force applied, the resistance that occurs, the force arm (the distance from where the force is applied to the pivot point), and the resistance arm (the distance from where the resistance occurs to the pivot point).

Leading arm: When arms work in opposition, the arm reaching farthest beyond the head. In the sidestroke, this is also called the bottom arm.

Lift: A force created by a body's shape and motion through a fluid, that acts perpendicular to the direction of the movement. Also the force of a diving board propelling a diver into the air (not the principle of lift in hydrodynamics).

Long axis: An imaginary line going through the center of the body from head to feet that divides the body equally into left and right parts.

Longshore currents: Currents that move parallel to the shore.

Mainstreaming: The process of including people with disabilities in the same programs and activities as the nondisabled.

Masters: A classification in some organizations for swimmers 19 years old and older and divers 21 years old and older.

Medley relay: A competitive event in which each member of a four-member team swims one quarter of the total distance and then is relieved by a teammate. The first uses a backstroke start and swims the backstroke, the second swims the breaststroke, the third swims the butterfly, and the fourth swims freestyle.

Mental function: Intelligence and the capacity to reason, process and store information.

Metabolic rate: The amount of energy produced by the body in a given period.

Motor function: The brain's ability to direct both reflexive and voluntary movements.

Open turn: A simple turn used in noncompetitive situations.

Open-water swimming: Any competition that takes place in rivers, lakes or oceans.

Overload: A fitness principle based on working somewhat harder than normal so that the muscles and cardiovascular system must adapt.

Passive drowning victim: An unconscious victim face down, submerged or near the surface.

Physics: The science that studies matter and energy.

Physiological: Relating to the physical processes and functions of the human body.

Pike position: A basic diving position during flight with the body bent at the hips and the legs straight.

Pike surface dive: A technique for moving under water from the surface by bending at the hips and descending headfirst with legs kept straight.

Plummet: A line from the midpoint at the tip of a diving board to the bottom of the pool.

Power phase: The stage when the arm or leg stroke is moving the body in the desired direction.

Press: A diver's downward push on a diving board before the upward recoil.

Progression: An ordered set of steps, from the simplest to the most complex, for learning a skill; in an exercise program, gradually increasing frequency, intensity or time so that an overload is produced.

Prone: On the front, face down.

Propulsive: Causing motion in the desired direction.

Psychological: Referring to the way the mind works and the attitudes, behaviors and beliefs reflecting a person's state of mind.

Push leg: The leg that pushes down on the board on the step before the hurdle.

Racing start: A long, shallow entry from starting blocks used by competitive swimmers.

Recovery: The phase of a stroke when the arms or legs relax and return to the starting position.

Rehabilitation: Process of providing and directing selected tasks to enhance, restore and reinforce performance.

Rescue breathing: A technique of breathing for a non-breathing victim.

Rip currents: Currents that move straight out to sea.

Rotary kick: A kicking technique used for treading water; sometimes called the eggbeater kick.

Safe diving envelope: The area of water in front of, below and to the sides of a diving board that is deep enough that a diver will not strike the bottom, regardless of the depth of the water or the design of the pool.

SCUBA: Self-Contained Underwater Breathing Apparatus.

Sculling: A propulsion technique for moving through the water or staying horizontal using only the arms and hands.

Sensory functions: Sight, touch, taste, smell and hearing.

Set: A prescribed series of swims in a particular pattern or sequence.

Shallow dive: A dive for entering the water headfirst at a shallow angle with great forward momentum.

Spatial orientation: The understanding of one's location in space and position with reference to other objects.

Specific gravity: The ratio of the weight of a body to the weight of the water it displaces.

Specificity: The principle that states that the benefits of exercise relate directly to the activity performed.

Spinal cord: The bundle of nerves from the brain at the base of the skull to the lower back, inside the spinal column.

Spoon-shaped pool: A pool with a bottom that is rounded upward from the deepest point to all the sides.

Starting block: A raised platform from which competitive swimmers begin a race. A bar or handhold is usually attached for backstroke starts.

Straight position: A basic diving position of the body during flight with the body straight or arched slightly backward and the legs straight and together.

Streamlined position: A body positioned so that as it moves through the water, it pushes the least amount of water, receiving the least amount of resistance.

Stroke frequency: The number of complete arm cycles in a set period.

Stroke length: Distance traveled in one complete cycle of the arms.

Stroke mechanics: The application of the hydrodynamic principles to understand and improve swimmer performance.

Supine: On the back, face up.

Swim meet: A competitive event in swimming; may be a contest between teams or between individuals.

Synchronized swimming: Rhythmical water activity of one or more people performed in a pattern synchronized to music.

Tactile impairment: Partial or total loss of the sense of touch.

Takeoff: The propulsive part of a dive in which a diver's feet leave the deck or the end of a diving board.

Taper phase: The 1- to 3-week period in a training season before a peak performance, in which the person in training decreases distances but raises the intensity almost to racing speed.

Target heart rate range: The ideal heart rate range for an individual to maintain during exercise for greatest cardiovascular benefit.

Track start: A competitive start often used from starting blocks for a fast takeoff. Differs from grab start in initial foot placement.

Trailing arm: The arm that rests on the hip in the glide phase of the sidestroke. Also called the top arm.

Training effect: An improvement in functional capacity of a system (cardiovascular, respiratory, muscular) that results from an overload of that system.

Trauma: Physical injury caused by a violent action.

Treading water: A skill using arm and leg movements to stay vertical in the same location with the head out of the water.

Triathlon: A sporting event made up of three different activities, usually swimming, biking and running, in that order. Triathlons often start with an open-water swim.

Tuck position: A basic diving position during flight with the body pulled into a tight ball with knees drawn up to the chest and heels drawn to the buttocks.

Tuck surface dive: A technique for moving headfirst from the surface with the hips and knees flexed to under water with the hips and knees extending.

Undulate: To move in a wavy, sinuous or flowing manner.

Vision impairment: Partial or total loss of sight.

Wave drag: Energy loss due to generation of waves as a body moves along the surface of the water.

Sources

American Alliance for Health, Physical Education, Recreation and Dance. *Safety Aquatics*. Sports Safety Series, Monograph #5. American Alliance for Health, Physical Education, Recreation and Dance, 1977.

American College of Sports Medicine. *Calculating Your Exercise Heart Rate Range*. Available at http://www.acsm.org/pdf/Guidelines.pdf. Accessed September 2003.

American College of Sports Medicine. *Fit Society Page Newsletter, January-March 2001*. Available at http://www.acsm.org/pdf/01fitsoc.pdf. Accessed October 2003.

American College of Sports Medicine. *Guidelines for Healthy Aerobic Activity*. Available at http://www.acsm.org/pdf/Guidelines.pdf. Accessed September 2003.

Anderson, B. *Stretching*. Bolinas, California: Shelter Publications, Inc., 1980.

American National Red Cross. *Adapted Aquatics: Swimming for Persons with Physical or Mental Impairments*. Washington, D.C.: The American National Red Cross, 1977.

American National Red Cross. *Basic Water Rescue*. Yardley, Pennsylvania: StayWell, 1998.

American National Red Cross. *Community Water Safety*. Yardley, Pennsylvania: StayWell, 1995.

American National Red Cross. *Lifeguard Training*. Yardley, Pennsylvania: StayWell, 2001.

American National Red Cross. *Responding to Emergencies*. Yardley, Pennsylvania: StayWell, 2001.

American National Red Cross. *Small Craft Safety*. Yardley, Pennsylvania: StayWell, 1995.

American National Red Cross. *Swimming and Diving*. Yardley, Pennsylvania: StayWell, 1992.

Armbruster, D.A.; Allen, R.H.; and Billingsley, H.S. *Swimming and Diving*. St. Louis: The C.V. Mosby Company, 1968.

Auerbach, P.S. *A Medical Guide to Hazardous Marine Life*. Jacksonville, Florida: Progressive Printing Co., Inc., 1987.

Besford, P. *Encyclopedia of Swimming*. New York: St. Martins Press, 1971.

Bigelow, J., editor. *The Works of Benjamin Franklin*, Vol. 4. New York: G.P. Putnam's Sons, 1904.

Brems, M. *The Fit Swimmer: 120 Workouts & Training Tips*. Chicago, Illinois: Contemporary Books, 1984.

Brems, M. *Swim for Fitness*. San Francisco: Chronicle Books, 1979.

Burgess, G.H. "Shark Attack and the International Shark Attack File," in Gruber, S.H., editor. *Discovering Sharks*. Highlands, New Jersey: American Littoral Society, 1991.

Clayton, R. D., and Thomas, D.G. *Professional Aquatic Management*. Champaign, Illinois: Human Kinetics, 1989.

Clayton, R.D., and Tourney, J.A. *Teaching Aquatics*. Minneapolis: Burgess Publishing Company, 1981.

Collis, M., and Kirchoff, B. *Swimming*. Boston: Allyn and Bacon, Inc., 1974.

Colwin, C.M. *Swimming Into the 21st Century*. Champaign, Illinois: Leisure Press, 1991.

Cooper, K.H. *The Aerobics Program for Total Well-Being*. New York: Bantam Books, 1982.

Counsilman, J.E. *Competitive Swimming Manual*. Bloomington, Indiana: Counsilman Co., Inc., 1977.

Counsilman, J.E. *The Science of Swimming*. Englewood Cliffs, New Jersey: Prentice-Hall, Inc., 1968.

Edwards, S. *Triathlon: A Triple Fitness Sport*. Chicago: Contemporary Books, Inc., 1983.

Firby, H. *Howard Firby on Swimming*. London: Pelham, 1975.

Sources

Flewwelling, H. "Sparging System," in Gabriel, J.L., editor. *U. S. Diving Safety Manual.* Indianapolis: U.S. Diving Publications, 1990.

Ichthyology at the Florida Museum of Natural History. *Reducing the Risk of Shark Attacks.* Available at http://www.flmnh.ufl.edu/fish/Sharks/Attacks/relariskreduce.htm. Accessed August 2003.

Forbes, M.S. *Coaching Synchronized Swimming Effectively.* Champaign, Illinois: Human Kinetics Publishers, Inc., 1988.

Gabrielsen, M.A. *Diving Injuries: A Critical Insight and Recommendation.* Clayton, R.D., editor. Indianapolis: Council for National Cooperation in Aquatics, 1984.

Gabrielsen, M.A. *Diving Injuries: Prevention of the Most Catastrophic Sport Related Injuries.* Presented to the Council for National Cooperation in Aquatics, Indianapolis, 1981.

Hay, J.G. *The Biomechanics of Sports Techniques.* Englewood Cliffs, New Jersey: Prentice-Hall, 1985.

Jonas, S. *Triathloning For Ordinary Mortals.* New York: W.W. Norton & Co. Inc., 1986.

Katz, J. *Swimming for Total Fitness: A Progressive Aerobic Program (2nd edition),* New York: Bantam Doubleday Dell Publishing Group, 1993.

Katz, J. *The W.E.T Workout.* New York: Facts on File Publications, 1985.

Knopf, K.; Fleck, L.; and Martin, M.M. *Water Workouts.* Winston-Salem: Hunter Textbooks, Inc., 1988.

Krasevec, J.A., and Grimes, D.C. *HydroRobics.* New York: Leisure Press, 1984.

Leonard, J., editor. *Science of Coaching Swimming.* Champaign, Illinois: Leisure Press, 1992.

Maglischo, E.W. *Swimming Faster.* Palo Alto, California: Mayfield Publishing Company, 1982.

Maglischo, E.W., and Brennan, C.F. *Swim for the Health of It.* Palo Alto, California: Mayfield Publishing Co., 1985.

McArdle, W; Katch, F.; and Katch, V. *Exercise Physiology: Energy, Nutrition and Human Performance (2nd edition),* Lea & Febiger, Philadelphia, 1986.

McEvoy, J.E. *Fitness Swimming: Lifetime Programs.* Princeton: Princeton Book Company Publishers, 1985.

Messner, Y.J., and Assmann, N.A. *Swimming Everyone.* Winston-Salem: Hunter Textbooks, Inc., 1989.

Montoye, H.J.; Christian, J.L.; Nagle, F.J.; and Levin, S.M. *Living Fit.* Menlo Park, California: The Benjamin/Cummings Publishing Company, Inc., 1988.

National Heart, Lung, and Blood Institute. *Facts About Cystic Fibrosis.* Available at http://www.nhlbi.nih.gov/health/public/lung/other/cystfib.htm. Accessed October 2003.

National Institute of Neurological Disorders and Stroke. *Amyotrophic Lateral Sclerosis Fact Sheet.* Available at http://www.ninds.nih.gov/health_and_medical/pubs/als.htm. Accessed October 2003.

National Institute of Neurological Disorders and Stroke. *NINDS Cerebral Palsy Information Page.* Available at http://www.ninds.nih.gov/health_and_medical/disorders/cerebral_palsy.htm. Accessed October 2003.

National Institute of Neurological Disorders and Stroke. *NINDS Multiple Sclerosis Information Page.* Available at http://www.ninds.nih.gov/health_and_medical/disorders/multiple_sclerosis.htm. Accessed October 2003.

National Institute of Neurological Disorders and Stroke. *NINDS Stroke Information Page.* Available at http://www.ninds.nih.gov/health_and_medical/disorders/stroke.htm. Accessed October 2003.

National Safety Council. *Injury Facts.* Chicago, Illinois: National Safety Council, 2002.

National Spa and Pool Institute. *American National Standard for Public Swimming Pools.* Alexandria, Virginia: National Spa and Pool Institute, 1991.

Paralympic Games. *Paralympic Games.* Available at http://www.paralympic.org. Accessed October 2003.

Report of the 16th Annual Meeting, Council For National Cooperation in Aquatics, 1966.

Special Olympics. *Sports Offered—Aquatics.* Available at http://www.specialolympics.org. Accessed October 2003.

Swimming Pools: A Guide to Their Planning, Design, and Operation. Champaign, Illinois: Human Kinetics Publishers, Inc., 1987.

United States Coast Guard. *Lifejackets and other Personal Flotation Devices.* Available at http://www.uscg.mil/hq/g-m/mse4/pfd.htm. Accessed September 2003.

United States Synchronized Swimming. *About USA Synchro.* Available at http://www.usasynchro.org/#. Accessed September 2003.

USA Diving. About USA Diving. Available at http://www.usadiving.org/USD_03redesign/about/about.htm. Accessed September 2003.

USA Swimming. *USA Swimming News & History.* Available at http://www.usa-swimming.org/media_services/. Accessed September 2003.

USA Triathlon. *About USA Triathlon.* Available at http://www.usatriathlon.org/. Accessed September 2003.

USA Water Polo. *USA Water Polo.* Available at http://www.usawaterpolo.com/. Accessed September 2003.

Ward, A.W.; Trent, W.P.; et al. *The Cambridge History of English and American Literature.* New York: G.P. Putnam's Sons, 1907–21; New York: Bartleby.com, 2000.

Available at http://www.bartleby.com/cambridge/. Accessed September 2003.

Williams, M. H., *Nutrition for Fitness and Sport.* Dubuque, Iowa: William C. Brown Company Publishers, 1983.

YMCA of the USA. *Principles of YMCA Competitive Swimming and Diving (2nd Edition),* Champaign, Illinois: Human Kinetics Publishers, Inc., 2000.

YMCA of the USA. *The Parent/Child and Preschool Aquatic Program Manual.* Champaign, Illinois: Human Kinetics Publishers, Inc., 1999.

YMCA of the USA. *The Youth and Adult Aquatic Program Manual.* Champaign, Illinois: Human Kinetics Publishers, Inc., 1999.

Index